HERMANN AND ALBERT GOERING

THE NAZI AND THE RENEGADE

JAMES WYLLIE

The
History
Press

Cover illustrations: Hermann (left) and Albert Goering.

First published 2006
This edition published 2021

The History Press
97 St George's Place, Cheltenham,
Gloucestershire, GL50 3QB
www.thehistorypress.co.uk

British Library Cataloguing in Publication Data.
A catalogue record for this book is available from the British Library.

ISBN 978 0 7509 9787 4

Typesetting and origination by The History Press
Printed and bound in Great Britain by TJ Books Limited, Padstow, Cornwall.

Trees for L♀fe

Contents

Acknowledgements

This book would not have been possible without the dedication, skill and belief of my sister, Dr Barbara Wyllie, author, academic, researcher and editor, and Adam LeBor, author and journalist, who together discovered the forgotten story of Albert Goering and set about trawling the archives for the truth. Their labours resulted in a feature length piece in the *Sunday Times* (1998) and a sixty-minute documentary for Channel 4 produced by 3BM TV (1998). Both Barbara and Adam continued to unearth material and provided the bulk of the raw data on Albert. Since I embarked on this project they have offered their full and enthusiastic support for which I will be eternally grateful.

I am equally in debt to the individuals who were kind enough to take the time to share memories of Albert with me: Jacques Benbassat, George Pilzer, George Staller, Elsa Moravek Perou de Wagner and Dr Christa Hartnigk-Kummel.

I would like to thank Dan Korn and his team at 3BM TV for their cooperation and Ann Williams for her expertise. An American researcher, Robert Fink, has provided invaluable assistance throughout. Professor Dennis Deletant at the School of Slavonic and East European Studies offered expert advice on the complexities of Romania's involvement in the Second World War. I look forward to his forthcoming biography of Marshal Antonescu.

My editor at Sutton, Jonathan Falconer, has been nothing but positive ever since he read my proposal, as have all the staff at the company. Without my agent of many years, John Rush, who retired earlier this year, I would never have got this far. Thanks to Amanda Preston for being a fan of the book and guiding me through the deal making process, and thanks to my current agent at Sheil Land Associates Ltd, Emily Hayward, for stepping in so effortlessly.

The constant and unquestioning support of my mother and father has been nothing short of miraculous. To all my friends and family I extend my love and gratitude. Finally, three cheers for the History Department at Latymer Upper School, *circa* 1977–84, for taking a hungry adolescent mind and teaching it how to think.

James Wyllie

PART ONE

Nobody knows the real Goering. I am a man of many parts.

Hermann Goering, 27 May 1946

Just name any subject to me and I will be glad to give you all the information at my disposal. I swear by God I am not trying to hide anything.

Albert Goering, 25 September 1945

Every morning as we woke up, every night as we lay down to sleep, we cursed Death who had vainly beckoned us to his mighty banquet. And each of us envied the dead. They were at rest beneath the soil, and next spring violets would grow from their bones. But we returned home, fruitless and inconsolable, crippled, a generation dedicated to death, by death disdained.

Joseph Roth, *The Emperor's Tomb*

CHAPTER ONE

Siblings

Stockholm, 1925. Hermann Goering, future head of the Nazi war economy, commander-in-chief of the Luftwaffe and chosen successor to Adolf Hitler, was a morphine addict and refugee from German justice. His chances of recovery depended on his Swedish wife, Karin. Her wealthy family had agreed to pay for his treatment at a private clinic. After attacking a nurse he was put in a straitjacket and deposited in a lunatic asylum. There was no guarantee he would see the outside world again. However, with Karin at his side, he quit the morphine and regained his health.

This was significant, not only for the Nazi movement but also for his brother Albert. Two years Hermann's junior, Albert loathed Hitler from day one. Had Hermann not achieved immense power, Albert's feelings about the Nazis would have had little consequence. As it was, he saved hundreds, perhaps thousands of people across Europe from persecution, spending nearly a decade working against his brother's regime, rescuing humble shopkeepers and heads of state, running escape routes, hauling prisoners out of concentration camps, influencing policy and assisting the Resistance.

But none of this would have been possible without Hermann. During preparations for the Nuremberg trials, Albert informed his sceptical Allied interrogators that, 'Hermann Goering often saved his life and never tried to curtail his Samaritan activities, only cautioning him to have some consideration for his position.'[1]

* * *

On 8 May 1945, as the Second World War ground to a halt, Albert Goering walked into the Allied Command Centre in Salzburg and was immediately detained by the Americans. They had located a base there in response to rumours that German troops might attempt to regroup in that mountainous region and launch a rearguard action. Large numbers of soldiers were fleeing in that direction seeking safety, clogging roads already jammed with civilian refugees.

Among their number was Hermann Goering, who had set off towards inevitable capture in the style of a warlord embarking on a triumphal procession through his homeland. Surrounded by his close family and attendants, sporting his array of medals, trailing a conspicuous amount of luggage, he passed through the throngs of defeated and dispossessed, their morale momentarily lifted by the sight of the Reichsmarschall in all his brazen glory, seemingly unaffected by the disasters that had befallen him. Some 30 kilometres south of Salzburg, he was taken into custody by First Lieutenant Jerome N. Shapiro. The young American officer could not believe his luck. He had been fruitlessly scouring the region only to run into Hermann, full of bonhomie and delighted to be arrested.

When Albert turned himself in a few hours earlier he was seriously ill. Suffering from inflammation and swelling of the liver, compounded by heart problems, he had dragged himself off his sick bed in order to fulfil what he considered to be his duty. As the brother of one of the most influential men in the Third Reich he believed it essential he set the record straight at the earliest opportunity.

Both brothers regarded the Americans as potential saviours. Neither felt guilty of any crimes and expected fair treatment. They were equally mistaken, failing to grasp the victors' determination to set a precedent for future conflicts. In Albert's case the miscalculation was understandable given that he had resisted the Nazis in any way he could. For Hermann it was symptomatic of the degree of delusion and denial he was capable of.

Their geographical proximity when arrested was an example of the strange synchronicity that existed between them. Despite having had no contact for months, no information about each other's whereabouts, or of their fate, both sought refuge in the familiar surroundings of their youth.

* * *

When Hermann Goering entered the world on 12 January 1893, his family had been in the service of the Prussian state for over 200 years. His earliest ancestor on record was an economic administrator for Frederick the Great. His father, Heinrich Goering, worked in the consular service. As a young man Heinrich had fought in the wars against the Austro-Hungarian Empire and the French which had made possible the unification of a disparate federation of states and principalities into a single Germany under the dominance of Prussia and its mercurial chancellor, Bismarck.

Its territorial integrity secure, the new Germany looked to expansion, eyeing jealously the global empires of its main rivals. The options available for realising Germany's imperial ambitions were already disappearing fast as its established competitors made their own headlong dash to wrest control of the remaining bits of the map from their indigenous populations. Africa was the focus of much of this attention, having only recently been opened up to the European.

The fear that Germany might miss out altogether was not shared by Bismarck, who was always suspicious of the actual value of colonies, having declared them to be 'good for nothing but supply stations'. But, ever the opportunist, in 1884 he seized a broad strip of West Africa, encompassing an area that today includes Namibia and Cameroon, on the flimsy pretext that Germany's main trading outlet at Angra Pequena needed some extra protection.

During the spring of 1885, Heinrich Goering was posted to Windhoek, designated capital of German South-West Africa. He was accompanied by his second wife, Fanny. His first wife had died not long before he had received the appointment, having borne him five children. Fanny, a mere nineteen years old, had captivated Heinrich with her startling blue eyes.

As Resident Minister, Heinrich was expected to create conditions under which Germans could prosper. First an accommodation had to be reached with the two dominant tribes in the region, the Herero and the Nam. Heinrich had no military support to speak of and therefore relied on their goodwill. They also controlled the cattle trade, which dominated economic activity in the province. Heinrich set about drawing up conditions that would respect their autonomy.

In exchange for the right to trade freely without harassment and control over foreign policy, Heinrich agreed to honour the sanctity of their laws, customs and property. These treaties helped secure peace for the rest of Heinrich's stay – not that this was entirely down to his efforts. The tribes were preoccupied with a long-running war between them, while the actual number of Germans in the colony remained tiny. In any case, much of the territory under Heinrich's management was nothing but desert. In effect he had very little to administer.

Then his young bride became pregnant. In hostile conditions of unbearable heat and dust, aggravated by poor sanitation, Fanny and her unborn child were at considerable risk. However, help was at hand. Offering good company, comfort, and his expert counsel was the doctor who became a formative influence on Hermann and Albert Goering, Hermann von Epenstein.

Epenstein was a charismatic, eligible bachelor from Berlin. Something of a playboy, he was an established figure on the international circuit that catered for the cream of European society – St Petersburg one week, Cairo the next. Though not conventionally handsome and given to corpulence, he had an imposing voice, extravagant clothing and dashing demeanour, described as 'swashbuckling'. In acknowledgement of his service to the crown as Prussian court physician he had been ennobled, signified by the addition of 'von' to his name.

Not long after the birth, the Goerings returned to Europe. Sources suggest Heinrich's departure was less than dignified. Though he had an agreement with the Herero tribe, their chief was in secret dialogue with the British in the Cape, who were keen to destabilise this new German dominion on their doorstep. With no garrison of any kind and threatened with revolt, Heinrich allegedly fled with his tail between his legs.[2]

Increased German involvement in the region, combined with crude racist attitudes, eventually caused the Herero people to rise up. In 1904, the German Army launched an extermination campaign against them: 'Within the German boundaries every Herero, whether found armed or unarmed, with or without cattle, will be shot.'[3] This order from General von Trotha drove the Herero into the deserts, cutting off their food and water supplies. Having left sufficient time for them to die of 'natural' causes, troops were sent in to finish off the survivors.

* * *

Heinrich's diplomatic career had reached a critical juncture. His next appointment, a posting to Haiti, was a definite step down. Haiti had been in Germany's sphere of influence for centuries as a minor trading centre and there was some talk of it as a springboard into South America, but formal occupation was ruled out and policy was restricted to occasional sabre-rattling in defence of German interests. The job was an exercise in killing time.

Once again his young wife packed her bags for a tropical destination. While they were there Hermann was conceived. For health reasons Fanny went home and booked into the exclusive Marienbad clinic. A couple of days after Hermann was born Epenstein arrived to check on their progress. Within a week he had decided to become Hermann's godfather. Fanny rejoined her husband and Hermann was left in the care of a Bavarian family in the small town of Fürth.

Three years later, Heinrich had completed his duties in Haiti and faced the prospect of early retirement. His finances were in a poor condition. Civil service pay was meagre in comparison to other professions. To serve the state was reward enough. His reunited family based themselves in Berlin. It was here that Heinrich began to unravel. He began drinking heavily to dispel the melancholia that enveloped him. Just fifty-six, he appeared much older.

Epenstein took this as his cue to ride to the rescue. He offered to take the whole family under his wing and provide for their needs. Whether his generosity was prompted by the start of his affair with Fanny, is hard to establish. It did coincide with the birth of Albert Goering in March 1895. This inevitably raises the question: was Epenstein Albert's biological father?

The consensus of many who knew them was that Albert was Epenstein's son. They cite the facial resemblance between them – both were dark haired and shared a Central European physiognomy while Hermann was fair and blue eyed – and the glaring differences in personality between the brothers.

For Hermann and Albert it was never an issue. Both were well aware of the nature of their godfather's relationship with their mother. As a close family friend observed, 'Everyone accepted the situation and it did not seem to trouble Hermann or Albert at all.'[4] As far as they were concerned they were united as siblings. Even years later, when it would have been incredibly convenient for Albert to claim his 'real' lineage, he resolutely stuck with the Goering name.

* * *

Epenstein divided his time between two medieval castles. Castle Veldenstein was a stone fortress built on a cliff high above Neuhaus, a beer-producing town about forty kilometres north of Nuremberg. The original buildings may well have been constructed as early as 918 but the castle only entered the historical record in 1269. Epenstein bought it in 1897 for 20,000 marks. He spent the next seventeen years and 1.5 million marks restoring its former splendour. Today the castle is host to a successful hotel and restaurant business.

His other acquisition was Castle Mauterndorf, built around the end of the first millennium, former home of the local feudal lord, situated to the south of Salzburg and just east of Innsbruck. An imposing structure, set deep in the mountains, the castle towers over the small village that carries its name. Epenstein took over in 1894 and began redecorating. Nowadays the castle is a medieval theme park, with its own tour guides and adventure activities.

The Goering family went back and forth between both castles, often having Veldenstein to themselves for long periods. At Mauterndorf, Epenstein installed them in lodgings built in the grounds. They were free to roam except when Epenstein entertained visitors. Then only Fanny was allowed to show her face, taking the part of lady of the manor, which in effect she was, while the others remained elsewhere. She would then retire to Epenstein's bedchamber and not return to her family until the next morning.

Given that Epenstein's lavish dinner parties were almost a nightly occurrence, this embargo made Heinrich a virtual exile. He retreated further into depression and alcoholism, resigned to the fact that his wife was his benefactor's mistress. At a glance it seems odd that there was not some kind of scandal. The rise of mass media had created a public arena for salacious gossip, and tales of the sexual misdemeanours of the ruling class were guaranteed to shift newspapers. The courts then dealt with the sensational litigation that followed the headlines.

Prince Philip Eulenberg, former ambassador to Vienna and one of the Kaiser's closest friends, was accused by a newspaper of being part of a homosexual clique that operated at the highest level of society. The libel trial lasted two years, 1907–9, and held the nation's interest every sordid step of the way. It revealed, among other things, details of orgies held at an elite cavalry officers' club in Berlin. The Goerings were spared this kind of indignity. Their domestic arrangement barely raised an eyebrow.

Epenstein, Fanny and Heinrich maintained their masquerade for nearly fourteen years. Then, in 1912, Epenstein fell hopelessly in love with Fraulein Lilli, an engaging beauty in her twenties who knew exactly how to twist him round her little finger. At sixty-three years old the confirmed bachelor was ready to marry. Lilli left him little choice, refusing to succumb until her wedding night. Heinrich and Fanny were unceremoniously ejected from their quarters in the spring of 1913, the old man mumbling darkly about this 'betrayal of friendship'.

At the time Hermann was nineteen and Albert seventeen. Neither boy was there to witness the end of the affair. Hermann had just received a regimental commission and Albert was away at school. A few months later Heinrich died. He was already ailing and the shock of moving to a rented house in Munich in such degrading circumstances was enough to kill him. He was buried in the grand Waldfriedhof cemetery.

Though there was some bitterness felt towards Epenstein in the immediate aftermath, particularly by Hermann, the family crisis was quickly overshadowed by the advent of the First World War. The damage was soon repaired. Lilli was just as keen as Epenstein to maintain contact with his godchildren. When Hermann was granted convalescent leave from his fighter squadron in 1916 he chose to spend it at Mauterndorf.

* * *

Though not born to it, Epenstein flaunted his newly earned aristocratic pedigree with all the energetic enthusiasm of a self-made man who had reinvented himself in the pursuit of respectability. For Epenstein was Jewish. This was not an absolute block on advancement, but Epenstein still decided to become a Roman Catholic.

The pitfalls of being a successful Jew were exemplified by the life of the financier Bleichröder. As Bismarck's personal banker he helped pay for the wars that delivered unification and, in 1872, was the first Jew ever to add the coveted 'von' to his name. Bleichröder also backed Bismarck's overseas expeditions. In 1885, at the same time that Heinrich Goering was Resident Minister in Windhoek, Bleichröder set up the German South-West African Colonial Company to handle commerce in the region. However, his wealth left him open to bribery. A legal battle that lasted throughout the 1880s began with an accusation by a wronged mistress, who felt entitled to a share of his fortune. She took him to court. The case was dismissed but the scandal sheets got a whiff of it and made sure the whole thing snowballed into an anti-semitic witch hunt, orchestrated by state officials who wanted to charge Bleichröder with perjury. Though he avoided another trial, the mud-slinging continued right up to his death in 1893.

Epenstein side-stepped such prejudice and was not alone in seeking total assimilation, despite legislation passed in 1871 that removed the last legal restraints on the Jewish community in Germany, which then numbered around 600,000 people, about 1 per cent of the population. During the nineteenth century over 22,000 converted to Christianity. Epenstein never looked back. He remained a dedicated Roman Catholic for the rest of his life, making great show of his devotion.

Though the Goerings were Protestant, the brothers' main exposure to the ritual of weekly worship was through Epenstein. Every Sunday, either at Mauterndorf or Veldenstein, he led a parade of pious observance, taking his extended family and guests to Mass at the village church where rows of pews were reserved for them. Hermann had little interest in religion. He paid his respects to a generic God and avoided churches. A British Tory MP later observed that, 'There is something un-Christian about Goering, a strong pagan streak.'[5] Sentenced to death at Nuremberg, Hermann did not seek absolution from the prison chaplain, or forgiveness from the Almighty. Instead he 'launched into a tirade on the homosexuality of the Catholic clergy', and the affairs of 'the priests and the nuns. The nuns are "brides of Christ" you know, what a set up!'[6] Albert took religion seriously and grew up to adopt a broad spiritual awareness based on tolerance and fundamental humanism: 'I am a Protestant by confession, but I have been in Orthodox churches, in synagogues, I have been to Buddhist and Brahmin services, and it does not make any difference to me. There is only one God.'[7]

* * *

Daily life at Mauterndorf resembled that of a medieval court. The castle staff were expected to bow and scrape before their master. The arrival of food was signalled by a blast on a hunting horn. On special occasions Epenstein would hire a band of minstrels and musicians to play in the gallery of the main hall. He strode round his domain wearing regal costume, issuing commands, laying down the law: 'We had to stand to attention while he was talking to us and we were not allowed to address him without permission.'[8]

Hermann was seven when his family moved to this world of turrets and dungeons, and already obsessed by tales of ancient Germanic heroes and their exploits. The dramatic setting made a lasting impression on him; as his sister Olga remarked years later, 'You must come and see Castle Veldenstein, then you will understand him better.'[9] He quickly took to re-enacting skirmishes with Roman legions.

Epenstein encouraged Hermann's natural inclination towards adventure. When he was only five Epenstein gave him a hussar's uniform. As soon as Hermann was old enough to hold a gun he joined Epenstein on hunting trips into the forests to stalk game. He was a natural, and in later years, when he had the necessary power and wealth, he would indulge his passion for the sport on a grand scale.

Hermann was also a particularly fearless climber, intent on scaling the area's most dangerous peaks. Aged ten he took on the sheer cliff face that Castle Veldenstein had been carved out of. Three years later he reached the peak of the 3,800-metre-high Gross Glockner by the most hazardous route available. Hermann showed a barely concealed contempt for the risks involved: 'I have no fear of heights. They stimulate me. Besides, any danger is worthwhile if you reach the top of the mountain. You know you will have a view few men will ever see.'[10]

In 1906, aged thirteen, Hermann was enrolled at Karlsruhe military academy, after Epenstein had pulled a few strings to get him into this exclusive training camp. The Army was virtually a state within a state, commanding huge respect and influence. Though the Army had doubled in size between 1880 and 1913, the aristocracy's monopoly on leadership remained intact. On the eve of the First World War, 48 per cent of all German infantry officers were nobles. This proportion rose to 80 per cent in the cavalry. By securing a place for Hermann at the academy Epenstein had given him the best possible start towards a distinguished career. Hermann repaid his efforts by excelling. He became an 'exemplary pupil'. An unruly, difficult child in all the conventional schools he had attended, Hermann had finally found an environment which inspired him and drove him to achieve.

At sixteen he had no problem graduating to the elite Gross-Lichterfelde officer cadet school after getting excellent grades in all his academic subjects and displaying leadership qualities. In his final report it was noted that Hermann had 'developed a quality that should take him far: he is not afraid to take risks'.[11] When he left he was able confidently to say, 'I am the inheritor of all the chivalry of German knighthood.'[12]

Hermann was referring to the period of expansion masterminded by the Teutonic knights. This holy order was a contemporary of the Templars and the Knights of Malta. Organised around a hard core of military monks, the knights spread from their power base in southern Germany through pagan Prussia and into the Baltic States. During the thirteenth and fourteenth centuries they waged a succession of wars to consolidate and extend their gains, defended by a network of castles and fortifications. Christian knights, landowners and merchants were drafted in to assist the monks as they imposed their social organisation on the natives. Their armies were constantly replenished by crusaders, mercenaries, robber barons and peasant conscripts. The Teutonic knights fell from grace at the Battle of Tannenberg, 15 July 1410, annihilated by a combined force of Poles and Lithuanians. As a military outfit they were finished. Deprived of further support for their endless war, the order withered away, only to be resurrected as one of the most potent ingredients of German nationalism. The defeat at Tannenberg became a pivotal moment in the collective memory.

In late August 1914 the Teutonic knights were finally avenged by a week-long counter-offensive against Russian armies that had advanced to the German border near the scene of the monks' original downfall. The onslaught broke the Russian line and it collapsed. The tsar's troops were surrounded and crushed as they tried to retreat. Such was the scale of the triumph that the German generals, Hindenburg and Ludendorff, were quick to give this series of battles a suitable name: Tannenberg.

The original battle continued to exert a hold on the German psyche. In 1927 a memorial was raised in honour of the fallen knights at a massive ceremony with speeches broadcast on the radio. It was attended by a crowd of military and political figures, including Hindenburg, who was by then president of Germany. When Hindenburg died in 1934, Hitler insisted that he was buried at the site of his most famous triumph.

To establish feudal rule across the lands of their historic enemies, purged of all undesirables, was a cherished dream of the Nazi faithful. Alfred Rosenberg, the movement's self-appointed philosopher, wrote in his theoretical tome *Der Mythus* about the need for 'an association of men, on the lines of the Teutonic Order'.[13] Hitler first expressed his ideas on the subject in the second edition of *Mein Kampf*: 'We take up where we broke off 600 years ago. We stop the endless German movement to the south and the west, and turn our gaze to the east.'[14]

In 1913, ready and willing to lay down his life for the Fatherland and hoping to die a warrior's death, Hermann joined the Prinz Wilhelm Infantry Regiment. A year later he wrote in a letter to his sisters, 'If war breaks out you can be sure I will do credit to our name.'[15]

* * *

Albert was a shy, introverted, sensitive child, given easily to tears. These were not attributes that appealed to Epenstein. Aged five, Albert was sent to a boarding school in Hersbruck to toughen him up. A young man was expected to have steel in him. At a time when over 95 per cent of German children ended their formal education at the age of eleven, Albert started attending a Realschule in Munich, a specialist form of grammar school that concentrated on scientific and technical training. The Realschulen were linked to Technische Hochschulen, tertiary level institutes with a strong reputation for academic and research excellence. By the late nineteenth century there were twelve Technische Hoch-schulen across Germany. Their syllabuses were geared to the needs of industry, which had quickly recognised that technological innovation, and therefore scientific education, was the key to future prosperity and success in the world economy. Each Technische Hochschule was connected to a major firm which recruited directly from the student ranks. Most courses offered on-the-job training. As long as Albert did well at Realschule he would join this new elite. Though not quite as prestigious as a military career, his chosen path was no less respectable and potentially more lucrative.

Albert was a competent, if unexceptional student. Alongside his school work, he showed enthusiasm for arts and culture. His interest was met with approval by Epenstein who believed that an appreciation of the finer things in life was vital. Even Hermann, who had no particular aptitude, developed a well-trained eye: 'I never could paint or draw but from my earliest youth I was an emphatic lover of art. I liked bright colours such as blue, red and green.'[16]

Albert had a real talent for music. He was a decent pianist with a good singing voice. He shared this love with Epenstein, as did a great number of Germans. Music was everywhere, with opera houses, concert halls, academies and orchestral societies in every major town. It was a national hobby that bordered on an obsession. Albert was allowed to join Epenstein for late-night recitals at the piano where they would romp through entire operas. Albert's affection for an impromptu sing-a-long stayed with him forever.

The count was a big Wagner fan and made sure he always had excellent seats at Bayreuth, not far from Castle Veldenstein, where regular festivals dedicated to the composer took place. These were gala nights. The cult of Wagner attracted the great and good from across Europe. The young Albert would have watched sparkling carriages pull up and unload their gilded cargo – women in their extravagant finery escorted by their impeccably suited companions. The spectacle continued inside the auditorium. Performances were enlivened by spectacular sets and stunts. During some productions a real horse frolicked on stage.

Music was not their only mutual passion. Albert grew up to have a similar attitude to the opposite sex to that of his mentor. Though discreet, Epenstein was an inveterate womaniser. If a lady took his fancy he would woo her, regardless of his other commitments. He had an excellent bedside manner. How much of this he consciously passed on to Albert is difficult to gauge, as is the degree to which Albert absorbed his methods of seduction. What cannot be disputed is Albert's own varied and busy sexual history. Married four times, he was a consummate ladies' man: 'He loved to have nice women around him. Everybody had a crush on him.'[17]

* * *

Hermann's and Albert's education was designed to instil core values in them that represented the moral currency of the majority of society, regardless of class, and informed the consensus of what constituted a decent citizen. Loyalty, duty, honour, a willingness to serve the greater good, selfless courage in the face of adversity: these were virtues to be exercised with absolute conviction.

The importance European civilisation placed on these notions of duty and unquestioning obedience was evident in the response that greeted the opening of hostilities in 1914. Though many were nervous at the prospect of war and the left was quick to voice its concerns, there was little organised resistance. The call to arms was answered in droves. A patriotic war was, by definition, a just one. The bonds of loyalty that wed the masses to their leaders' suicidal policies held firm.

The code that nourished this commitment to arms was found wanting and inadequate when subjected to the horrors of industrialised, mass produced warfare. All the countries involved experienced serious repercussions.

Imperial Germany was already riven by contradictions. The ruling elite clung to the old verities and extolled them in the face of huge technological, demographic, material, political and intellectual challenges, whilst trying to exploit these for their own benefit and preservation.

The degree, scale and speed of transformation was unprecedented. Between 1870 and 1913 the German population grew by 25 million. This increase was concentrated in urban areas. While 64 per cent of Germans had lived in small rural communities of fewer than 5,000 people at the time of unification, by 1910 this figure had dropped to 40 per cent. During the same time cities and towns with over 100,000 citizens had gone from only 5 per cent of the population to 21 per cent. The social landscape of Germany had irrevocably changed.

This process was driven by economic revolution. In 1872 Germany's GNP stood at 16 billion marks. By 1913 it had leapt to 55 billion. Agriculture was overtaken by industry. The factory worker replaced the field hand. Such a momentous shift reconfigured the division of labour and led to the thorough commercialisation and capitalisation of business practices and the emergence of a well organised working class. The aristocracy were reluctantly obliged to accommodate middle-class aspirations and relax the rules of membership.

Epenstein was as much a product of these upheavals as he was a throwback to days of yore. The very forces that threatened to topple the established order were responsible for his rise through the ranks. The loosening of feudal ties and obligations increased social mobility. Epenstein abandoned his Jewish roots and secured his status. Like many who travel upwards he had little time for reflecting on the journey. The fact that he was only able to assume the lifestyle of a medieval lord because he seized on the possibilities that modernity offered was an irony completely lost on him.

His spirited example was followed by Hermann: 'I have come to the conclusion that there was no difference between myself as a boy and as a man. I believe that the boy had all the markings which later on appeared in the man.'[18] However, as a prominent Nazi, Hermann saw fit to erase Epenstein from any discussions of his childhood. Though he inherited both Veldenstein and Mauterndorf castles, he was not prepared to publicly admit that his patron and mentor was a Jew as defined by the anti-semitic laws he had put his signature on.

Albert's professional life was quiet, conservative and uncontroversial. Only when his brother's political party set about destroying everything he believed in did Albert reveal the extent of his personal courage, conviction and incorruptibility: 'When Goering was asked why he undertook all this assistance to the Jews and other victims of Nazi persecution he replied that he was completely disinterested in politics, that he loathed all oppression and tyranny, and that he was doing in some small way, everything in his power to atone for the evil and brutality of his brother and all the leaders of the Nazi regime.'[19]

CHAPTER TWO

Cataclysm

By winter 1914 the Western Front had already solidified into the shape it would stay in, with only minute variation, until the last few months of the Great War. The British and French Armies had established a line of defence stretching from the Belgian coast to the Swiss mountains after managing to halt a massive offensive by the Germans which had been intended to end the conflict swiftly. The Germans dug in opposite them. Four years of trench warfare lay ahead, four years of mind-numbing slaughter.

In the early days of the war the pilots of the fledgling German Army Air Service were drawn largely from the cavalry corps and represented the social elite of the army. Their primary strategic function was reconnaissance, providing aerial photos of enemy positions and troop concentrations. Their daring caught the imagination of many, including Hermann. In the early days of the war his infantry regiment was stationed at Mülhausen (Mulhouse) on the Rhine, away from the main action. Having endured several weeks in cold, damp trenches, he was struck down with rheumatic fever and transferred to a hospital in Freiburg to convalesce. While there he met Bruno Lörzer, who was at air training school, and they embarked on a life-long friendship.

Erich Gritzbach wrote the 'authorised' biography of Hermann in 1938 with his subject's full cooperation. Gritzbach became Hermann's creature in the early 1930s, when he was private secretary to Franz von Papen, an establishment figure who considered himself a potential dictator of Germany. As Papen put it, 'Gritzbach . . . very soon joined the "winning side" and deferred to Goering more than he did to me. His reward was that he continued to remain in office for many years.'[1] In his book, Gritzbach described how Hermann joined the air service by stealing a plane and becoming attached to a squadron by default, only narrowly escaping a court martial. This story has since given rise to a slightly watered-down account that sees him effectively desert, though not by flying away, and evading a custodial sentence thanks only to the intervention of Epenstein.[2]

Military records reflect a more mundane reality. Hermann's initial request to join the air service was successful, helped no doubt by a recommendation from his new comrade Bruno Lörzer. By the end of October 1914 Hermann was on an observer training course with the 3rd Army Air Detachment. Once he had taken to the skies, he never looked back.

* * *

While a struggle of pitiless attrition was being waged on the ground, another, apparently more glamorous, battle was soon being conducted in the skies above. For the generals and politicians it was hard to create popular heroes out of the men in the trenches, whose countless acts of bravery, dragging a comrade to safety, clearing a trench, leading a frontal assault on a machine-gun nest, diminished in meaning against the sheer scale of the conflict and the catastrophic number of casualties. This lent a certain anonymity to the front-line infantryman or gunner. He was just one of a multitude. All the main combatants erected monuments in honour of the Unknown Soldier, marking the extent to which the heroes of the trenches remained nameless. By contrast, the air war was perfectly suited to creating legends.

High in the clouds the airmen manoeuvred against each other, machine guns blazing as they went head to head, close enough to see the expression on the enemy's face. They needed lightning-quick reflexes and nerves of steel. They had to contend with terrible weather, deal with faulty equipment and mechanical malfunctions, and face the ever-present threat of burning to death: 'If the fuel tank is punctured and the stuff squirts around the legs, the danger of fire is great . . . one drop and the whole machine will burn.'[3]

The extreme peril attracted mavericks and colourful personalities, which, added to the visual spectacle of the dog-fight, gave this form of warfare a powerful allure. It was quickly likened to medieval jousting. The pilots became knights who fought according to the rules of chivalry. To a population spoon-fed and reared on tales of old Germanic heroes this was inspiring stuff. This image of noble sparring between medieval lords was encouraged by the media: 'We perceive very strongly how much the old knightly gallantry has come alive again in the conduct of modern aerial combat.'[4]

In the spring of 1915 a French engineer fitted an aircraft with interrupter gear, which allowed bullets from a fuselage-mounted machine gun to pass between the blades of the propeller. A young Dutch engineer, Anthony Fokker, was convinced he could improve on the French design. He demonstrated his plane, equipped with rapid-firing machine guns, to the German Army on 15 May 1915, after lunch at a nearby château with a group of young pilots, one of whom was Hermann Goering.

* * *

Throughout the war, the Western Front was convulsed by a series of huge battles. Up to 1918 the onus remained on the Allies to attack, the Germans to defend. The aim was to smash the enemy's line by the sheer weight of assault, the concentration of men and firepower. This thinking applied increasingly to the air war.

The immediate effect was a reorganisation of the German Air Force. 1916 saw the formation of specialist fighter units, Jagdstaffeln, known as Jastas, which became attached to areas of the front in order to support the operations down below. An elite unit was set up for combat fighters, comprising men from Jastas 1 and 2. Minor skirmishes were replaced by battles between large formations of planes.

This only served to accelerate the arms race in design and manufacture. An interlocking process of increased production and expanding, multiplying squadrons – by spring 1917 there were thirty-five Jastas in the skies – meant casualties at an increased rate and continuous missions, day after day, for months on end. During the Battle of the Somme in 1916, the British lost 308 pilots. German losses were similarly severe. In 1917 this carnage was repeated again and again.

German industry struggled to keep pace. While Germany made 45,704 aircraft between 1914 and 1918, the British were able to produce 55,061. Take into account the French total of 52,146 and then add the potential of American factories, especially after the US entered the war in April 1917, and it is clear that the German air force was fighting an uphill struggle. Nevertheless, 800 of the new Fokker DVIIs, considered to be the best all-round fighter of the war, joined the last great offensives in 1918. Between 21 March and 29 April 1918, the Jastas destroyed 1,302 British aircraft. By then, what may have started as an 'honourable' contest between a small band of 'knights' had ended up as a relentless cull, another cog in a war machine that devoured men by the thousands. Chivalry was no longer an issue: 'War is not as the people at home imagine it, with a hurrah and a roar: it is very serious, very grim.'[5]

Nevertheless, compared to the slog of the trenches, the diving, swooping men in their brightly coloured flying machines remained highly appealing. The German war leaders desperately needed heroes to lift the morale of their troops. The fighter aces supplied that boost: 'When I fly out over the fortified trenches and the soldiers shout joyfully . . . often they forget all danger, jump out on the roofing, swing their rifles and wave at me.'[6] They also offered hope to the embattled home front, enduring economic deprivations, unprecedented social upheaval and the loss of loved ones. After 1916 the Allied blockade of Germany bit hard. Even the most basic foodstuffs, such as potatoes, were in desperately short supply: 'Hunger destroyed our solidarity; the children stole each other's rations.'[7] It is estimated that by the end of the war nearly half a million civilians had died due to dietary restrictions. In these increasingly harsh conditions, the exploits of dashing young pilots were seized upon as proof of Germany's inevitable victory.

Consequently a successful flyer had the world at his feet. He had access to the highest tier of German society and was honoured accordingly. He became a household name, celebrated wherever he went, front page news. Manfred von Richthofen, the infamous Red Baron, set the bar. Hermann aspired to that level of fame and nearly reached it. As far as his fellow Germans were concerned, he was cut from the same cloth and merited his share of hero worship.

Richthofen came from a long established family. His forebears were feudal lords who entered the Prussian aristocracy in the eighteenth century. His father had been a major in the cavalry. Hermann's father, Heinrich Goering, was also in the cavalry but of lower rank, because his ancestors carried less social clout. Aged five, Richthofen was packed off to an elite cadet academy, once attended by the infant Hindenburg. Hermann kicked his heels in a regular classroom. In 1909, Richthofen went to the Gross-Lichterfelde military school, the same one Hermann attended thanks to his godfather's influence. When Richthofen graduated he was privileged enough to go into a cavalry regiment. Hermann went into the infantry.

Richthofen shared Hermann's youthful passion for hunting. His mother claimed he shot his grandmother's ducks dead with his first rifle and his skill as a marksman translated into combat. He experienced the 'same feeling in the moment when the bull came at me, the same hunting fever that grips me when I sit in an aeroplane and see an Englishman'.[8] This rush peaked at the moment of victory: 'My heart beats a little faster when the opponent, whose face I have just seen, goes roaring down from 4,000 metres.'[9]

Richthofen's cavalry regiment was sent to the Eastern Front, where the vast, open plains left some scope for horses, before being transferred to the west. It was here he began his pilot training in May 1915, just a month before Hermann. Since joining his friend Bruno's unit as an observer in October 1914 and flying reconnaissance missions over the French fortress at Verdun, Hermann had made a name for himself. While Bruno was in the pilot's seat, Hermann was in charge of taking the photographs of the French positions. Flying very low, with soldiers on the ground shooting at him, Hermann would literally hang out of the plane to take the snaps, earning the nickname 'the trapezist'. Such was the quality of the pictures Hermann and Bruno provided that they were awarded the prestigious Iron Cross First Class on 25 March 1915. The Iron Cross had been introduced by the Prussian king during the Napoleonic Wars. It was designed to resemble the black cross on white background that was the symbol of the Teutonic knights, worn on their shields and tunics, flying from their pendants, as they went into battle.

Meanwhile Richthofen's career took off. Oswald Boelcke, one of the first flying aces and the brains behind German fighter tactics, became his mentor. By spring 1916 Richthofen was leading the fight against the British air offensive. During that summer and autumn he notched up fifteen kills. In 1917 he downed forty-eight planes. By then he was internationally renowned and a domestic superstar. His total number of Allied scalps stood at eighty when he was shot down and killed on 21 April 1918.

Hermann's record was modest in comparison, adding up to only a quarter of Richthofen's tally. Training complete, he joined Jasta 5 in October 1915. On 16 November he gained his first official kill. After the winter break, when weather made flying nigh on impossible, fighting began in earnest. By June 1916 his total had risen to three. Days later he was lucky to escape with his life when a Sopwith fighter attacked his plane. The wing was damaged and the fuel tank hit. Hermann had a bullet lodged in his thigh, which had splintered the bone. He was forced to crash-land in a cemetery. Fractions of inches and fractions of seconds decided Hermann's fate. Somehow he survived.

His injuries did put him out of action until the following spring, the first six months in hospital, the rest convalescing at Epenstein's Castle Mauterndorf. On his return he was posted to Jasta 26, which was under the command of good old Bruno Lörzer. During the Bloody April of 1917, that bled on throughout the summer, Hermann was in the thick of it. His reputation grew and he was promoted to command the newly formed Jasta 27. Between April and November he recorded a further thirteen victories and joined a handful of pilots who basked in the glow of Richthofen's fame.

1917 was a stellar year for the Red Baron. He was awarded Germany's most coveted medal, the so-called Blue Max. He became the centrepiece of a propaganda campaign to lift the nation's flagging spirits. He was given a substantial commission to write his memoirs by a Berlin publisher, and a stenographer to help type it. *Der Rote Kampfflieger* ('The Red Battle Flyer') came out that year. In 1918 his diaries were published posthumously. Other books compiling Richthofen's thoughts followed. They were all reissued during the Nazi years.

Postcard manufacturers mass-produced collectible portraits of the top aces for an eager market. A card autographed by one of these heroes could sell for hundreds of marks. Everywhere the Red Baron went he was mobbed. Crowds met him at railway stations and followed him down the street. He received honours from the kingdoms of Saxony, Bavaria and Württemberg, to name a few. He was even granted the privilege of hunting the rare European bison on the private estates of one of Germany's richest landowners. This immense wildlife reserve would become one of Hermann's private playgrounds after he became Master of the German Forests and Master of the Hunt in 1934.

Though Hermann may not have been exposed to the degree of adulation that Richthofen was, he still benefited from the limelight.

There were postcards with his face on them too. He was featured in magazine articles, his exploits reported in the press. He moved with ease in similarly elite circles, a regular in the officers' mess reserved for royalty. He relished dressing up and going on show. He was slim and handsome, with magnetic blue eyes that he had inherited from his mother. He had considerable charm and charisma. A member of the Prussian royal family wrote in his memoirs that Hermann 'displayed conspicuous dash and zeal'.[10]

Hermann enjoyed a raucous party as much as a genteel dinner. Lavish events were laid on at the best hotels for the pilots' entertainment by the aeroplane manufacturers: 'What they wanted most, and what we tried to give them, was gaiety, charm, diversion, the society of pretty girls, the kind of good time they had been dreaming about.'[11] Richthofen was uncomfortable at these events, anxious to get back to the world he understood: 'One could see that he was a front line soldier not a courtier.'[12] This assessment was echoed by his mother: 'He longed for the din of the propeller, the laughter of the machine gun . . . that was his nature.'[13] He had a pragmatic attitude to flying a plane. It was a means to an end, not an end in itself: 'As for flying . . . he did not care much for it. He has never made a loop out of sheer joy of sport.' It was strictly forbidden for his pilots to indulge in any 'acrobatic tricks'.[14]

Hermann, on the other hand, loved the buzz he got soaring above the clouds: 'I seem to come alive when I am up in the air and looking down at the earth. I feel like a little God.'[15] He became a skilled exponent of aerial gymnastics. After the war he briefly made his living as a dare-devil stunt pilot. Even so, he was not irresponsible in the line of duty. Richthofen wanted to 'draw a line between daring and stupidity', otherwise a brave but hot-headed pilot might 'pay for his stupidity with his life'.[16] The efficient fighter must be cold and calculating. He may have admired 'splendid daring', but he did not endorse it.

Hermann followed these principles to the letter. His official mission reports bear witness to his sober attitude. Here he is describing an apparent victory, 'I immediately closed in on the nearest hostile and loosed off a few short bursts at it. I then attacked the second Nieuport, which suddenly lost height and made off at low altitude', or reflecting on a near disaster, 'The Englishmen attacked me and shot out my rudder . . . I could not see what happened then as I had my hands full flying my plane without a rudder.'[17] This modest language is light years away from the kind of egomaniacal boasting that became second nature to Hermann the Nazi warlord.

As the war entered its final year, the Red Baron could not envisage a life for himself beyond the battlefield: 'I myself cannot think of a more beautiful death than to fall in aerial combat.'[18] Eventually he got his wish. Having crashed behind enemy lines he was buried by the Allies with full military honours. In 1925 his remains were returned to Germany and reburied at a formal state funeral in Berlin. Thousands came out to escort the coffin from the train station.

* * *

By the summer of 1918 Hermann had added a host of medals to his Iron Cross, including the Zahring Lion with Swords, the Karl Friedrich Order with Swords and the Hohenzollern Medal with Swords. Most important of all, for his prestige and public image, he was awarded the coveted Ordre Pour le Mérite, the Blue Max, by the Kaiser on 2 June 1918.

Not only did winning this medal guarantee a place in the hall of fame, it also meant access to the best and newest planes. In the early years of the air war eight kills were needed to win it. By 1918 a pilot needed twenty. Just over a month after Hermann had received this accolade he took over command of the Red Baron's Jasta 1. But he was not first in line. Von Reinhardt had that honour. Both men were involved in a series of test flights of new fighter designs in front of the top brass. On the agenda was an experimental biplane. Hermann could not resist trying it out. He did so in spectacular fashion. Reinhardt, not wishing to be outdone, took the plane up. It crashed and Reinhardt was killed instantly. Hermann was appointed as his replacement.

There was discontent in the noble ranks of Jasta 1 when the word came from on high that Hermann was their new commander. The source of this latent hostility was undoubtedly social snobbery. Hermann was seen as lacking in real pedigree, an 'upstart', an 'outsider'. His patron, Epenstein, may have been a count, his father a career diplomat, but he was of lower status than the majority of his comrades.

His first address to the squadron set exactly the right tone, 'I am sensible to the fact that there are no better fliers in the world than those I see before me now. I hope I shall be worthy of your confidence and your trust', ending on this sombre note, 'We will need to give our best, all of us, for there are grave times ahead. We will face them together for the glory of the Fatherland.'[19]

But the sniping continued, stimulated by the intensely competitive atmosphere the fighter pilots operated in. To be credited with a kill there needed to be some sort of independent confirmation. This was not easily done in the heat of battle. Interception of enemy communications provided some reliable figures, but there remained inevitable discrepancies and inconsistency. Such was the importance of getting a confirmation that Richthofen, whenever possible, followed his victim to the ground and collected a souvenir from the wreckage as proof positive.

Clearly there was room for exaggerated or false claims. Near-forensic examination of the available records indicates that, of the twenty-two kills recorded in Hermann's name, seven are highly questionable. At least three others are impossible to clarify. However, this was the norm rather than the exception. With promotions, medals and fame on offer, it was inevitable that a culture of casual deception flourished. Even the mighty Red Baron was subject to scrutiny and complaints that he took more than his fair share. Whatever the doubts, Hermann's 'knowledge of tactics was extensive' and he possessed the one essential characteristic shared by every ace: utter ruthlessness. Infinitesimal margins separated those who lived from those who died. There was no time for sentiment. Those lacking an element of cold-blooded cruelty were likely to perish fast.

Many people over the years would underestimate or not even recognise this ruthless streak in Hermann, often only realising too late his ability to act with great speed and brutality, to smile while organising a rival's downfall, with no hesitation or moral wrangling. He was able to project a bonhomie, a reasonableness, wear an accommodating demeanour that masked the killer instinct. As Albert Speer, the architect who took control of the Nazi war economy away from Hermann, confessed, 'I have to say that I too had a weak spot for Goering. I had known him as a charming and highly intelligent man ... more as an individualist, an eccentric, if you like, than as sick or evil.'[20]

Yet this duality between civilised sophisticate and heartless predator was a fundamental part of the day-to-day existence of a First World War German fighter pilot. For the necessary ruthlessness of these men was hidden behind the aristocratic codes of behaviour that permeated the squadrons, private clubs for gentlemen who abided by the 'ancient' rules of war and the etiquette of polite society. Hermann knew how to destroy another human being using the most advanced technology known to man by day and make the correct champagne toast at night.

* * *

While Hermann lived the high life, Albert Goering was having a very different kind of war. Called up in 1914, he found himself in a communications unit attached to an infantry division on the Western Front where he stayed until 1918 when he was shot in the stomach and invalided out of the army, having reached the rank of lieutenant. He was a technician in uniform, part of the support organisation behind the front line, operating just outside the main zone of battle, but still exposed to its dangers and sheer awfulness. Men like Albert were in constant demand, essential to the maintenance of trench warfare, educated, well-trained and hard to replace. Despite chronic manpower shortages at various key moments during the fighting, these units were only finally sacrificed by the German Army in the last months of the war.

As the deadlock on the Western Front persisted, tactics of defence in depth were developed. Two or three lines of trenches, separated by stretches of no-man's-land, heavily impregnated with barbed wire, formed the main barriers. A series of communication trenches then led back to the main command centres, often several miles away from the actual fighting. The size and complexity of the forces engaged, combined with the logistic requirements of mounting attacks and counter-attacks, meant that good, fast communications were essential. That the technology available was inadequate for the task was a major contributing factor to the problem neither side could resolve: how to turn a minor offensive advantage into a decisive victory. During the Battle of the Somme it took up to ten hours for a message to reach the front from the rear. This problem would consistently stall and limit progress. It also added to the pressures brought to bear on signals personnel like Albert.

At the time, radio was not yet sophisticated enough to relay voice messages. Flags were still used by the artillery divisions. Carrier pigeons did what they could. The bulk of information was conveyed by telegraph and telephone from army HQ to the trenches. In order to do this hundreds of kilometres of phone cable had to be laid to link the commanders with their men. At a safe distance from the enemy's artillery the cables could remain above ground. Once in range, the cables had to be buried up to two metres down. Much of the signal engineers' work was trying to keep this network up and running. The periodic lulls in fighting were the best time to carry out this mammoth task, even though engineers were still liable to be shot at by snipers.

During battle, cables were easily destroyed. They had to be mended as quickly as possible, even while the fighting raged, which meant dodging shells and bullets to try and do the repairs. Things were not much better for signalmen who sat in makeshift huts decoding and passing on instructions. They were also targets for artillery fire.

Albert may not have been a front-line soldier, but his duties brought him in close contact with the worst of the killing fields. He would have suffered similarly appalling conditions of flooded, vermin-infested quarters, witnessed first hand the obliteration of the countryside around him, a landscape stripped of all life, watched the daily convoy of corpses trundle by on carts.

* * *

When all else failed, or when a message was deemed too secret to risk broadcasting, runners were employed to pass them by hand. This was often akin to a suicide mission. These men were of the lower ranks, and often considered exceptionally brave. Hitler served as a runner continuously between 1914 and 1918 and was badly wounded three times. Nevertheless he regarded his years in the trenches as 'the greatest and most unforgettable time of my earthly existence'.[21]

It is unlikely Albert felt the same way about a conflict that left roughly two million Germans dead, and polarised the nation like nothing before, triggering collapse and civil war. Like his Allied counterpart, the German soldier found that his early enthusiasm was steadily replaced by grim despair, relieved only by the comradeship that grew out of such close proximity and the shared experience of death. Overriding everything else was the will to survive, the dream of making it home. That keeping hope alive meant killing and more killing was an inescapable fact. A German infantryman wrote in his diary, 'Courage has nothing to do with it. The fear of death surpasses all other feelings and terrible compulsion alone drives the soldier forward.'[22]

What is remarkable is how they held together, even though morale was slowly crumbling and there was no sign of relief from the hell being visited upon them by Allied firepower. Only when the High Command gambled on one last series of massive offensives in the spring and early summer of 1918, and lost, did discipline crack. As the Allies launched their counter-attacks Germans began to surrender in large numbers rather than die. Any residual faith in victory had gone: 'Every man here knows that we are losing the war.'[23] Nevertheless the leadership refused to accept the inevitable and poured all available reserves in to stem the Allied tide.

Signalmen were among those called up to the front line. Albert was sent into the killing zone and shot in the stomach during this desperate last stand. The gut wound was serious enough to end the war for him and never really healed. When he got out of hospital, Europe was in the grip of a decimating influenza epidemic, the Kaiser had abdicated and Germany was now a republic with a Social Democrat government. Food and basic goods were in dangerously short supply. The economy was in meltdown. When the German Army surrendered in November 1918, it not so much demobilised as dissolved. Hundreds of thousands of men, still in uniform, were suddenly redundant. From their ranks sprang two alternative responses to the crisis.

The first to emerge was modelled on the 'soviets' set up by mutinous elements of the Russian Army that quickly threw in their lot with the Bolsheviks and the industrial proletariat during the 1917 Revolution. After an initial outburst by sailors in the German port of Kiel, soviets popped up all over the country, often coordinating their actions with local workers' councils. A general strike was in the air. Berlin was effectively under the control of the far left.

Then their nemesis appeared: the Freikorps. Created 'for the maintenance of order within the Reich', they were a part spontaneous, part organised solution to the threat of revolution. They were volunteer regiments, often with a hard core of veterans, those who loved fighting and hated Communism in equal measure, paramilitaries given an official stamp by the embattled state. They took inspiration from the storm-trooper units that the Germans had introduced on the Western Front, a heavily armed elite trained to punch holes in the enemy line.

January 1919 saw the two forces clash on the streets of Berlin. The Freikorps crushed the revolt with bloody and merciless thoroughness, executing its leaders, indiscriminately murdering its supporters, setting a pattern for their grisly conduct over the next few years. But the movement for Soviet-style revolution would not be easily suppressed. The Ruhr fell briefly under its control. Hamburg and Munich were the scene of violent insurrection. In Berlin a general strike paralysed the capital. The barricades were mounted once again. The Freikorps arrived *en masse*. Between 12,000 and 15,000 people were killed in the unequal battle that followed, leaving the radicals decimated.

A period of relative calm did not put a stop to the Freikorps' activities; they simply went abroad. The Baltic states of Latvia, Lithuania and Estonia, the Teutonic knights' old stamping grounds, were caught up in the bitter civil war engulfing Russia. Some 15,000 Freikorps men set off to join the anti-Communists, including the young Rudolf Höss, future camp commandant of Auschwitz. Latvia suffered the worst excesses of this marauding outlaw army: 'We no longer had anything of human decency left in our hearts. We kindled a funeral pyre – there burned our hopes ... bourgeois codes, the laws and values of the civilised world, there burned everything.'[24]

Defeated, the Freikorps survivors limped home, the ignominy of their campaign quickly forgotten as they were once again called upon to stamp out left-wing insurrection. During the spring of 1920, a bungled right-wing coup, the Kapp Putsch, led to the formation of a Red Army 50,000 strong. The Freikorps were reassembled and let loose. Within forty-eight hours they had shot around a thousand 'rebels'.

This would prove to be the Freikorps' last bloody hurrah. The new administration was desperate to restore law and order under its own aegis. In the summer of 1920 the Freikorps were officially disbanded. A dedicated few turned to political assassination. Over a fourteen-month period they were responsible for 350 murders. The two most prominent victims were the Minister of Finance, Erzberger, who had the misfortune of negotiating Germany's surrender in 1918, and the Jewish Foreign Minister, statesman and Social Democrat, Walter Rathenau. Many other ex-Freikorps men would join illegal militias and later end up in Hitler's storm-troopers, the SA.

Albert was never a member of a Freikorps unit, nor did he join any Army soviets. By choosing not to become directly involved in the continuation of military action, by his rejection of both ideologies and their shock troops, Albert was like the majority of ex-soldiers who wanted nothing more than to return to their families and a semblance of normality. He headed for Munich, where his mother was living, and enrolled as a student of engineering. He at least was ready to embrace a new life.

Hermann found it less easy to make the transition to civvy street.

* * *

Hermann's actions during November 1918 showed an obvious reluctance to concede the fighting was over. Ordered to surrender, he declared he would 'neither allow my men or my machines to fall into the hands of the enemy'.[25] Hermann tried to trick his superiors by sending a few planes to French-held Strasbourg while the bulk of them headed for Mannheim in Germany, where the local Army soviet tried to commandeer them. Allegedly Hermann confronted them with his machine guns at the ready. The planes were swiftly returned.

A more credible, but no less dramatic, indication of Hermann's state of mind, was his appearance on the stage of the Berlin Philharmonic on 18 December 1918. A big meeting was being held to encourage Army officers to support the recently elected Social Democratic government. Those attending were requested not to wear any insignia or decorations on their uniforms. Hermann ignored this, showed up with all his medals, pushed his way onto the stage uninvited, and delivered a defiant speech that was greeted with wild applause: 'The ones who are to blame are the ones that stirred up the people, who stabbed our glorious army in the back. I ask everyone here tonight to cherish a hatred, a deep and abiding hatred for these swine who have outraged the German people and their traditions . . . The day will come when we will drive them from our Germany.'[26]

Defeat had unleashed a flood of highly charged emotions. Primary among them was anger, largely directed at the Versailles peace treaty. Germany was stripped of what it had taken from Russia in the east. Its borders with Poland were radically re-drawn. East Prussia was cut off from the rest of the country by the Danzig corridor. Germany also forfeited Alsace Lorraine, gained from the French in 1870, plus previously German territory on the banks of the Rhine. The Saar coal- and steel-producing region was placed under the control of the newly formed League of Nations.

All Germany's colonies in Africa and the Far East were seized. The armed forces were neutralised, reduced to a maximum of 100,000 men. The High Seas Fleet was dismantled. All military aircraft, tanks and vehicles were banned. In addition there was a bill for the war in the form of reparations that ran into billions and the promise of war crimes' trials to come. The majority of Germans, whatever their political inclinations, were aggrieved by these harsh terms and wanted some measure of pride restored.

Hermann voiced these feelings in a tearful speech he gave to comrades from his squadron at a last meal together, shortly after the 1918 cease-fire: 'Those same qualities which made the Richthofen Squadron so great will prevail in peace as well as in war. Our time will come again.'[27]

CHAPTER THREE

Munich

Post-war Munich was the scene of a brief family reunion between Hermann, Albert and their mother, before Hermann was forced to move on. As events in the city spiralled out of control, he was a potential target for the left-wing paramilitaries taking charge of the streets. A cycle of reprisal and counter-reprisal began when Kurt Eisner, a theatre critic described as 'an anarchist and a fool', declared Bavaria a republic and set about forming a revolutionary government. Soon Eisner decided to resign but before he could do so he was shot dead in broad daylight by a young aristocrat on 21 February 1919. In the aftermath of the assassination, law and order evaporated. The lunatic fringe took over, a motley crew consisting of two playwrights, an anarchist writer and a certifiable foreign minister, whose policy initiatives included declaring war on Switzerland.

They were quickly swept away by the emergent Bolsheviks, whose coherent strategy was backed by a Red Army of around 20,000 men. A revolt that had consisted of sporadic incidents of violence against the class enemy became a more coordinated campaign of hostage-taking. Anyone associated with the establishment was fair game. Hermann managed to slip out of the city and head for Berlin. His departure was somewhat hasty. The Bolshevik hold on power only lasted a few more chaotic weeks. By May 1919, a Freikorps army of 30,000 men had been gathered to retake Munich. They surrounded the city and unleashed their indiscriminate terror. Between 600 and 1,000 were killed.

This successful counter-revolution did not induce Hermann to return to his family. Instead he took the job offered to him by his wartime acquaintance, design guru of the German air force, Anthony Fokker, who had set up operations in Scandinavia to avoid the restrictions imposed by the victorious Allies. He asked Hermann to test-fly his new plane in Denmark. Hermann accepted.

His celebrity as a flying ace went with him. While the Freikorps were dealing out savage retribution in Munich, Hermann was acting as an advisor to the Danish government on its aircraft purchases. But he longed for excitement and mass adulation. With four other pilots from his old Richthofen squadron he put on a tour of acrobatic shows. These events were seen by thousands, who cheered, roared and held their collective breath as Hermann and his team of stunt flyers amazed with their gravity-defying, hair-raising exploits.

The media sat up and took notice. That summer his fame spread to Sweden, where he was featured in a string of glossy magazine and newspaper articles. Hermann was the toast of Stockholm. Staying at the top hotels, he embarked on a champagne lifestyle reminiscent of his days in the officers' mess. In early August 1919 he left Fokker after being head-hunted by the Swedish airline Svenska Lufttraffick.

He quickly lost interest in flying modest charter planes around Scandinavia and instead he talked occasionally of a career in politics. He fell in and out of love with actresses and society girls. The novelty of his acrobatic flying shows was beginning to wear off, not just for him but also for his public. Then, one stormy night, he found the person who would shape and mould his very existence, and exert a hold on him that nobody else would ever quite equal, not even Hitler.

On 20 February 1920, a wealthy Swedish explorer, Count Eric von Rosen, hired Hermann to fly him back to his isolated medieval castle, decorated with paintings and sculptures depicting legendary Nordic warriors, runic symbols and swastika flags. In the midst of a severe blizzard Hermann landed the plane on a frozen lake nearby and Rosen invited him to stay the night.

The other house guest was Countess Karin von Foch, Rosen's sister-in-law. At thirty-one and married with a seven-year-old boy, she was bored with her respectable life. Prone to ill-health, she possessed a refined, frail beauty that gave little indication of the passion burning within or her positive lust to serve destiny on some great quest.

Hermann and Karin started seeing each other and the relationship blossomed. During the summer of 1920 Hermann took Karin to

Munich to meet the family. Back in Stockholm tongues were wagging. Karin's husband refused a divorce and threatened to fight for custody of their son, Thomas. Her parents were shocked and dismayed. She was forced to go back and forth between Sweden and Germany, sometimes with Hermann, sometimes without. Regardless of these problems they remained consumed by love, their devotion to each other only increasing with each obstacle. But their relationship had little hope of acceptance in Stockholm so Karin agreed to make the break with her homeland. In early 1922 they headed for Munich, determined to build a life together.

* * *

During the vicious upheaval that shook Munich in 1919, Albert remained put. He endured urban civil war and conditions of near starvation. He had fewer options than his famous brother. But he did have a clear idea of where his future lay, which meant completing his training as a mechanical engineer at the Technische Hochschule. As long as Albert got his degree he was pretty much guaranteed a position at a leading firm.

Though he was among the privileged few, times were hard. Student grants were meagre and further devalued by Germany's dire economic problems. Albert's Army invalid pension did little to improve his standard of living. His mother had nothing to offer in the way of financial help. Epenstein continued to look kindly on his godson, but we do not know if this went beyond invitations to stay at his castles.

Social life at the college was dominated by student fraternities, beer swilling all-male societies whose culture revolved around extreme nationalist politics and duelling. Given Albert's antipathy towards far-right ideology and the fact that at twenty-five he was older than the majority of his fellow students, it is not surprising he did not get involved in their high jinks.

Much of the public discourse at both the Technische Hochschule and Munich University was a poisonous brew of anti-semitism, pan-Germanism, and demands to avenge 1918. Munich's academic institutions had become a breeding ground for Nazism. Hitler attended a lecture series in the summer of 1919 as part of his political education by the Army. Six months earlier, Joseph Goebbels, future Nazi Propaganda Minister, had spent a semester at the university. Rudolf Hess, one of the

Führer's right-hand men until his bizarre defection to Scotland in 1941, was there on a geopolitics course.

Heinrich Himmler enrolled at the Technische Hochschule to study agriculture in October 1919. To imagine that Albert might have run into or known Himmler while they were students and conjure up scenes of them debating the issues of the day or clashing over a sharp difference of opinion, would give their story an appealing dramatic unity. Twenty-five years later Himmler was the ultimate arbiter of Albert's fate. However, there is no evidence to suggest they were even aware of each other's existence. Himmler embraced the fraternity scene, joining one called Apollo, desperately hoping to prove his manhood in a duel. He was finally 'blooded' in the summer of 1922 when he clashed swords with another student and received five cuts that needed stitches, much to his delight. This kind of macho, semi-feudal ritual was anathema to Albert.

Not that the rest of Munich offered much alternative. Once the Freikorps were officially disbanded in 1920, the city acted as a magnet for hundreds of those unwilling to trade in their uniforms. Monopolising the beer halls, moving around in drunken packs, holding militaristic mass meetings, they were hard to ignore. To Albert the situation must have been deeply depressing.

However, all was not doom and gloom in his life. Albert found love and married the twenty-one-year-old Maria von Ummon on 16 March 1921. A couple of years later he was a guest at Hermann and Karin's wedding in Munich, on 3 February 1923, a week after they had married in a civil ceremony in Sweden. This time they did it in style, with the entire Richthofen squadron acting as guard of honour.

After the couple had settled back in Munich they drifted without much purpose. Karin was periodically unwell and preoccupied with her family problems back in Sweden. Hermann, somewhat inevitably, enrolled at Munich University. He rather arbitrarily chose to study economics, barely attended lectures and read only what he felt like reading. He was close to dropping out before the first semester was over. The person who would provide him the opportunity and the decisive motivation to quit was none other than Adolf Hitler.

* * *

Hitler was a coming player, a force to be reckoned with in the maelstrom of far-right extremism engulfing Munich. His face was on posters, he was a regular speaker at both small and large political gatherings and a prime mover in the nascent National Socialist Party. In late 1922 Hermann heard him giving a talk at the Café Neumann, where he had a regular meeting, on a subject close to Hermann's heart, 'The Versailles Treaty and the Extradition of the German Army Commanders'.

It is hard accurately to assess the true impact Hitler's performance had on Hermann that night. The idea that Hitler's oratory had the magical power to create instant devotees was a persistent part of his legend. People from all sections of society testified to the over-whelming, almost cathartic, effect his public appearances had, trans-forming their lives in a matter of minutes. This, of course, was not a universal reaction. But, even those who detested what Hitler had to say could not deny his ability once in front of a big audience, his skill at communicating directly to the assembled mass, drawing out and exploiting their darkest fears and wildest passions, fusing them into a state of raw, powerful emotion. This man, who by his own admission was socially dysfunctional – 'In a small, intimate circle I never know what to say'[1] – came alive on stage.

The 'Hitler effect' was even more acute for those who became his closest colleagues. After seeing him for only the second time Goebbels thought he was 'the born tribune of the people, the coming dictator!'[2] Six months later Goebbels felt 'completely bound to him'.[3] The highly educated, twenty-one-year-old Baldur von Schirach, future leader of the Hitler Youth, ran home to write a eulogy after watching him speak in 1926. He sent the poem in and got back a signed photo. Some, like Himmler, did not even need to see Hitler in person to be completely convinced of his 'genius'. Having read published extracts of his speeches, Himmler wrote, 'He is in truth a great man and above all genuine and pure. His speeches are marvellous examples of Germandom and Aryanism.'[4]

While in the dock at Nuremberg, Hermann recalled his first exposure to Hitler: 'The conviction was spoken word for word as if from my own soul . . . I told him that I myself to the fullest extent, and all I was and possessed, were completely at his disposal.'[5] This commitment took the form of an oath of loyalty, given with the full seriousness of a military man: 'When I had more insight into the personality of the Führer, I gave him my hand and said, "I pledge my destiny to you for better or for worse . . . in good and bad times, even if it means my life."'[6]

But in the privacy of his cell he gave a different version of events which suggested his decision was based on mutual respect rather than utter submission: 'I heard Hitler give an address in a Munich beer hall where he spoke about a greater Germany, the abolition of the Versailles Treaty, arms for Germany, and the future glory of the German people. So I joined forces with him and became a member of the National Socialist Party.'[7] In return, Hitler 'was honoured to have me as a fellow worker because I had some fame as the successor of the Richthofen Squadron'.[8]

Here we get a hint of an important facet of Hermann's complex relationship to his Führer. Though he knew Hitler could dismiss him at any moment and destroy his power, he did have a perception that the two of them were somehow equals, equals as men of vision, talent and strength, equals in the affections of the German people, and equals as statesmen in the eyes of the world: 'I am convinced that whether or not Hitler happened along, I would have been a leading statesman and military power in Germany and would have succeeded in winning a war.'[9]

He never resolved this tension between his craving to rule and his willingness to serve an individual capable of rejuvenating the German empire. In his cell at Nuremberg, he explained his predicament: 'When I give my oath of loyalty, I cannot break it. And I had a hell of a time keeping it too, I can tell you. Just try being crown prince for twelve years . . . always loyal to the king, disapproving of many of his policies, and yet not being able to do anything about it, knowing at any moment you may become king and having to make the best of the situation. But I couldn't plot behind his back with poison gas or sticking briefcases under his arse and cowardly tricks like that.'[10]

What can be said is that in 1922 Hermann made his choice without much evidence that the National Socialists would go anywhere or amount to anything. So what led Hermann to become attached to this diminutive ex-corporal and former tramp? In 1918 he had lost everything his life had revolved around. The Versailles Treaty had deprived him of his reason for being on the planet. In the air it seemed like his manifest destiny had been fulfilled. To have died in combat would have been a perfectly appropriate end. 1918 denied him this glory and offered only defeat in exchange. His beloved air force was torn apart. His next few years were aimless, lacking focus or direction, with no means of recapturing or redeeming his military past, like so many attracted to the right-wing fringe groups of which the Nazis were one. Was he canny enough to understand that in the new democratic Germany, Hitler represented the best chance for the nationalist right? It could simply be that, at the age of thirty, Hermann felt he did not have time to delay; he had to jump or be left on the fence. This was a man for whom inaction was a kind of slow death.

It is important not to underestimate the decisive effect Karin's overwhelmingly positive reaction to Hitler had on Hermann. Her family background in Sweden had exposed her to ideas of Aryan superiority and the quasi-religious mission of the Nordic race. This, coupled with rabid anti-semitism, made her extremely receptive to Hitler's world view. Her hatred of the Jews was never far from the surface, popping up in casual conversation and letters to her family: 'I would rather die of hunger a thousand times than serve a Jew.'[11]

She was also drawn to Hitler personally, to 'his wonderful, noble character and intellect',[12] feeling an intense devotion and, for want of a better word, love for the Führer that had a strong spiritual dimension. Hitler inspired this kind of semi-worship from women of all social classes, an emotional response devoid of sexual connotations. There was nothing Hitler liked better than to bask in this kind of female adulation, especially when it came in such an attractive and well-bred package as Karin Goering.

While Hitler had quickly realised that Hermann was a potential asset – as he rather caustically put it, 'a war ace with the Pour le Mérite, imagine it! Excellent propaganda! Moreover he has money'[13] – Karin wanted to ensure that the two men became close friends. In her mind's eye she had immediately constructed a picture of an unshakeable alliance between them, a shared date with history. At Karin's instigation the Goerings' small villa in the suburbs of Munich became the scene of regular political soirées attended by Hitler and a coterie of right-wing plotters and socialites. Her sister described a typical evening: 'After the earnest conferring would come the warm, cheerful hours which filled Karin with such joy. Hitler's sense of humour showed itself in gay stories, observations and witticisms, and Karin's spontaneous and whole-hearted reaction to them made her a delightful audience.'[14] Her wilful intervention guaranteed that Hermann's immediate future lay with Hitler. As a consequence a wedge was driven between Hermann and Albert which would define the parameters of their relationship.

* * *

Albert was probably exposed to Hitler before Hermann, and took an instant dislike to him. As he repeatedly told his American interrogators at Nuremberg, 'From the beginning I was the strongest and most active fighter against National Socialism.'[15]

In the 1920s it was easy enough for many educated bourgeois Germans to dismiss Hitler as a crank; it became a lot harder to hold that line when he was master of Europe. Albert never changed his mind about Hitler, never deviating from his initial conclusion that the man was a menace and his ideology repugnant: 'He detested the Hitler crowd and foresaw a bitter end for Germany.'[16] Albert believed in freedom and justice. Whether he thought that politicians could deliver a more civilised world is open to question. His anti-Nazism was not based on any strong party affiliations. He answered to a more timeless ethical agenda: 'The things I did, I did because it was my humane and religious duty to do so.'[17]

As children Hermann and Albert had spent the majority of the time apart, both away from home at different schools and academies. Hermann enjoyed hunting, climbing and dressing up in uniforms, while Albert was more studious and orientated towards cultural pursuits. The First World War widened the gulf between them. Hermann concluded that Albert 'was always the antithesis of me. He was not politically or military interested.'[18]

Considering that their common ground was limited anyway, Hitler's emergence could have marked the point of no return. Hermann recalled that, 'For twelve years we never spoke to each other because of Albert's attitude to the party.'[19] He was referring to the years 1923 through 1935. The brothers were geographically quite separate and there is no documentation that mentions them meeting during this period. But we must be wary of accepting Hermann's remarks at face value. He was almost pathologically incapable of not manipulating facts to create a version that suited him.

What seems likely is that contact between Hermann and Albert was restricted to family occasions, weddings, baptisms and suchlike, and celebrations such as Christmas and New Year. Relations, however strained, remained cordial. There was no spite or ugly recrimination. As Hermann observed, 'Neither of us was angry at each other. It was separation due to the situation . . . he was not a bad fellow, Albert.'[20]

Albert echoed these sentiments during Allied questioning, choosing to distinguish between Hermann 'as a private person, as my brother' and

Hermann 'the statesman', going on to add, 'As brothers we were very close together, and we had the usual relationship brothers would have inside a family. I have had no relations with him as a statesman.'[21]

This was not the same thing as denying the strength of their disagreement: 'Albert talked openly about the fact that he and Hermann did not see eye to eye in political terms.'[22] Hermann told Albert, 'not to mix into affairs of state, and affairs of history, because I had no political knowledge whatever: his very words were, "You are a political idiot."'[23] Albert could be equally damning: 'I have a brother in Germany who is getting involved with that bastard Hitler and he's going to come to a bad end if he continues that way.'[24]

When this fundamental clash of ideas first reared its head, as 1922 turned into 1923, neither Albert nor Hermann had sufficient influence over the other to win the argument. The events of that year would only serve to magnify the seriousness of their dispute and render any kind of understanding between them a distant possibility.

* * *

Hitler rewarded his newest recruit by putting him in charge of the SA (Sturmabteilung – 'Storm Section'), the brown-shirted bully boys. Formed in November 1920, from a nucleus of bouncers and heavies, they were nurtured by Ernst Röhm, a former front-line soldier. Röhm had strong Army and Freikorps connections and access to weapons and ammunition. Hardly an intellectual, he was a self-declared enemy of any philosophy that did not celebrate violence: 'Since I am an immature and wicked person, war and unrest appeal to me more than bourgeois order.'[25]

For tactical reasons Röhm remained independent of the National Socialist Party, leaving the way clear for Hermann to assume control of the SA. Hermann threw himself into his work – 'Often I was on the go until 4 a.m. and was back in the office at 7 a.m. the next day. I didn't have a moment's respite'[26] – determined to fashion what was an ill-disciplined mob into an efficient fighting machine, which Karin would describe as 'a band of eager Crusaders'.[27]

An acid test of his achievements was not far off. 1923 saw Germany plunged into a crisis as serious as anything that occurred in the immediate post-war period. Hyper-inflation was running wild, laying waste to day-to-day life, causing such damage that any 'normal' activity became ridiculous, pointless and impossible. Germany's inflationary problems began to get out of control after 1914, due to the government borrowing heavily to finance the war. The only way to repay these mounting debts was through military victory. The defeat of 1918 removed that option. The rapid devaluation of the currency then began in earnest. At 1919 rates, the dollar was worth 47 marks. By late 1921 it was worth 263 marks. One year later it was worth 3,000 marks. Not only was money losing its meaning, it was doing so at escalating speed. In April 1923 the exchange rate stood at 24,000 marks to the dollar. In July, it took 353,000 marks to redeem that same dollar. The figures became astronomical. By September a dollar cost 25,260,000,000 marks. In financial terms this was nothing less than apocalyptic. Prices had risen to a billion times their pre-war level.

Society was drowning in worthless bank-notes. People transported their wages in wheelbarrows. A British correspondent reported, 'In the shops the prices are typewritten and change hourly . . . a copy of the *Daily Mail* purchased on the street yesterday cost 35,000 marks, but today it cost 60,000.'[28]

A loaf of bread cost 163 marks in January 1923; by November a loaf was 78 million, while a kilo of butter was retailing at around 168 million marks. Bartering became commonplace, as did looting and food riots. Crime levels soared, whether it be theft, prostitution or murder, as did the numbers of homeless and destitute. The black market flourished.

Political upheaval went hand in hand with economic collapse. There were attempted Communist coups in Saxony and Thuringia. After the government defaulted on its reparation payments French troops moved in to occupy the Ruhr, sparking a campaign of passive and not so passive resistance, giving an excuse for the old Freikorps regiments, supplemented by young volunteers, to mass once again. By September 1923 80,000 were in southern Germany waiting to strike. Though a deal was struck with the French and they withdrew, the assembled Freikorps, re-dubbed the Black Reichswehr, were in no hurry to disband.

Hermann captured the mood of approaching Armageddon: 'Over here life is a seething volcano, whose destructive lava may at any moment spew forth across the country . . . strife and deprivation ravage the land and the hour is not far off when we must take responsibility for the future.'[29]

This day of reckoning preoccupied Hermann, Hitler and their right-wing allies. Benito Mussolini's 'March on Rome' the previous year, when he assumed control of Italy at the head of his Fascist black-shirts, seemed a plausible model to copy. The plan was hatched to seize power in Munich first as the prelude for a March on Berlin. After a promising, if confused, start in a beer-hall on the evening of 9 November 1923, during which Goering was called upon to calm the agitated crowd, the insurrectionists settled in to await the coming dawn with some confidence. Back-stage Hitler had harangued his dubious and reluctant co-conspirators, Gustav von Kahr, state governor, Seisser, chief of police, and General von Lossow from the Army, into accepting his leadership.

Next morning it was clear the Nazis had bungled it. Important civic buildings and public utilities had not been taken over. Crucially the forces of law and order did not jump to join the putsch. Instead they stood firm behind the notables that Hitler thought he had hitched to his bandwagon. Inexplicably, Kahr, Seisser and Lossow had been allowed to go home the previous night. Instead of going quietly to their beds they proceeded hotfoot to the safety of the local barracks and notified the press and the radio that, though Hitler's putsch was under way, they were still in control.

With Hitler in the front rank and Hermann immediately to his left, around 2,000 putschists marched on the Bavarian War Ministry, where there was a brief confrontation between them and the police, who had no qualms about opening fire. Their first volley was enough to win the day. Hitler fell and dislocated his shoulder. Hermann was hit twice in the thigh, one of the bullets piercing his groin. Badly wounded, he was spirited away from the scene and into Nazi folklore.

* * *

The Munich Beer Hall Putsch became one of the central symbolic pillars of the Nazi regime. Each year on 9 November, Hitler would attend a mass ceremony to honour the sixteen 'martyrs' who died that day. The importance to him of this event, and the personal attachment he felt to the veterans of the putsch, was considerable: 'What would my life be without you! The fact that you once found your way to me and believed in me gave your life new meaning and a new goal! The fact I found you was the prerequisite for my own life and my struggle.'[30] However, his goodwill was not sufficient to spare many of the survivors of Munich from the reckoning of the Night of the Long Knives in June 1934.

The SA were the main victims of this purge. Ernst Röhm, who had spent much of the 1920s training the Bolivian Army, returned to take control of the brown-shirted paramilitaries in November 1930. A year later membership had tripled. By 1934 the SA had swelled to around 400,000 men. This street army had been instrumental in the repression of Nazi rivals after Hitler became chancellor in 1933 and was not content to limit itself to a bit of spring cleaning. Röhm and his associates thought the time was right to push forward with a root and branch clear-out of society: 'The SA will not allow the German revolution to fall asleep or be betrayed half-way.'[31]

Hitler was well aware of the negative publicity the SA's 'excesses' generated both at home and abroad. Ordinary Germans were anxious about the continued violence and upheaval. Hitler had promised stability; the actions of Röhm's cadres gave the lie to that promise. The SA were a thorn in his side, 'a haven of riff-raff and scumbags'.[32] Confrontation seemed increasingly likely. Hermann played a key role in the accumulation of 'evidence' which suggested Röhm was planning a coup against Hitler, backed by a few disaffected political luminaries.

Using his existing power base as Prussian Interior Minister, which gave him effective control over the largest police force in Germany, Hermann had developed his own network of spies and informers and gained a monopoly on the latest in telephone bugging technology, which enabled him to listen in on Röhm and company, on members of Hitler's first cabinet, on former chancellors like General Kurt von Schleicher and Franz von Papen, on Army generals, foreign embassies, and Goebbels's conversations with his mistresses. All this information was sifted until there was enough for a dossier to present to Hitler.

Whether there actually was a fully formed conspiracy by the spring of 1934 is debatable. Certainly the SA sensed a showdown was coming and many, including Röhm, actively welcomed the prospect: 'The SA is and will remain Germany's destiny.' Significant establishment figures were contemplating using the brown-shirts to overthrow Hitler. What this uneasy alliance lacked was a coherent strategy, an agreement over ends and means, a sensible division of labour and some kind of timetable.

Hitler decided to act. His weapon of choice was the SS. Set up in 1922 as Hitler's personal bodyguard, the Schutzstaffel (Protection Formation) was a tiny, elite force of a mere 290 men when Himmler took charge of it on 6 January 1929. He quickly expanded the SS to 3,000 men and added the distinctive, universally feared black uniforms and macabre insignia. The SS recruits were expected to match Himmler's absolute obedience to Hitler: 'For him I could do anything. Believe me, if Hitler were to say I should shoot my mother, I would do it and be proud of his confidence.'[33]

Himmler's aim was to build the SS into a valid alternative to the existing police forces, the SA and eventually the Army. What he lacked in manpower he made up for in intelligence-gathering. At the beginning of 1932 he set up the Sicherheitsdienst (Security Service), the SD, as a separate department within the SS, dedicated to amassing information on suspect individuals, an extremely broad category encompassing communists, homosexuals, pickpockets, giants of industry, parliamentary deputies, intellectuals of all kinds, churchmen of every denomination and, of course, Jews.

Running the SD, initially from his tiny Berlin flat, was the young Reinhard Heydrich, a man who would later feature prominently in Albert's life, an ex-Navy intelligence officer obsessed with the world of espionage. The SD was divided into five sections, each run by an academic. 'V' men were recruited to work undercover as spies. By January 1933 Heydrich had twenty-three agents on the payroll and 200 unpaid informers. By 1937 there were 50,000 'volunteers' snooping for the SD, mostly drawn from the middle classes.

Pooling their considerable intelligence resources, Hermann and Himmler, the fighter ace and the chicken farmer, were able to pick the most appropriate date to strike while certain of retaining the element of surprise. As the spring of 1934 turned to summer, and the SS expanded from 25,000 to 40,000 men between April and June, Hitler gave the green light. The condemned, identified on a list drawn up by Hermann, began their annual holidays unaware they were about to die.

On the Night of the Long Knives, 30 June 1934, as many as 250 people may have been dragged from their beds and murdered. Around 80 corpses were accounted for but, considering many victims were hacked or beaten to death, and their bodies very thoroughly disposed of in swamps, lakes and deep forests, the higher estimate is probably nearer the truth. All those in the SA leadership structure who were loyal to Röhm were wiped out, including dozens of the fabled 'old fighters' from the Munich days. Schleicher, a former chancellor, was shot dead in front of his wife, who was then dispatched the same way. Scores were settled. Gustav von Kahr, the Bavarian politician that had pulled the rug out from under Hitler's feet during the 1923 Putsch, was killed with a pickaxe. Gregor Strasser, Hitler's former number two, who had been edged out the previous year after voicing criticisms of Hitler's apparent abandonment of the party's socialist principles, and had quietly agreed to remove himself from political life, was also brutally slain by nocturnal visitors. In several cases the wrong people were assassinated. As Hermann casually put it, 'Of course in the general excitement some mistakes were made.'

Hermann and Himmler coordinated the bloodbath, ensconced together in an operations room set up in Hermann's study, glued to the phones as they received information and issued instructions. During the course of seventy-two hours they dealt with over 7,000 phone calls, while assistants delivered messages and sandwiches. The self-congratulatory air of a job well done – 'Goering exudes an air of cheerful complacency' – was occasionally punctured by him bellowing, 'Shoot them down! . . . Shoot them down!'[34]

After being held in custody until Sunday 1 July, a full day after the killing had stopped, Röhm was given the option of suicide. He refused it and was gunned down in his cell. That evening Goering held a champagne reception and a extravagant feast to celebrate the success of the purge, playing host to Himmler, Heydrich and their SS cronies. The mood was boisterous and rowdy, though Himmler would later endeavour to paint a more sombre and sanctimonious picture of the emotions felt by his SS hit-men: 'not a victory but the hardest day that can be visited on a soldier in his lifetime. To have to shoot one's own comrades . . . is the bitterest thing that can happen to a man.'[35] The true attitude towards their victims was one of breathtaking callousness, summed up by the decision to post the ashes of the dead to their relatives in cardboard cartons. Only Gregor Strasser's family were privileged enough to get his remains sent to them in an urn.

* * *

For those who survived the cull, participation in the Munich Putsch remained a badge of honour, untainted by association. As the years passed, its commemoration became more ostentatious and overblown, carefully orchestrated to resemble a pagan sacred rite dedicated to the ancient gods awaiting the 'old fighters' in Valhalla.

Hitler would first give an informal talk to selected comrades, Hermann included, at the beer hall where it all started. They would then proceed through flame-lit streets to pay homage to the coffins of the fallen, draped in swastika flags and blood-stained relics, and sing their nostalgic battle songs. The next morning, Hitler and Hermann would walk side by side, evoking their original, futile march on the War Ministry, while the coffins, with the sound of drums and cannon fire ringing in the air, were led to the newly built temple that acted as their resting place, where Hitler solemnly laid a wreath to sanctify the dead.

Hermann had a special place in the pantheon. He had taken a bullet for Adolf. Back in 1923, this may have seemed a dubious honour. As the smoke cleared, the putschists scattered and the arrests began, Hermann was a seriously wounded fugitive, famous enough to be recognised anywhere. Having been given rudimentary treatment close to the scene of the debacle by a Jewish doctor, he was smuggled out of Munich and driven seventy kilometres south of the city with Karin to the villa of a friend near the Austrian border.

Next morning they attempted to cross and were apprehended by customs guards. A warrant for Hermann's arrest had already been issued. The local police escorted him to a hospice and then left to get the correct paperwork, Hermann having sworn faithfully not to abscond, which he immediately did. His driver had been waiting round the back with the engine running. That night they crossed into Austria along treacherous roads through the snow-bound mountains; Hermann was wrapped in blankets in the back seat and a doctor sat in the front. Karin waited until the next day to join her husband.

So began four years of exile, that saw Hermann reach the lowest depths of poverty and drug addiction. This degrading experience did much to empty him of his reserves of compassion and humanity, almost totally eliminating his moral sense. He became capable of real cruelty and outright criminality. Previously, he had stayed broadly true to his own code of ethics. He may have lied when it suited him, or taken advantage of situations, but he was never systematically corrupt. His years on the run, culminating in destitution and madness, left him ravenous for power.

CHAPTER FOUR

Going Up, Going Down

By the time Hermann and Hitler launched their putsch, Albert had graduated from the Technische Hochschule and gone to Dessau, an industrial town beside the River Elbe just south of Berlin, to take a job as a mechanical engineer. His departure coincided with family tragedy. Fanny Goering collapsed suddenly and died, aged fifty-seven, in August 1923. She was buried next to her husband in a ceremony attended by both Albert and Hermann. The abruptness of their mother's death was a deep shock. This upheaval was magnified by serious complications in Albert's love life. His first marriage to Maria von Ummon had failed to satisfy him and he had now fallen for someone else, Erna von Miltner, a mature Munich woman, who, at thirty-seven, was nine years older than Albert and already married with two young sons. She abandoned her family and became a social outcast to marry Albert, attesting to her passion for him and his disregard for convention. After barely two years of marriage, he divorced Maria and wed Erna on 10 September 1923.

According to a confidential memo written by an American intelligence officer on 9 May 1945, 'From 1923 to 1926 he, Albert, worked for the firm IG Farben in Dessau'.[1] Created in 1925 out of an amalgamation of six major companies and a host of subsidiaries, IG Farben was the biggest corporation in Europe and the fourth largest in the world, a giant of chemical engineering based on turn of the century innovations in the manufacture of dyes, and later experiments with nitrogen and ammonia that led via fertiliser to the mass production of explosives for the German war effort in 1914–18. Like all major companies built by science, it had close links with the Technische Hochschulen.

But Albert never worked for IG Farben. In 1924 the conglomerate did not even exist and it had no subsequent presence in Dessau. Albert had not studied as a chemical engineer, so there would be no obvious role for him at the company. We know that from 1926 he was working for the Junkers company, which had been in Dessau since 1892. It was their town. Logic dictates the conclusion that Albert was at Junkers from the start.

The intelligence officer probably made a genuine mistake. The importance of IG Farben's contribution to the Nazi war effort made it a prime target for Allied investigators. It provided Hitler with a host of necessities: explosives, synthetic fuel and rubber, pharmaceuticals, photographic equipment and the poison gas Zyklon-B, which was manufactured by its factories at the Auschwitz-Birkenau camp complex and used in the death chambers. No wonder Albert's interrogator had IG Farben on the brain.

His error reveals an attitude that would colour Albert's subsequent treatment by the Allies: an assumption of guilt. The officer ended the hasty memo by recommending that Albert 'be forwarded to Seventh Army Headquarters CIC detachment . . . It is felt that the subject has various important information that would interest the proper authorities in a higher echelon.'[2] Four days later Albert was transferred. A report based on further questioning reeks of barely concealed contempt: 'The results of the interrogation of Albert GOERING brother of the REICHSMARSCHALL Hermann, constitutes as clever a piece of "whitewash" as SAIC has ever seen. Albert GOERING's lack of subtlety is matched only by the bulk of his obese brother. His career almost matches the rise of the Nazi Party.'[3]

* * *

Dessau was well placed to benefit from the rapid expansion of German industry that gathered pace from the mid-nineteenth century. By 1841 it had a railway link to Berlin and by 1860 it was an established factory town. Albert's employer was the inventor and entrepreneur, Professor Hugo Junkers. Like Albert, he had studied mechanical engineering at a Technische Hochschule and, as a professor from 1897, he had taught at the school in Aachen until 1912.

He set up experimental laboratories during the 1890s and designed the Kalorifermeter, a machine that could accurately measure the thermal flow of gases. His innovations resulted in the first gas-driven warm-water heaters or boilers. A company, the Kaloriferwerke, was formed in 1904 to deal exclusively with this new technology. By 1911 his heating systems were in mass production. In 1914 the Kalorifer-werke moved to Dessau, joining Junkers's other factories. When Albert became one of Junkers's heating engineers in 1924 the company had already begun to diversify into construction, searching for materials flexible enough to accommodate anything from large buildings to kitchen furniture.

These experiments chimed nicely with Professor Junkers's involve-ment with the Bauhaus movement. The revolutionary design collective, famous for its distinctive aesthetic credo, took up residence in Dessau in 1925. The Kaloriferwerke collaborated closely with several artists on experimental metal structures, offering know-how and manufacturing capability. Albert, however, remained a boiler man throughout his five-year stay in Dessau.

The fate of the Kaloriferwerke, and all of Junkers's other concerns, rested on his aircraft business, which had grown out of his interests in engine design to dominate the enterprise during the First World War. The shackling of the industry by the Versailles Treaty hit Junkers hard. Having outlawed all military aircraft, the Allies imposed severe restrictions on the number, design and capacity of planes made for civilian use, including intermittent bans on their production. Between 1918 and 1921 the work-force at Junkers's aircraft factories dropped from 2,000 to just 200. But the professor was determined to carry on, firm in his belief that: 'The aeroplane will be the instrument of a fortunate human race: one which will bring its blessings to all peoples and nations.'[4]

In 1925, desperate for orders and on the verge of bankruptcy, Junkers got involved in the German Army's secret operations to rebuild an air force. This covert rearmament programme, and the strategic thinking that lay behind it, would have an important influence on the composition, tactics and priorities of Hermann's Luftwaffe. Negotiations with Soviet Russia had resulted in the Treaty of Rapallo, signed in 1922, that allowed the German military to have an air base for training pilots in Russia. In exchange for this support, the Soviet aircraft industry would get the benefit of superior German technical assistance. A Junkers factory, built in Dessau, was to be located south of Moscow. The cost of the venture was mitigated by an up-front payment from the German Army and a preliminary order from the Soviets for 100 Junkers planes.

Ernst von Brandenburg, former flying ace and now head of aviation at the Transport Ministry, wanted to bring the entire German aircraft industry under state control. The Lufthansa airline was set up with government sponsorship and a domestic monopoly. The new operations director was the thirty-eight-year-old Erhard Milch, a former head manager at Junkers's Dessau offices, whose experience of flying was limited to a spell in a police air squadron. Somewhat characterless, his real talents lay in administration, organisation and forward planning. A few years later he would become Hermann's patron and then his reluctant servant.

Only Professor Junkers resisted amalgamation and fought to keep hold of his company. But the Soviet factory was haemorrhaging money. The government threatened to halt his subsidies and put pressure on the banks to stop his credit. By January 1926 he could hold out no longer and control of the majority of his aircraft and airline business passed to Lufthansa and Erhard Milch.

These machinations did not directly impact on Albert's job at the Kaloriferwerke or affect the demand for its heating systems. His position as a technician was secure for the time being. With Junkers teetering on the brink of personal ruin, his gas boilers were one of the few things keeping him afloat.

* * *

Albert's modest, comfortable, respectable life in Dessau was light years away from the lower circles of hell that Hermann was moving through after the Munich putsch.

Once they had escaped across the Austrian border, Hermann and Karin stayed in Innsbruck at a hotel whose owners were sympathetic to their cause, giving them a 30 per cent discount. This was small comfort to the stricken Hermann, whose bullet wounds had become badly infected, filling his leg with poison. In the local hospital the doctors attempted to drain the pus and started giving him two injections of morphine a day. Hermann lay there in the grip of a high fever, his suffering vividly described by Karin: 'It hurts so much he lies there and bites the pillow, and all I can hear are inarticulate groans . . . His mind wanders, he weeps, he has nightmares of street fighting, and all the time he is in indescribable pain.'[5]

Their stay was abruptly terminated when the authorities, under some pressure to return Hermann to Germany, advised them to move on. Sweden seemed to be the obvious destination. However, due largely to Karin's unshaken belief in Hitler – 'This first misfortune will make the final victory deeper, richer and more serious . . . He will win, I feel it, I know it, we have not seen the end yet'[6] – and her determination that Hermann stay in his orbit, she secured an important task for her ailing husband: to open dialogue with Italy's Fascist dictator, Benito Mussolini.

Hermann and Karin arrived in Venice during May 1924. His mission was to raise 2,000,000 lire for the Nazi Party and discuss the South Tyrol, an area with a German-speaking majority that Italy had gained in 1919 at the expense of the defeated and dissolved Austro-Hungarian Empire. Hermann's point of contact was the diplomat Giuseppe Bastiani. For the next ten months Bastiani was on the receiving end of a barrage of letters, documents and requests from Hermann, that led absolutely nowhere.

Some biographies of Hermann say he met Mussolini. In fact, at no point was Mussolini prepared to grant him an audience. The Nazis were small fry, beaten, apparently scattered, a regional insignificance. Even though Mussolini was a keen aviator and an admirer of First World War fighter pilots, he still showed no interest in a sit down with Hermann, whose social position, war record, and relative fame were suddenly irrelevant. For all his persistence, the doors of power were closed to him; he was not even given the status of a messenger boy by his potential benefactors.

The idea that he held high level discussions with Il Duce at this time comes to us from Karin's letters: 'Have I told you about our meetings with Mussolini? It is a wonderful thing to be with him . . . Hermann has to work with Mussolini himself on all the agreements and negotiations . . . this is a huge responsibility for him. But I believe it's all going far better than even Hitler imagined in his boldest dreams.'[7]

Whether this was a calculated lie or, in her own over-heated mind, what she believed to be the truth, it is impossible to say. This was a woman driven by a burning faith that, even in her more sombre moments, never left her: 'But even though it sometimes seems as if the world's entire misfortune is about to descend upon Hitler's work and us, I have a firm belief that everything will turn out all right.'[8] Part of her motivation may have been tactical. She was Hermann's only link to the

Nazis, visiting Hitler in prison and on his release in 1925, and needed to maintain a positive front. Hermann would have lost all credibility if Hitler had known the real story of the Italian mission.

Hermann encouraged her delusions. Right up to their departure in the spring of 1925, he pretended that everything was going well. Back in the real world, as their situation became desperate, Hermann went over Bastiani's head to the more powerful Negrilli, begging and threatening him to intercede on his behalf: 'I am convinced that Mussolini will be very upset when he hears how we have been given the run-around . . . If only I can speak with Mussolini, I shall be able to work everything out.'[9]

Hermann's final pleas achieved nothing. Having received their travel expenses from Karin's mother, the couple left for Sweden, Hermann's diplomatic humiliation quickly forgotten and rarely mentioned. Of more immediate concern was his addiction to morphine, acquired in hospital, which had flourished while they were in Italy going from Venice to Rome and back to Venice, staying at cheaper and cheaper hotels, borrowing what money they could to survive, close to starvation.

By the time they left, Hermann was injecting himself four to six times a day. His weight had also ballooned. His mood swings became increasingly savage and unpredictable, total lethargy alternating with wild rage. At night the pain from his wounds kept him awake. Karin's poor health persisted. A dose of tuberculosis she picked up at Fanny Goering's funeral kept recurring, putting her close to critical on a number of occasions.

Hermann was suicidal. Some years later he admitted as much to Thomas von Kantzow, Karin's son by her first husband: 'I remember once standing before the Trevi fountain at three o'clock in the morning and wondering what everyone would say if they found me lying at the bottom of it instead of three coins . . . Then I decided the water was too shallow to drown in.'[10] What kept him going through his Italian torment was Karin's indefatigable willpower, which belied her weak physical constitution. As Hermann wrote to her mother, 'For one year we have grappled with our singular fate. Often we are in despair, but . . . Karin is so brave, so sweet to me and such a great comfort that I cannot thank her enough'.[11]

* * *

Sweden seemed to offer a chance to turn things around. Karin had managed to sell their villa in the Munich suburbs and they were able to afford a modest apartment in Stockholm. Hermann even landed a job as a pilot for a local airline. But his hunger for morphine did not abate, dominating every waking hour. After a few weeks he lost his job. Karin had to pawn their furniture, while her sister sold her piano to help pay for Hermann's drugs. His volatile, aggressive outbursts got so extreme that Karin fled to the safety of her parents' house.

Hermann could not bear life without her. His need for her was far stronger than his need for morphine. A regular visitor to their flat observed that, 'Her wish was his command. He was not her slave, but almost. Goering was clearly even more deeply in love than she was.'[12] So, when Karin and her family physician suggested he enter a withdrawal programme, Hermann, without protest, registered voluntarily at Aspuddens Nursing Home on 6 August 1925.

Having to make do with small doses of a morphine substitute pushed Hermann close to the edge. After ten days he went over. According to a nurse, 'He broke open the medicine cupboard and took two shots of the 2 per cent Eukodal solution himself. Six nurses could do nothing to stop him and he behaved in a very threatening manner. Goering's wife was afraid he might even kill someone in his frenzy.'[13] Finally, after some sedatives and a few doses of morphine, he calmed down.

Within a matter of days Hermann was on the loose again: 'He jumped out of bed, got dressed and shouted that he wanted to get out and meet death somehow, since somebody who had killed forty-five people had no other choice than to take his own life.' Then, 'He ran up to his room and armed himself with a cane which turned out to contain some sort of sword.' The nursing staff did not hesitate and called both the police and the fire brigade. Hermann 'tried to resist but it was futile'.[14]

He was trussed up in a straitjacket and taken, via hospital, to the Langbro asylum where he was deposited in a padded cell, certified insane. Five weeks of cold turkey followed. Today we are all too familiar with the mental and physical horrors associated with this unforgiving process. The stomach cramps, the night sweats, the terrifying hallucinations, limbs aching, bones hurting, every single molecule screaming out for a fix. For Hermann there were no reference points for what he was going through, no pervasive drug culture to explain away or mediate his condition. He faced it alone.

Hermann's medical notes give the impression that all his darkest thoughts, primal urges, malicious fantasies and tawdry human failings spilled out in a black spew of emotions, 'depressed . . . weeping . . . constantly demanding . . . irritable, dejected, talkative . . . egocentric', with 'thoughts of suicide . . . hysterical tendencies, inflated self-esteem', while seeing 'visions' and hearing 'voices'.[15] Mixed in were wild anti-semitic rants and torrid dreams of a conspiracy against him which featured Abraham, the 'most dangerous Jew that ever existed', who was 'driving a red hot nail into his back', and a Jewish doctor who 'wanted to cut out his heart'. At one point he 'smuggled a weight in as a weapon', and made a 'suicide attempt by hanging'.[16]

One doctor made the much quoted comment that Hermann was 'a sentimental person, lacking in fundamental moral courage'.[17] Nevertheless Hermann endured. On 7 October 1925 he was released with a clean bill of health. This crisis apparently over, Hermann and Karin were plunged into a nasty custody battle over her son which they promptly lost.

In an effort to help reverse the judgement, and having already slipped off the wagon, Hermann returned to the asylum on 22 May 1926 for another enforced cure. A month later he was out, declared 'completely free from the use of all types of opium derivatives'. To strengthen their case further Hermann got a concession to sell BMW aircraft engines in Sweden. Despite this, custody was once again refused. The future stayed bleak.

Then, a general amnesty was declared by the German government that wiped out the criminal charges against Hermann dating back to the Munich putsch. He saw his chance to return to the Nazi fold. Leaving Karin in Stockholm temporarily, Hermann headed for Berlin.

Arriving in January 1927, without any means of support, he took to dossing at a friend's place in a seedy district of the city. It did not take long for him to slip back into drug abuse, a fact confirmed by a letter from Karin urging him to quit: 'Make a real and mighty effort to liberate yourself before it's too late . . . to be a morphinist is to commit suicide.' Her devotion was perhaps never more clearly expressed than in these desperate words, written to rescue him from destruction: 'You are a great spirit and a fine man, you dare not succumb. I love you so strongly, with my whole body and soul, that I could not bear to lose you . . . you are ruled by an evil spirit or force, and your body gradually wastes away. Save yourself and with you, me!!!'[18]

Hermann took heed. He spent three weeks of September 1927 at the Langbro asylum in Stockholm, getting clean. This time when he left, there would be no going back. He returned to Germany with Karin at his side, his addiction beaten.

* * *

Hermann's battle with morphine was a defining moment in his life, a point of no return. He had grown up surrounded by lavish wealth; he had ascended the heights of German society as a fighter ace and come to regard himself as a natural leader of men. Morphine made a nonsense of all that. The drug interacted with the worst elements of Hermann's character, invigorated his demons and brought out his monstrous and slothful aspects. It dragged him into squalid rooms and fleabag hotels, made him fat, erratic, lazy and homicidal.

The assumption that Hermann continued to seek refuge in morphine throughout his years in power, and almost chronically during the war, was perpetuated by his contemporaries, who were not shy to point the finger, and has passed into the folklore about him. Friends and enemies would observe him dozing off at state funerals, or greeting them 'wearing a white toga and a glazed, trance-like expression', and draw the obvious conclusions, adding grist to a rumour mill that had by 1944 ensured that Hermann was the most notorious dope fiend in Europe.

There is no real evidence to suggest he ever used again after his spells at the Langbro asylum but, as a result of the side effects of his addiction, Hermann became a pill popper. The first hangover from the morphine years was the weight gain. The once slim, athletic fighter pilot had bloated out of all proportion, piling on the pounds as he sated his cravings by gorging on food. Then there was the insomnia, extremely common among recovering junkies. Unable to sleep he started to take pills to knock himself out. Meantime he began using slimming pills to combat his eating disorders.

In 1937, suffering from severe toothache, he sat in Professor Hugo Blaschke's dentist's chair enjoying the effects of a painkilling sedative, paracodeine, a mild morphine derivative. After the session the professor gave Hermann a bottle of them and advised him to take two every two hours. A week later, though the dental pain was gone, he went back for more pills. By 1938 he was taking ten a day.

When the Americans arrested him at the end of the war he was carrying 2,000 and taking twenty a day. As the US colonel in charge of prisoners bluntly put it, 'He was a simpering slob with two suitcases full of paracodeine. I thought he was a dope salesman. But we took him off his dope and made a man out of him.'[19] A doctor was drafted in to oversee his progress. His task was made easier by the fact that the narcotic component of Hermann's pills, dihydro-codeine, contained only trace elements of morphine: 'I can testify that his addiction was not very severe. If it had been, I could never have taken him off the drug in the manner which I did ... I used a simple, straight withdrawal method, whittling down the dosage each day until no more drug was allowed.'[20]

Locked up in conditions not dissimilar to those he experienced at the Langbro asylum, deprived of belts, braces and shoelaces, in a windowless room with no mirror or electricity, Hermann kicked the habit. Not only that but he lost eighty pounds of flab. An unintended consequence of him being forced to go straight was his appearance in the dock at Nuremberg sober and fighting fit. Instead of being an incoherent, vague and passive witness, he was firing on all cylinders, restored to something like his charismatic best.

* * *

Hermann's years in exile marked him profoundly. It taught him how transient and fragile success and material wealth could be. However, this insight did not make Hermann a wiser person. Instead it made him perpetually insecure, tortured by the knowledge that everything can be taken away overnight. No amount of money or palaces or titles, not even a personal empire stretching across Europe, was enough to dispel this fear.

His suffering had sharpened his loathing for the system and the society that had abandoned him. It had reinforced the iron in him and hardened his contempt for weakness. Some have argued that his addiction demonstrates his lack of inner strength and inability to handle set-backs, but this view obscures the root cause of his addiction which was the legitimate treatment he received for the pain from his injuries. Hermann did not seek out morphine for thrills or recreation. It also neglects the fact that in the period immediately after his stay at the Langbro asylum, he bounced back with a vengeance. For the next decade or so his energy levels were phenomenal, his drive relentless. Hermann carried a workload and lived to a timetable that would have buried a lesser individual. Given a second chance, with Karin egging him on, he seized it with both hands.

Without doubt, by 1943, he was spending long periods in a haze, his mind foggy, the world fuzzy. But compare this to how other Nazi leaders were affected by the stress of war, particularly as defeat loomed. Hitler was a walking medicine cabinet on a comprehensive daily diet of pills, afflicted with nervous tics and trembling hands. Himmler suffered from crippling stomach problems that were largely psychosomatic and meant that he was accompanied everywhere by his personal masseur and healer. Ribbentrop, the Nazis' foreign minister, would spend weeks lying in a darkened room, paralysed by nervous exhaustion.

In this context, Hermann's flight from reality was par for the course. He wrapped himself in a cloak of self-deception and wishful thinking that shielded him from his own depravity and the terrible consequences of his actions. As far as he was concerned, 'Mostly I had the highest ethics and the highest aims.'[21]

* * *

It is extremely unlikely Albert had any meaningful contact with Hermann during his exile. Whatever joy Albert may have felt at his homecoming was quickly quashed as his brother gravitated straight towards Hitler and a mildly resurgent Nazi Party. When Albert was given the chance to leave Germany in 1928 he took it, once again putting distance between himself and Hermann's political activities.

The move arose when Albert was offered the job of export director for the Kaloriferwerke, based in Vienna. He was happy to accept. This was definitely a step up for Albert, trading in his white lab coat for a business suit. The location made the offer doubly attractive. His childhood memories of Austria were fond ones and Vienna was one of Europe's great cosmopolitan centres, a multi-cultural hub, with a centuries-old imperial history dramatised by the majesty of its architecture and unique musical heritage. Dessau paled in comparison. It was an industrial town, built around factory complexes, not a wonder of civilisation. And Albert may already have seen the writing on the wall. In 1930 the Nazis gained a majority on the town council. A year later, the Bauhaus, which the Kaloriferwerke had been closely involved in, was forcibly shut down.

The signs for Junkers as a whole were not good. Milch continued to try and harass Junkers out of existence and complete Lufthansa's domination of the air industry. After the May 1928 Reichstag elections, he decided to bribe some deputies and buy their support in the debating chamber. Hermann was selected as a potential mouthpiece, having won a seat as a Nazi candidate, one of only twelve to do so.

Hermann received his first payment in June of that year, enabling him to cover the deposit on an apartment. Lufthansa forked out for his office. Milch entered Hermann's social circle and converted to Nazism. When a cheque for 10,000 marks was deposited in Hermann's account at the Deutschebank, Milch wrote a covering letter explaining the transaction: 'As far as Deputy Mr Goering is concerned . . . he was a paid consultant in the American sense.'[22] That their business relationship was more akin to the workings of the Chicago mafia than Wall Street was a cause for anxiety. In the summer of 1929, Milch suggested they suspend the arrangement 'for the time being',[23] pacifying Hermann with a one-off payment of 100,000 marks.

In the spring of 1933, after Hitler became chancellor, Hermann was appointed Reich Commissar for Aviation. He chose Milch as his deputy. Armed with a prospective budget of 1.1 billion marks, they launched an aggressive rearmament programme aimed at hugely increasing aircraft production, thereby reversing the slump that had hit the industry and reduced annual turnover from $4.76 million in 1930 to a mere $952,000 in 1933.

Professor Hugo Junkers was in their sights. He was asked to hand over all his patents to the government. He refused. Urged on by Milch, the local Dessau court investigator threatened him with arrest. On 2 June 1933 he signed them over. Next they went after his personal shares. The 1926 debacle over Junkers's Russian factory was dragged up as evidence of treason. He gave away 51 per cent of his stock but clung on to the rest. He was ordered to leave Dessau. On 3 February 1934 he was placed under house arrest in Munich. By September, with his health deteriorating, he had handed over the entire company. Hermann ignored his letters of protest and pushed ahead with the take-over. Deprived of everything he held dear, Professor Junkers died five months later.

The factories, laboratories and research facilities of the Junkerswerke in Dessau became the Luftwaffe's main development and production centre. Even when defeat was inevitable aircraft kept rolling off the assembly lines. But on the night of 7/8 March 1945, after a series of small Allied raids, 526 RAF Lancaster bombers destroyed the town. The torment for the survivors lasted right up until the final day of the war as the remnants of the German Sixth Army fought their way across the Elbe, retreating away from the advancing Red Army and towards the Americans. Unfortunately for Dessau, when the shooting stopped, it fell within the Soviet zone of occupation. What remained of the Junkerswerke was dismantled and transported to the Soviet Union.

PART TWO

I rearmed Germany until it bristled! I am only sorry we did not rearm more.

Hermann Goering, 11 December 1945

Although millions adored Adolf Hitler, he was a lonely man . . . I met no one who was close to him – perhaps Goering was the sole exception. Goering was able to achieve a great deal with Hitler.

Joachim von Ribbentrop, *Memoirs*

He told me if I wanted to protect the Jews and wanted to help them, that was my affair, but I would have to be more careful and tactful about it, because I made endless difficulties for him.

Albert Goering, 25 September 1945

CHAPTER FIVE

Power

On the morning of 30 January 1933, Adolf Hitler was sworn in as Chancellor of Germany, making him the second most powerful man in the state behind President Hindenburg, the aging hero of Tannenberg. Hitler's power was not yet complete. In his first cabinet, Hermann Goering was the only Nazi given a key position, as Prussian Minister of the Interior.

That afternoon he was entrusted with the task of announcing Hitler's appointment to the foreign and domestic press: 'In this mood Goering was charming, captivating, far removed from the turmoil of the streets.'[1] In the evening he went on the radio and compared the events of the previous twenty-four hours to 'that great day in August 1914 when there also rose a nation', and said that he was confident that '30 January will go down in history as the day when the nation found itself again.'[2]

When Hermann had limped back to Germany in 1927 the prospect that, six years later, he would have such a prominent place at the Führer's side and such a crucial role in German politics must have seemed impossibly distant, even in Karin's wildest dreams. But, like in 1923, when hyper-inflation encouraged the Nazis to attempt a putsch, it was an economic disaster that raised their profile. This time, it was not a form of temporary financial insanity that gripped Germany but a long-term collapse that broke the will and patience of the already dissatisfied, volatile and fearful population, opening the flood-gates to Hitler's movement.

The piecemeal recovery of the economy in the mid-twenties was built on wobbly foundations. A series of agreements fixing reparations to the Allies at a sustainable rate and a massive injection of American capital helped obscure the real weakness. Demographic pressures were swelling the workforce at a moment when unemployment was on the rise, standing at $2\frac{1}{2}$ million in the winter of 1928–9. Both agriculture and heavy industry were suffering. Then came the Wall Street Crash.

Panic selling on the New York stock exchange began on 'Black Thursday', 24 October 1929. Five days later, on 'Black Tuesday', 10 billion dollars was wiped off the share value of America's leading companies. The effect was calamitous and plunged the world economy into a depression that had barely lifted when the Second World War began. Germany was particularly vulnerable. US banks began calling in the country's debts. By 1932 one in three workers was out of a job. When Hitler became chancellor the official unemployment figure was 6,013,612. The true total may have been as high as $8\frac{1}{2}$ million. Roughly half the available labour force was either unemployed or on restricted working hours. The republic's welfare system ceased to cope. By the end of 1932 between a quarter and half a million men were homeless.

For those clinging to a job things were not much better. Wages were reduced and fixed at their 1927 level. Profits shrunk as exports dried up and the domestic market contracted rapidly. Chronic insecurity stalked every sector of the economy. Crime soared. Breadlines grew and soup kitchens appeared across the land. Aggressive deflationary measures pursued by the government only made matters worse.

The Nazis were able to make inroads into the mass unemployed, but it was the Communists who benefited most from the mobs of disaffected, hungry and bored young men loitering in parks, many of whom had never had a job. When the Wall Street Crash hit, membership of the Kommunistische Partei Deutschlands (KPD), formed in December 1918, was a paltry 117,000. By 1932 it had risen to 360,000. The party's leader was Ernst Thalmann, an ex-labourer and front-line soldier who had impeccable working-class credentials and an aversion to 'intellectuals'. The KPD slavishly followed the line handed down by Moscow, rejecting parliamentary democracy and any form of alliance with the largest party in the republic, the Social Democrats, who were the traditional partners of the trade unions. To the KPD they were class traitors, as much an enemy as the Nazis.

The KPD's paramilitary organisation, the Red Front-Fighters League, pitched itself against both the police and Hitler's SA, fighting an incessant battle of intimidation, confrontation and provocation. Action taken by the Red Front-Fighters League to prevent Hermann speaking at a meeting in Bremen represented the norm. After about a hundred communists broke in: 'A terrifying melee followed. Blackjacks, brass knuckles, clubs, heavy buckled belts, glasses and bottles were the weapons used . . . women fainted . . . dozens of heads and faces were bleeding . . . the storm-troopers fought like lions . . . the band struck up a martial tune. Hermann Goering stood calmly on stage, his fists on his hips.'[3]

Berlin was the main battleground as political violence once again became endemic, rising to fever pitch in 1932, the year of elections – two for the Reichstag, one for the federal state assemblies and one for president. In the first seven weeks of the campaigning season there were 82 deaths and 400 injured during waves of rioting. As Germany voted during June and July, 105 people died in bitter fighting. This was the tip of an iceberg that featured torture, vandalism, extortion, public brawling and a state of general mayhem that convinced many Germans that all-out civil war was just around the corner. Exploiting this widely held perception, and actively fanning the flames, were the Nazis, who by now had leapt from an unimpressive 2.6 per cent of the vote in 1928 to 37.4 per cent in the July 1932 Reichstag election.

The great depression and the consequent rise of the KPD were the vital components of Nazi success in this breakthrough period. Hitler was able to heap the blame for the failing economy squarely onto the republic and its politicians, something they made it easier for him to do by their inept reaction to the crisis. At the same time the spectre of Communist revolution justified all the excesses and violence of his own activists. He was tapping into very real fears, shared almost universally by the middle class, the upper class, the church and the ruling elite, not only in Germany but all over Europe.

Nazi rhetoric and propaganda ceaselessly twinned Bolshevism with the Jews; as Karin put it, 'Every day the Communists parade with their crooked noses and red flags with the star of David',[4] portraying them as the ultimate bogeyman, simultaneously responsible for the Soviet Union, the iniquities of finance capital, high prices in department stores and modernist art. However, it was the war against Communism that spoke most directly to the German electorate. Anti-semitism won the Nazis few votes. Their attacks on the KPD won them millions.

* * *

The year 1930 marked the arrival of the Nazis as a significant parliamentary bloc within the Reichstag. At their helm was Hermann, already a deputy after being chosen as one of a dozen Nazis to enter the chamber in 1928, 'like the wolf into the sheep flock'.[5] Hermann's return to the limelight was courtesy of Hitler's decision to pursue a 'legal' path to power, using the ballot box to bring down democracy. According to Hermann, 'This tactical change to the legal struggle did not at all mean renouncing the idea of revolution.'[6]

The strategy was predicated on winning the support of business, industry and the traditional elite, partly to elicit much needed funds for sustaining a mass organisation, but also to gain leverage with the power brokers in German society with whom the Nazis would have to work if they were to rule the country effectively and realise their ambitious plans for empire. How successful the Nazis were at achieving a relationship of mutual understanding with these groups remains a contentious issue, revolving around questions of who was using who, and to what degree the business tycoons, bankers, generals and land-owning nobles actually subscribed to Hitler's ideas. What is certain is that Hermann was the pivotal figure in these negotiations. His fame as a First World War flying ace and his solid family credentials, given further gloss by Karin's breeding, made him the obvious choice for such a mission, particularly compared to the other leading Nazis.

Goebbels had established a reputation as an aggressive rabble-rouser who aimed his rhetoric at the Berlin workers and dispossessed, lacing his propaganda tirades with the language of radical socialism. Himmler was as yet a nobody. Hess was too much in Hitler's shadow. Strasser was a party functionary par excellence, not a social gadfly. Hermann was the only man for the job.

Once the Lufthansa money started rolling in via Milch, supplemented by Hermann's salary as a Reichstag deputy and a variety of commissions, he and Karin were able to set themselves up on the exclusive Badenschestrasse. Fritz Thyssen, the Ruhr coal and steel magnate, met Hermann in the late 1920s and immediately befriended him: 'At that time Goering seemed a most agreeable person. In political matters he was very sensible.'[7] Thyssen called Karin an 'exceedingly charming woman', and paid for 'improvements' to their new apartment to the tune of 150,000 marks.

The entertaining began in earnest, filling the Goerings' home with guests: 'I don't think there is a single meal we have had alone, there are always people there, never less than three.'[8] Two early scalps were the former Kaiser's second son, Prince August Wilhelm, and the Prince and Princess Victor zu Weid, who opened connections to the aristocracy of central Europe: 'The Weids want everyone they know to become interested in the Hitler movement . . . Hermann is bombarded with questions . . . he must explain and answer, elaborate to an exhausting degree . . . but . . . the circle around us is constantly growing.'[9]

A good example of how well Hermann and Karin mixed business and pleasure is their social diary for the Christmas/New Year period, 1930–1. Buoyed by the Nazis' recent electoral windfall, the couple had much to celebrate. On Christmas Eve Goebbels and his wife came round. On the day itself they had fourteen guests, including Prince August Wilhelm and the Weids. On 5 January they held a New Year party, attended by Hitler, to serve as a point of introduction between him and Fritz Thyssen. Also invited was Doctor Hjalmar Schacht, an ex-president of the Reichsbank who was on the board of governors at the Deutschebank, and destined to be the Nazis' first economics minister. A few weeks earlier Schacht had been introduced to Hermann at a dinner hosted by another member of the Deutschebank board.

The atmosphere Hermann and Karin created was perfectly tailored to assuage the worries these men might have about the revolutionary intentions of the Nazis. Schacht remarked on their 'pleasant middle class home', and found Hermann an 'urbane companion', without 'anything that might have been described as irreconcilable or political radicalism'.[10]

The allegiance of these two men paid off almost as soon as Hitler stepped into the chancellor's shoes. On 20 February 1933, Hermann held a private party at his official residence for members of the Reich Association of German Industry. Hitler was the guest speaker, Schacht the host. Aside from Thyssen, there was Krupp, the legendary arms baron, Bosch from the electronics sector, Schnitzler from IG Farben and Voggler of United Steel.

Precise records do not exist of Hitler's 1½-hour-long address, or of Hermann's closing remarks but, according to Krupp, 'Goering led his argument adroitly onto the need for those circles not engaged in the political arena at last to make some financial sacrifice.'[11] By the end of the evening three million marks had been pledged to the Nazi Party.

* * *

Had Hermann merely been a conduit to an establishment that the Nazis still intended to overthrow, his use to Hitler would have remained limited, if essential. But Hermann also had popular appeal; he was able to make his way 'through the people with complete confidence and with a clear aim'.[12] Though not an original speaker, he was effective, relaying a crude message peppered with key words, phrases, and emotional triggers, endlessly repeated during a performance that built to a rousing crescendo. He developed a winning persona, the bluff, sometimes coarse, often jovial, ex-flying ace, a 'big' character, always dressed to the nines in a dazzling array of uniforms, speaking his mind, no bullshit.

Germans responded positively to this image simply because he did not need to cultivate or fabricate it very much; people sensed that the barn-storming, flamboyant character who appeared on the hustings was genuine, without pretence or artifice. This cut across class barriers, making Hermann not only instantly recognisable, but also approachable. The British ambassador noted that, 'None of the Nazi leaders except Goering had any sort of hold on the people, and some of them . . . were cordially disliked and distrusted.'[13]

As a result Hermann found himself on a never-ending speaking tour. Writing to her mother on 21 February 1929, Karin's described his packed schedule: 'Today Hermann gives his first big speech in the Reichstag . . . Tonight he speaks at Berlin University before students from all different parties . . . Tomorrow he speaks in Nuremberg and then he goes off on a twelve-day trip to East Prussia to make twelve different speeches in twelve different places.'[14]

Hermann was careful not to ignore his own constituency. He did not mind 'slumming' it, being quite able to speak the depraved language of the most vile, vulgar anti-semites and bloodthirsty ex-Freikorps killers. He opened his home to Nazi Party members in need of food and lodging on trips to Berlin. A humble farm labourer could find himself sitting down to eat next to a crown prince.

That Hermann could operate with ease in such a variety of different worlds gave him a unique place in Hitler's entourage, though to a perceptive observer it revealed a man of immense contradictions, 'torn between a blustering and rowdy revolutionary and the visionary grand seigneur – between the SA's brown shirt in the afternoon and the snug-fitting dinner jacket at night'.[15] But these were also the contradictions of the Nazi movement as it attempted both to seduce and terrorise Germany into submission.

By 1933, in the eyes of the German public and the world, Hermann was visibly Hitler's number two. They were not quite a double act, yet each was sustained by the other. Hermann represented the human, fallible side, the one you could have a beer and a laugh with, while Hitler was more than human, untouchable and unknowable by virtue of his greatness. Hermann was fully aware of this dynamic: 'Let me explain the difference between me and Hitler . . . The German people called him "my Führer". They addressed me as "Hermann". I was always closer to the hearts of the people.'[16]

The cultivation of the Hitler myth, which placed him in a different realm from his subjects, had developed steadily from his image as the 'drummer' of the movement, to being its 'leader', to being Germany's man of destiny. The potential pitfalls of this process of deification, that would lead Hitler further and further from the masses he claimed to understand instinctively, are apparent in Hermann's book, *Germany Reborn* (1934).

On the one hand Hitler is 'an unknown soldier of the world war, a man of the people, without rank or possessions or connections, a plain, simple man',[17] on the other he exudes 'something mystical, inexpressible, almost incomprehensible'.[18] Demi-god or regular guy? The two identities could not coexist indefinitely. When Hitler became supreme ruler of Germany he could no longer, even if he had wished to, sustain the fiction of his ordinariness, which left Hermann to assume the mantle of 'the second man in the Reich' for over a decade.

* * *

Between 1930 and 1933 democracy ceased to function in Germany. An authoritarian clique around President Hindenburg sought to side-step the Reichstag and rule without having to resort to the messy business of forging parliamentary coalitions, winning debates, votes or party consent for their policies. The constitutional device they used was Article 48, rule by emergency decree, which allowed the chancellor to suspend the Reichstag indefinitely and assume its powers. This sweeping measure was fundamentally limited by the fact that the Reichstag retained control of the budget. Hindenburg and his co-conspirators still had to pay lip service to parliament.

Nevertheless, their intention to manage without it was clear. The first emergency cabinet of 'experts', set up in 1930 with Heinrich Brüning at its head, was formed without the participation of the Social Democrats, the largest party in the Reichstag. During the 1920s the deputies had met a hundred times a year. Thanks to Article 48 they met for a total of seventy-four days between October 1930 and July 1932. Between then and Hitler's appointment as chancellor six months later, they met only three times.

When the Reichstag did actually sit in session both the Nazis and the KPD were determined to foul up proceedings. With 107 and 77 deputies respectively after the 1930 elections, out of 577 in all, they had sufficient muscle to bring things to a halt. As chief of the Nazi contingent, Hermann acted as a wrecking ball, imposing himself on the chamber and orchestrating a chorus of disapproval.

The pressure on the democratic system intensified during 1932. Brüning, dubbed the 'hunger chancellor', having failed miserably to alleviate the effects of the depression, resigned in May, to be replaced by Franz von Papen, a deeply unsympathetic character without any kind of following. The July Reichstag elections saw the Nazi vote double, giving them 230 seats, only 75 short of a majority. Hitler's run against Hindenburg in the presidential elections, where he secured 30 per cent on the first ballot and 37 per cent on the second while Hindenburg hovered round 50 per cent, underlined the perilous state of the conservative coalition founded on the old war hero's name.

The Reichstag ceased to function altogether on 12 September 1932, the day Hermann was elected president of the chamber. This coincided with, as Hermann dryly put it, 'the famous scene . . . in which Herr von Papen wished to dissolve the Reichstag, but I . . . sought to prevent him doing so'.[19] Papen had walked into the chamber with a dissolution order, drawn up to avoid further elections and signed by Hindenburg on 30 August. However, at the same time the KPD leader, Thalmann, had put forward a vote of no confidence in Papen's government.

Always happy to exploit an opportunity to cause trouble, Hermann decided the Nazi bloc should support the proposal. He was about to start the vote when Papen tried to speak. Hermann deliberately ignored him and carried on. Papen lost his temper, slapped the dissolution papers in front of Hermann and stomped out to boos and cat calls. The vote of no confidence was passed by 512 votes to 42, with five abstentions and one spoiled ballot. As a result of this farce new elections were called for November.

These did not significantly alter the parliamentary landscape. The Nazi vote had dropped a little, from 37.4 per cent to 33.1 per cent, but they remained the dominant party with 196 seats compared to 121 for the Social Democrats. Extremism gained at the expense of moderation. The middle of the road, mainly Roman Catholic, Centre Party now had fewer seats than the Communists.

Throughout this period, those close to Hindenburg had been attempting to bring Hitler into the equation on their side. The first of several clandestine meetings between the president, Hitler, and Hermann, was held on 31 October 1931. Hitler knew Hindenburg would feel less ill at ease with Hermann. The ex-commander of the Richthofen Squadron was more palatable than an ex-corporal.

These sessions foundered on Hitler's insistence on becoming chancellor and not settling for the lesser positions he kept being offered. As 1932 came to an end Papen was replaced by 'the most pitiful' Kurt von Schleicher, who continued to hope it was somehow possible to govern without a parliament and without any popular support. It was not. Given the fact that Hindenburg and Schleicher had no interest in a democratic solution, their options had narrowed to Hitler. But Hindenburg could not quite bring himself to bite the bullet. Hermann and Hitler wooed his son Oskar, who brought further pressure to bear on the eighty-four-year-old incumbent. Finally he relented. Hitler got what he wanted.

* * *

The vital role Hermann played in Hitler's journey from relative obscurity to the chancellorship was summed up in an entry Goebbels made in his diary. Known for his acid tongue and for not giving praise lightly, except in reference to Hitler, Goebbels described the events surrounding 30 January 1933 as, 'the finest hour in Goering's life. For years he had been smoothing the diplomatic and political path for the Führer by exhausting negotiations. His prudence, his strong nerves, and above all his force of character and loyalty to Hitler were sincere, strong and admirable.'[20]

Certainly these were glory days for Hermann, making him indispensable to Hitler. But the one person with whom he would have most dearly liked to share the spoils was no longer with him. Karin passed away before he could fulfil the dream she had nurtured, fostered and never let die even when all seemed lost. Her health had started on a steady decline in the summer of 1929 when she was hospitalised due to influenza. She recovered and recuperated at home, not yet fit enough to accompany Hermann on his travels: 'It's so empty when Hermann's not here, and I have a constant yearning for him.' She sought solace in his cause: 'It's only when I think of how I can help him or the Hitler movement, in some way or other, that strength comes to me from above.'[21]

By June 1931 her heart was weak, her pulse faint and she was close to comatose as she went in and out of sanatoria in East Silesia. Her time was running short. After Hitler gave Hermann a brand new motor car and two weeks' holiday, he decided to take his wife on one last trip. Karin managed to raise herself sufficiently to make the journey down into Bavaria and then across into Austria, where they went to stay at Castle Mauterndorf. Karin met Epenstein, Hermann's fairy godfather, for the very first time. Lilli persuaded Epenstein to throw an impromptu banquet for his guests in the main hall, with minstrels playing medieval tunes, just as they had done when Hermann was a boy.

On 25 September, Karin's mother died. Though Karin's doctor's warned her that going to Sweden for the funeral might kill her, she was determined to be there. Hermann went with her. They were met at the station in Stockholm by Thomas von Kantzow, Karin's son by her first husband, who remembered greeting them on the platform: 'My mother had always looked most beautiful when she was most seriously ill and she never looked lovelier than she did when I first saw them.'[22]

That evening Karin collapsed. Hermann remained at her bedside for four days and nights: 'He would only steal away to shave or bathe or snatch a bite to eat ... otherwise he spent all his time on his knees at her bedside, holding her hand, wiping the perspiration from her face or the moisture from her lips'.[23]

His vigil was cut short when he got an urgent message from Hitler to return to Berlin immediately. Hermann did not know what to do.

As usual, Karin put the needs of the Nazi movement above her own, 'begging, pleading, even ordering him to obey Hitler's call'. Hermann could not disappoint her, even though it was tearing him apart: 'After a time he began to sob and she took his hand and laid it on her breast, as if it was he who was in need of comfort'.[24]

Less than a day after Hermann left her bedside, at 4.00 a.m. on 17 October 1931, Karin died. Hermann returned for the modest funeral. She was buried in the tiny chapel of the Swedish castle where she and Hermann first met. Devastated by her death, he poured every ounce of energy into his work, desperate to achieve the Nazi victory that would allow her to rest in peace.

Having attained this goal, Hermann wanted to pay proper tribute to his beloved wife and create something worthy of her memory. Now he had the power to do it on a grand scale. By 1934 he was executive in charge of all Germany's forests, wild animals and plant life. He hand-picked an area about two hours north-west of Berlin, known as the Schorfheide, a region covered in forests, lakes and moorland, claimed a 40,000 hectare chunk, banned all building on it and reserved it as a sanctuary for rare breeds of deer, buffalo, elk and flowers. His ministerial duties and philanthropic impulses satisfied, Hermann added a game park so he could go hunting whenever he liked, and found a spot for the construction of a country residence.

The site for Karinhall, as Hermann called it, was an enchanted space nestling on the shores of a small lake surrounded by trees. Two architects were drafted in to work on its original, somewhat modest design, based on a Norse timber lodge. Next to it an imposing mausoleum was built out of Brandenburg granite. Hermann was bothered by the fact that his wife was buried in Sweden. He wanted her brought home. On 17 June 1934, Karin's coffin was removed and transported from Sweden by ferry and then train, with her son Thomas, her parents and an armed escort.

As they travelled through Germany all the stations were draped in black and the locals were given a day's holiday to line the route and mourn her passing: 'On all sides there were black obelisks and flaming torches, in every village the church bells tolled.' The coffin was led in a sombre procession to Karinhall. At the re-interment Hermann was joined by Hitler, all the leading members of the Nazi hierarchy, and hundreds of politicians and eminent figures. Mist billowed in from across the lake, conjuring up visions of warrior kings and queens.

'Once Karin's sarcophagus was brought into the open place muffled drums sounded a tattoo, and then came the sound of the funeral march from the "Gotterdammerung". The Führer's great wreath was then brought in as a last tribute to a woman who had been so stout and true to the Third Reich, in whose cause she died. Then came the service. Hardly was it over when from the far side of the lake came the sounds of the hunting horns of the foresters sending forth their tribute.'[25]

With this solemn memorial Hermann sought to enshrine Karin as a great heroine of the Nazi movement, his very own Lady of the Lake. At the same time, when all the ceremonial pomp had been stripped away, it was an expression of the very deep love he had always and would always feel for her. She alone, of all the people in Hermann's life, truly captured his heart.

CHAPTER SIX

Ski Bunnies and Bolsheviks

Across the border in Austria, the citizens of Albert's adopted country watched the events of 1933 unfold with some trepidation. Though during the 1920s many Austrians were in favour of *Anschluss* – political and economic union with Germany – the prospect of living under Nazi rule was not a welcome one. When Albert arrived in 1928, Austria was just as unstable as the Germany he had left behind; if anything it was more sharply polarised than its neighbour. Defeat in the First World War had proved terminal for the Austro-Hungarian Empire, splitting it apart. On 12 November 1918 the Austrian republic came into being after the emperor had abdicated the previous day.

The state he bequeathed had shrunk drastically in size. Before the collapse, the Austrian part of his realm had held around 30 million people. As a result of territorial losses underwritten by the Allies the Austrian population was reduced to 6 million. A land mass that had covered 470,000 square kilometres had been cut up to leave only 130,000. In this precarious situation union with Germany was high on the agenda.

The former Allies had no intention of allowing the creation of the greater Germany they had fought to prevent. *Anschluss* of any kind was banned. The new Austrian republic would have to fend for itself. When it quickly became clear that it was too weak to survive the battering of post-war inflation the Allies bailed it out with huge loans. This was a stop-gap measure that did little to alleviate Austria's problems. The reconstituted nation suffered from a lack of proportion; it was a misshapen entity that was critically divided between Vienna, the great urban centre that was home to a third of the population, and the countryside around it.

Vienna had swollen during the second half of the nineteenth century, boosted hugely by immigration. It expanded 2½ times in size, its growth rate outstripping both Paris and London. By 1900 it had 1,674,957 residents, only half of whom had been born there. The city's splendidly wealthy and imperial inner core was surrounded by staunchly working-class suburbs, poor Jewish ghettos and a thriving criminal underclass.

After 1918 it became known as 'Red' Vienna, where a cradle to grave network of labour organisations and socialist clubs catered for the vast urban proletariat that lived almost exclusively in fortified housing projects. Their political party, the Social Democrats, pursued a thoroughly Marxist line. Participation in parliament was purely tactical: 'With our class enemy, we shall never go into coalition, never conclude an alliance or come to a truce of any sort.'[1]

The 'enemy' inhabited the rural, Catholic heartlands. Their party, the Christian Socialists, buttressed with support from the old ruling class, the state bureaucracies and the justice system, was able to hold power from 1920 onwards by forming coalitions with far-right groups. The atmosphere in parliament was unremittingly hostile; debates degenerated quickly into shouting matches.

Both sides developed their paramilitary wings. The left had the Schutzbund, the right, the Heimwehr. By 1930 they numbered around 30,000 men each. Local clashes were frequent, causing occasional eruptions of mass violence like 'Black Friday', 15 July 1927. After the Vienna High Court saw fit to acquit the murderers of two Schutzbund men, 'Red' Vienna marched on government buildings. By the end of the day eighty-four were dead, mostly protestors, and 500 wounded. Civil war was an ever present possibility. The effects of the Wall Street Crash almost made it a reality.

Living in Vienna, Albert was at the eye of the storm. Nevertheless, it would be fair to say that these years were among the happiest and most carefree of his life. His job for the Kaloriferwerke granted him access to a cosmopolitan business world that mixed naturally with the social and cultural elite of Europe: 'He always said he felt most comfortable in the triangle between Vienna, Prague and Budapest, at the time the very hub of Europe . . . It was his world . . . he fitted in very well there.'[2]

He was helped by the fact that he was 'charming, bright and amusing',[3] and Vienna offered him his favourite pastimes in abundance. He soaked up the music, the café culture – 'Albert was an eager consumer of good coffee in large quantities'[4] – and the city's decadent atmosphere. 'He enjoyed life, he liked the good things.'[5]

Albert formed lasting friendships. His loyalty to his friends went beyond the norm: 'Albert asked me once for my definition of friendship. I told him that it meant enjoyment of another's company, sharing of interests, etc., the usual. He smiled and shook his head. "It is much more, a friend is someone who will risk his fortune, his safety, even his life when you need him."'[6]

He met Albert Benbassat, a Jewish businessman, when he delivered a crane to a building site Benbassat was running. They hit it off instantly: 'They were both young, and they were both fond of Viennese music, of good wine and a good time. And they became very good friends.'[7] After the Nazi occupation of Austria in 1938, conditions became perilous for the Benbassats and they moved to Bucharest. During the war the situation became deadly. Albert arranged papers for them to get out of Romania and to neutral Spain via Italy, saving the entire family from extinction. Benbassat is fourth out of thirty-four names on a list Albert drew up for his Allied captors to identify some of the prominent individuals he helped escape Nazism.

After the war they remained in touch and Albert befriended Benbassat's seventeen-year-old son, Jacques: 'He seemed to enjoy my company, in spite of my young age.' Jacques talked to him about women – 'Albert shared this interest most intensely' – and admired the spirit of 'this very human, life-loving man'.[8]

Albert also made a close connection with two English businessmen, Leonard Bickford-Smith and his second-in-command, Major Frank Short MBE. Leonard had moved to Austria to oversee factories run by his company, a family firm stretching back to the 1830s which was based on the inventions of William Bickford. He had designed a 'safety' fuse for explosive charges that would burn at a uniform rate. The fuse became the global standard. In 1844 the company built a factory in Austria at Wiener-Neustadt.

By 1914 Bickford-Smith was part of a larger corporation founded by the Swedish inventor and entrepreneur, Alfred Nobel. In 1864 Nobel formed the Nitro-Glycerine Company. Ten years later he had factories across the world, including one in Hamburg. Though Nobel's Explosives Company acquired Bickford's Swansea factory in 1909, the Austrian outlet was still independent when Leonard Bickford-Smith arrived there. Just before war broke out he married an Austrian accountant and during 1914–18 he was technically under house arrest in Vienna as an enemy national, though little was done to enforce the curfew.

His business was equally unaffected by the hostilities, thanks to the Reich's Custodian of Alien Property Law. This measure applied to companies in Germany and the Austro-Hungarian Empire in which British or American firms held a majority share. On the declaration of war, they were seized and run by German management. However, once the conflict was over, these same companies, and any profits they made, would be handed back to their British and American owners perfectly intact. Years later, the Nazis would make use of this law when it suited them.

When Nobel Industries Ltd was set up in 1920, it owned 75 per cent of Bickford-Smith. Two years later Leonard's Austrian operation was renamed Nobel-Bickford AG and acquired a factory in Bratislava. This expanded concern was a subsidiary of Nobel's German company, Dynamit AG. But the treacherous post-war economic climate and the intense competition for markets brought Nobel Industries Ltd to crisis point. In response to the threat posed by the creation of IG Farben, the British chemical engineering sector formed Imperial Chemical Industries (ICI) in 1926. This massive combine included all Nobel's interests along with Bickford-Smith. ICI and IG Farben struggled to find a business arrangement that suited them both. Aside from some share transfers, negotiations had ceased by 1930. In the meantime IG Farben acquired Dynamit AG, which was still technically Bickford's parent company.

Nevertheless, under the wings of ICI Leonard was able to gain a foothold in the Czech company Explosia. He retired in 1936, moved back to England and set up a £15,000 fund for Austrian refugees from Nazism. It is distinctly possible that Albert helped distribute this money, but we cannot be sure. Albert knew Leonard well, but his constant travelling meant that Albert was closer to his man in Vienna, Major Frank Short.

The major was married to the Austrian ballet star, Gusti Pichler, a prima ballerina at the world famous Vienna Opera who had also appeared in several films. By 1939 the climate of Nazi terror was too hot to handle. The major was English, his wife was Jewish, her celebrity as a dancer offering no protection. Albert stepped in, sorted out the necessary travel documents, visas and tickets, and got them out of Europe to Cairo, where the major enlisted in the Royal Engineers. He appears as the twenty-ninth name on Albert's Nuremberg list.

By 1940 the factories in Austria and Bratislava had been taken over by Dynamit AG, and therefore, IG Farben. What was left of Bickford's firm was salvaged by Albert: 'I received 1,000 marks per month from a British company, whose President I was. The name . . . was Bickford and Co Ltd, of Vienna . . . This was headed by a Major Frank Short, who left Vienna for Cairo when all this Nazi trouble came up, and he asked me to take over the company for him and take care of his interests until after the war.'[9]

Albert took the responsibility seriously. As his Allied interrogators noted, Albert was 'so conscientious that he not only had himself assigned as a trustee for the Bickford Co through the Reich's Custodian of Alien Property, and prevented its amalgamation into some other German firm, but he even claims that he can show a profit for his six years of management.'[10]

The company survived the war fully functioning. It was finally wound down by ICI on 23 May 1946 and absorbed into its explosives division. Albert had repaid the major's trust in full. That Frank Short chose Albert to be guardian of the Bickford Company in Vienna is typical of the faith people, from all walks of life, put in him, believing he had the courage, character and moral strength to stand firm, regardless of any danger to himself.

* * *

One of the few things that united Austrians during the fractious years after the First World War was skiing. The sport initially attracted the elite but developed at great speed into a mass leisure pursuit, making the Austrian Alps Europe's winter Riviera, and centre of a burgeoning tourist industry.

Austria produced the sport's first superstar, Johann Schneider. During the First World War he trained Austrian troops. In 1919 he set up a school for skiing instructors, concentrating on the technique he had perfected, known simply as Arlberg. It became the most successful academy of its kind in the world. Schneider was also a movie star, having pioneered the ski film, combining stunt action sequences on the snow with simple plot lines, anticipating the first ten minutes of most Bond films. His first international hit was in 1922. His last box office smash was *White Ecstasy*, a romantic comedy on skis, starring the young Leni Riefenstahl as the love interest. The movie brought her to Hitler's attention. She went on to make the infamous Nazi propaganda film about the 1936 Olympics, *Olympia*, and may have had a hand in getting Schneider arrested in 1938, though he managed to flee to America a year later.

Albert became a real skiing enthusiast. He loved nothing better than to get out on the slopes, revelling in the freedom and exhilaration of testing himself against nature, keen to share the thrill: 'In the winter we skied with him . . . when the full moon was there he took us out and he said, "You have to have this experience", he was that type of guy.'[11] No doubt he also enjoyed the après-ski scene, which grew in tandem with the sport. The best resorts were magnets for women, so much so that the expression *skihasserl* ('ski bunny') was coined at the time, and inspired a popular hit song, with the chorus, 'Yes, you've got to have a bunny, Without her skiing is no fun!' Albert probably had his fair share. Whether his wife knew about his affairs is impossible to say. She did write a poem in 1937 that expressed bitter feelings towards Albert. Nevertheless they stayed together. He was so content with life that he became an Austrian citizen, registering his disgust at the direction Germany was taking.

* * *

'I welcome the opportunity of presenting to the English-speaking peoples a few of my ideas about the struggle of the German people for freedom and honour. I hope these words will also be accepted by my opponents as a frank expression of my boundless love for my country, to whose service alone I have pledged my life.'[12] So, rather pompously, began Hermann's *Germany Reborn* (1934), written primarily for a British and American audience. The Nazis had ruled the roost for a year and their gaze was turning outwards. Hermann set out to offer his own explanation of what Nazism was all about.

It showed, in clear, layman's language – as opposed to the tortured pedantry, verbosity, and convoluted metaphysics of official ideologues like Alfred Rosenberg – how Hermann's viewpoint often placed him closer to the traditional nationalists than his more radical Nazi colleagues,

including Hitler. His affinity with their ideas was most clearly demonstrated in the first section of the book, where he discussed German history.
To him, it was 'a long tale of cruel wars',[13] fought to defend a nation with
'no natural boundaries . . . protected only by the bodies of its men'.[14] The
argument that Germany was not a habitual aggressor, but perpetually
under attack, was popular among mainstream, patriotic opinion, making
Germany the victim rather than perpetrator.

Hermann applied this interpretation to the First World War. In
1914 Germany was 'threatened from all sides', and 'had the sword
thrust into her hand . . . guiltless of the outbreak of this greatest of
wars'.[15] As a result, 'For four years the German people endured and
suffered grievously as in a besieged city.' Defeat came in 1918 because
'This best of all armies had its backbone broken from behind.'[16] The
Versailles Treaty was 'more devilish than the mind of a Dante could have
imagined',[17] and the 'destruction of Carthage was nothing compared to
this shameful peace'.[18]

Hermann's analysis differed from the main tenets of Hitler's
philosophy, outlined in *Mein Kampf*, which reduced all human history
to a biological race war between the Aryan and the Jew. This eternal
struggle could only be resolved by the utter destruction of one by the
other. The victor would then inherit the earth. Nowhere did Hermann
even allude to this theory. It is possible he felt it was too extreme to
present to a wider public, but the truth seems to be that Hermann
did not share Hitler's vision on this vital point. In *Germany Reborn*, he
restricted his anti-semitic remarks to a repetition of insults that were
common among the nationalist right.

It was his militaristic mind-set, his contempt for the existing order
and his post-war experience on the margins, which meant he never
became an integrated member of society, that set him apart from the
conservatives. While the circle around President Hindenburg sought
to preserve the establishment, Hermann sought to overthrow it. This
meant 'the tearing away of what is old and rotten and the breaking
through of new forces which are strong and young'.[19]

During the crisis of 1918–20, the Freikorps did 'their duty', staking
their lives 'for patriotism and honour'.[20] But they were not a solution
to the 'decadence and decay' of the Weimar Republic and the 'complete
bankruptcy of middle-class leadership', with its 'snobbery and self-
conceit'.[21] A fresh alternative to the right/left divide was required, and

Hitler supplied it: 'He took the symbols from both parties and melted them into the crucible of our philosophy to make a new synthesis', National Socialism, thereby proving the two were not 'mutually exclusive'.[22]

Hermann had little attachment to the socialist aspects of Nazi thinking, which were mainly the work of Gregor Strasser. He referred to 'German workers who, as loyal Storm Troopers, went to their death for their convictions and country'.[23] There was no mention of labour rights, social and economic policy or the redistribution of wealth. Hitler was similarly non-committal, happy to see Strasser terminated on the Night of the Long Knives.

Hermann's uncompromising nationalism formed the main plank of his ideology: 'All principles that tend to further the recovery and position of Germany we alone recognise as points in our programme; all other things which may be damaging to our country we condemn and they are to be destroyed.'[24] After the Munich putsch, 'The seed sown in blood began wonderfully to put out shoots.'[25] The movement grew. The Nazis 'were white hot with fanatical love for our people'.[26] A rolling tide of popularity washed away the ailing republic and its conservative coalitions and swept the Nazis to power.

* * *

Which brings us to Hermann's central theme, the crux of the book, the war against Communism: 'The leader gave me the Prussian Ministry of the Interior, above all things, in order to overthrow and crush Communism.'[27] Throughout the text he identified it as the greatest single threat to Germany's future: 'Where Communism raises its head a people is destroyed',[28] along with 'culture, morals, the church and industry'.[29]

Also implicated were the Jews, whose connection to Communism was exemplified by 'the Jew Karl Marx'.[30] Consistency was not an issue here. Hermann described the Jew as 'looking at us with the satiated middle-class face of a Marxist politician and then again with the hate-distorted features of a Communist from the underworld',[31] and had no problem further muddying the waters by suggesting a 'close connection between Marxism and liberalism'.[32] The only clear point to emerge from this hateful muddle was that Communism, in all its myriad incarnations, had to be defeated: 'If the Soviet star had been victorious, Germany would have perished in a bloody Communist reign of terror and the whole of the Western world would have followed Germany into the abyss.'[33]

Hermann went on to explain, with considerable satisfaction, his systematic efforts 'to use all the powers at my disposal in order ruthlessly to wipe out this plague'.[34] Rather than trying to conceal or deny the terror he unleashed during 1933, he took full responsibility for the blood on his hands, even congratulating himself on the modest amounts spilt: 'We must admit that this German revolution for freedom was one of the most bloodless and most disciplined of all revolutions in history.'[35]

His remarkable honesty on this subject stemmed from his belief that his actions would be applauded, and his virulent anti-communism warmly received by the book's intended audience: 'Hitler's mission is important for the history of the whole world because he took up the war to the death against Communism and therefore raised a bulwark for the other European nations.'[36]

His position in Hitler's first cabinet gave him *de facto* control of law and order in Prussia: 'It seemed to me of the first importance to get the weapon of the criminal and political police firmly into my own hands.'[37] He immediately set about 'reforming' them: 'Out of thirty-two police chiefs I removed twenty-two. Hundreds of inspectors and thousands of police sergeants followed in the course of the next month.'[38] Once sympathetic personnel were in place, he set out 'to inspire the police with an entirely new spirit',[39] and 'demanded' they 'devote all their energies to the ruthless extermination of all subversive elements'.[40]

To help achieve this goal, 'new men' were recruited. These auxiliary units, the Hilfspolizei, were made up of SA and SS hard nuts, and soon numbered 50,000 men. Hermann had no hesitation in giving them license to kill: 'Every bullet fired from the barrel of a police pistol is my bullet. If you call that murder, then I am a murderer. Everything has been ordered by me.'[41] They went straight on the attack, disrupting KPD marches and meetings, trashing KPD premises and banning its newspapers. The Social Democrats also came under fire. On 5 February 1933, less than a week after Hermann took up his ministerial post, a Social Democrat mayor was gunned down. The Centre Party received similar treatment.

On the 23rd, the KPD HQ in Berlin suffered a massive police raid, which, according to Hermann, uncovered evidence of a planned Communist uprising. He was looking for any excuse that would legitimise an escalation of the terror. A Dutch anarchist, Marius van der Lubbe, was about to provide it. What exactly was going through this young man's mind on the night of 27 February, when he broke into the Reichstag buildings and set fire to the curtains in the debating chamber, will never be known. All the evidence points to him acting alone. Two days before he had tried to burn down a welfare office, then a town hall and a former royal palace. He was determined to make a dramatic statement. This time he succeeded.

Hermann, whose official Berlin residence was linked to the Reichstag by a tunnel, was one of the first on the scene: 'As I opened the door I was all but drawn into the flames by the hot draught . . . I saw self-igniting fire-lighters on the benches and chairs . . . that had eaten through the leather upholstery and set them on fire.'[42] Hitler and Goebbels arrived and joined him to watch the German parliament go up in smoke. Van der Lubbe was arrested nearby. Despite his insistence that he was not part of a wider conspiracy, Hermann and the others were quick to jump to that conclusion. As he wrote in *Germany Reborn*, 'The fire was to be the signal for a general reign of terror by the Communists, for a general rising and a civil war.'[43]

Others, given what happened next, pointed the finger at Hermann, a charge he always firmly denied: 'I suppose they think that, dressed in a red toga and holding a lyre in my hand, I looked on and played while the Reichstag burned.'[44] Though Hermann was innocent, van der Lubbe's act of arson was immensely convenient. It provided the justification for Hermann to launch an all-out war on the left: 'That night I gave the order for the arrest of 4,000 Communist officials; I knew that before dawn the Commies would have lost a great battle.'[45]

On the 28th Hitler and Hermann convinced Hindenburg to sign a blank cheque for dictatorship, an emergency decree whose first paragraph suspended rule by law: 'Thus restrictions on personal liberty, on the right of free expression of opinion, including freedom of the press, or the right of assembly or association, and violations of the privacy of postal, telegraphic and telephonic communications, and warrants for house searches, orders for confiscations as well as restrictions on property rights, are permissible beyond the legal limits otherwise prescribed.'[46]

A few days later the Communist leader Ernst Thalmann was taken prisoner. During March and April 25,000 people were arrested in

Prussia alone. By the end of the year around 100,000 Communists had been locked up. Hundreds were murdered. Elections held on 5 March, in which the Nazis won 51.9 per cent, were used as justification for shutting down parliament completely. With Hermann overseeing proceedings, flanked by armed storm-troopers, the Reichstag deputies voted themselves out of existence on 23 March. The KPD representatives were not allowed to take part. Only the Social Democrats resisted.

Those who could, fled. A series of laws passed in April began purges of the civil service, the justice system, and the medical and educational professions. These purges targeted Jews and anybody with anti-Nazi sympathies. The trade unions were hit by the SS and SA on 2 May. On the 10th, the Social Democrats had their property and assets seized by court order. On 21 June the party was banned altogether and 3,000 members were promptly arrested nationwide. By 14 July all political parties, apart from the Nazis, had been outlawed. The Weimar Republic had been eradicated in a matter of months.

* * *

One of Hermann's tools of oppression was the Geheime Staatspolizei (Secret State Police), or Gestapo. In *Germany Reborn*, he took full credit for its existence: 'I alone created on my own initiative, the State Secret Police Department. This is an instrument which is much feared by the enemies of the state.'[47] Shortly after Hermann assumed his Prussian mandate he put Rudolf Diels in charge of this fledgling organisation. At thirty-two, and sporting several duelling scars, Diels was a senior figure in the already existing secret police. He set about Nazifying it, drawing on its records to build a database of 'subversives'.

Apart from intelligence-gathering, Diels's men were expert torturers. The Gestapo's official HQ was 8 Prinz Albrecht Strasse, Berlin. This address was one of the most feared in Germany, its basement the scene of horrific cruelty. Many of those arrested during the spring and summer of 1933 would spend a few days there before being released, their spirit broken, their flesh ruined.

What to do with the thousands who remained in captivity was something of a challenge. There were just too many of them. Improvised holding centres appeared across Prussia in all manner of locations, the conditions primitive, the justice brutal. Ships were requisitioned to take the overflow of prisoners. Hermann rationalised the problem by setting up formal concentration camps at Oranienburg and Papenburg. They quickly spread.

Hermann fielded a host of outraged complaints and pleas for mercy in individual cases. He made a big show out of temporarily releasing Ernst Thalmann, the KPD leader, meeting him in person, giving him clean clothes and assuring him he would come to no further harm. But his compassion ran barely skin deep. In *Germany Reborn* he explained that, 'It was only natural that in the beginning excesses were committed. It was natural that here and there beatings took place.'[48]

Based in Munich, Himmler had been appointed Provisional Police President of Bavaria. On 20 March he announced to the press that a camp for 'political' prisoners was going to be located at Dachau and run by the SS. Himmler saw it as the first step towards taking over the whole camp network. Hermann resented any SS presence in Prussia. Units of his Hilfs-polizei marched on a camp at Osnabrück and were fired at by SS guards. He felt threatened by efforts to centralise the federal police force. Hermann confessed his fears to Diels: 'I cannot hand over the police. Never! Otherwise I'm simply a bogey, a minister-president without territory.'[49]

Matters came to a head during January 1934. There followed a series of Byzantine manoeuvres between Hermann, Himmler and Hitler, leaving a tangle of lies, false clues and mixed motives that is almost impossible to unravel. Only the result is clear. Diels lost his job. Himmler's SS took over the Gestapo on 20 April 1934, while his deputy, Heydrich, was made head of the Office of the Prussian Secret State Police (Gestapa). A day earlier their SS and SD men had occupied 8 Prinz Albrecht Strasse.

Hermann was prepared to strike a deal with Himmler. The coming showdown with the SA was an important factor in his decision. He needed Himmler to launch any kind of action against them. Their team effort came to fruition on 30 June, the Night of the Long Knives.

But he did not concede everything. He held on to his intelligence agency, the Forschungsamt, dedicated to code-breaking and wire-tapping, which he had launched with Hitler's blessing and a guaranteed monopoly on all electronic surveillance in early 1933. At first the operation was modest, beginning with only four code-breakers. By July there were twenty. Over the next decade the staff would expand to 35,000 employees. Their base was a nondescript house in Berlin. On the top floor were the code-breakers. Elsewhere hundreds of phone taps were monitored twenty-four hours a day, divided into categories according to the language spoken. Foreign embassies were bugged. International cable networks were hacked into. Frogmen tapped into the underwater lines that linked continents round the globe. Fifty teleprinters in the basement churned out the information collected, which was analysed, edited, put in a brown folder, 'the Brown Pages', and shown to Hermann every morning. Crucially, Himmler and Heydrich, for whom phone-tapping had obvious importance, needed to get Hermann's express permission if they wanted to bug somebody's line.

As it was, the 1934 arrangement over the police and the execution of the SA leadership, led to a *modus vivendi* between the two men. This did not mean they were friends or allies in a conventional sense; their temperaments, obsessions and habits were totally different. Like all those close to Hitler they were perpetual rivals for his attention and approval, jostling for a greater share of the spoils of victory. However, Hermann and Himmler did, by and large, stay out of each other's way. They clashed most over economic issues.

After 1936 Hermann steadily acquired a monopoly of control over most of Germany's, and later occupied Europe's, heavy industry and raw materials. Meanwhile the SS wanted their own manufacturing empire. Himmler's aspirations relied on the labour of concentration camp inmates. With their blood, sweat and tears the SS established the German Earth and Stone-Works Company, a herb and spice plantation at Dachau, and control over the mineral water trade. During the war they got into furniture, textiles and construction. Between 1943 and 1945 Nazi in-fighting was at its most bitter. Hermann's power declined while Himmler's grew. Even so, Hermann believed, 'Himmler never had anything against me personally – it was just political rivalry.'[50]

* * *

A good example of how the two cooperated for mutual benefit was the Blomberg–Fritsch affair. General Werner von Blomberg was the Minister of Defence, Werner Freiherr von Fritsch, the Army Commander-in-Chief. Both had appeared lukewarm to Hitler's ambitious plans for European war at a meeting on 7 November 1937. This seemed to confirm the traditional Army leadership's lack of radicalism. More pragmatically, neither Hitler, Hermann, nor Himmler would rest until the military had been brought to heel.

Blomberg wanted to marry a young typist, Erna Guhn. As she was merely a commoner, Blomberg asked Hermann if he and Hitler would bless the union by attending the ceremony, which they did on 12 January 1938. What Blomberg did not know was that Erna had worked as a prostitute and posed for semi-pornographic photos when she was in her late teens. On 21 January this information reached Hermann. In his 'Brown Pages' was a record of an anonymous call to Army HQ that accused Blomberg of marrying a whore. Then a Gestapo file on Erna landed on his desk. Heydrich's agents wanted confirmation that the girl in the compromising pictures was indeed Erna. Once Hermann identified her he personally presented the dossier to Hitler.

At almost the same time another classified Gestapo file, which Himmler had first shown to Hitler in 1936, popped back into circulation. This concerned allegations that Fritsch had had an assignation with a male prostitute, Otto Schmidt, in a Berlin railway station. Hitler met with Hermann and Himmler on the 26th to discuss both sets of revelations. They decided that Blomberg and Fritsch would have to resign to avoid the scandal that they had largely concocted. Blomberg went quietly, Fritsch also resigned but was determined to clear his name. At a fractious meeting that evening in the Führer's library, Hitler and Hermann demanded the truth. Fritsch denied all, even when his accuser, Schmidt, was brought into the room.

An Army court of honour was arranged to settle the matter. Unfortunately for the prosecution Schmidt was a blackmailing fraud, his accusations a pack of lies. Hermann, who presided over the trial, knew this already. Not wishing to turn Fritsch's case into a *cause célèbre*, Hermann pardoned the general (but he was not reinstated), got a confession out of Schmidt, and protected the 'reputation' of Himmler's secret police: 'Both during the examination of the witnesses and his oral findings, Goering was at pains to justify the conduct of the Gestapo.'[51]

Hermann's understanding with Himmler had far-reaching consequences. It meant passive acquiescence to Himmler's ghastly mission, and complicity in the Final Solution. Hermann had no qualms about handing jurisdiction on the Jewish question over to the SS in order to safeguard his own power base. At Nuremberg, Hermann vehemently denied any knowledge of the death camps or any part in the extermination of European Jewry.

The terror he launched against Communism was a different matter. His anti-communism, that leapt from the pages of *Germany Reborn*, was as strong as ever in 1946, a principle he never compromised or diluted: 'I hate the Communists bitterly because I hate the system. The delusion that all men are equal is ridiculous ... In the German state, I was the chief opponent of Communism. I admit freely and proudly that it was I who created the first concentration camps in order to put Communists in them.'[52]

* * *

Foreign policy received scant attention in Hermann's book. Austria was not mentioned at all. This did not mean the Nazis had abandoned plans for *Anschluss*; he was merely trying to conceal them: 'Germany also has no future desire to rob or humiliate any other nation.'[53] But immediately the Nazis came to power Hitler began tightening the screws. On 29 March 1933 he put a 1,000-mark levy on travel visas to Austria, hoping to stop the millions of Germans who went there every year, mostly on skiing holidays. This measure further damaged the limping Austrian economy, that had seen its banking system collapse under the strain of the depression.

The Austrian Legion was formed in Bavaria as a paramilitary force made up of around 15,000 Austrian Nazis, divided into thirteen commando units. It specialised in cross-border raids, sabotage and minor acts of terrorism. After a series of bomb attacks on civilians, Chancellor Dollfuss banned the local Nazi Party, the SA and SS cadres, and attempted to unite his nation. Born the illegitimate son of a peasant woman, Engelbert Dollfuss had trained as a Catholic priest, distinguished himself as a soldier, pioneered health insurance and pension schemes for farm labourers, became Minister for Agriculture and Forestry in 1931, and Chancellor of Austria in May 1932, the fifth in only three years.

The constitutional crisis, and the chronic divisions within the Austrian parliament, mirrored their German counterparts. Dollfuss felt compelled to use Hitler's own methods. On 4 March 1933, after the Social Democrats had initiated a vote of no confidence, Dollfuss suspended parliament altogether and invoked an emergency act of 1917 to ban mass meetings, political gatherings and bring in press censorship.

He produced his own variant on Fascist ideology, incorporating a large dose of Catholicism. Under the slogan of 'Austria Awake' he created the Fatherland Front 'as an internally independent, vast patriotic movement'[54] with a historic mission: 'Here the Avars and the Turks ran into a brick wall, here Bolshevism found an impenetrable barrier . . . This country has always been a bulwark of Christian German culture, and will always remain so.'[55]

Of course, the left were not included in his vision. They knew it, and were armed and ready. The showdown occurred during February 1934. The Communist militia, the Schutzbund, had its weapons' dumps in Linz raided on the 11th. They fought back, and three days of running battles ensued, leaving over a hundred dead on both sides. Dollfuss decided to prevent the trouble spreading to Vienna, where the Schutzbund numbered 17,500, and launched a pre-emptive strike. On the 12th the largest working-class housing project in the city, and a suspected armoury, was ordered to open its fortified iron doors. When they stayed shut five light howitzers opened fire. The bombardment went on for three days. Some 1,500 arrests were made. Nine prisoners were executed, their sentences passed by the Jesuit lawyer and future chancellor, Kurt von Schuschnigg.

This may have removed the threat to Dollfuss from the left; it did nothing to stop the far right fomenting a putsch. Theo Habicht, head of the Austrian Nazis, planned a coup for 24 July. A revolt in the countryside was to coincide with an attack in Vienna, where the cabinet were to be taken hostage and the main communication centres seized. Hitler discreetly gave the go-ahead.

SS Standarte 89, a commando unit, led the assault on Vienna. Given a last-minute warning, Dollfuss broke up his cabinet meeting and took refuge in an ante-room next to his office. He was found and promptly shot twice, one bullet severing his spinal cord just above the neck. He died a few hours later, having chosen Schuschnigg to succeed him. However, by early evening the SS hit squads, outnumbered and lacking support, had surrendered.

In the countryside fighting was widespread and continued into August. The Army was called out as the Nazis took over regional towns, having signalled their intentions with an extensive bombing campaign, blowing up railway lines, bridges, viaducts, power lines and the odd market square. In total 269 lives were lost. As a confidential Austrian Ministry of Defence report noted, 'It was a case of overpowering a well-equipped army, highly trained in the use of weapons.'[56]

Hitler acted quickly to save face. On 7 August the Austrian Nazi Party was dissolved. In the spirit of reconciliation, the conservative Catholic, Franz von Papen, who had barely survived the Night of the Long Knives a few weeks earlier, was appointed the new German ambassador to Vienna. These gestures were purely cosmetic. The Nazis were biding their time.

Standing in the way of outright invasion during this period was Benito Mussolini. His commitment to Austrian national integrity had kept the wolf at bay: 'Austria knows that, in its defence of its independence as a sovereign state, it can rely on us.'[57] He admired Dollfuss – 'In spite of his minuscule size, he is a man of ingenuity, possessed of real will'[58] – and disliked the Nazis. As early as 1931 Hermann had visited Il Duce to try and seek concessions. This time Mussolini did actually see him on a number of occasions but refused to alter his position. A much heralded first meeting with Hitler in Venice, 14–15 June 1934, did little to change Mussolini's mind; Hitler reminded him of 'a plumber in a mackintosh'.[59]

However, on 30 December 1934, Mussolini issued a directive concerning 'the problem of Italo-Abyssinian relations', which had become 'a problem of force' to be resolved by 'the use of arms'. He was hell-bent on an African colonial adventure: 'Having opted for war, the aim can only be the destruction of the Abyssinian armed forces and the total conquest of Ethiopia.'[60]

Mussolini's ambition was to avenge the humiliation suffered by the Italians at the Battle of Adowa, on 1 March 1896. In 1895 the Italian Army had marched from the coastal colony of Eritrea over the border into Ethiopia, where the emperor united his various clans and led 70,000 men north to meet the Italian invader. After several months' fighting, stalemate set in. The Italians decided to strike a decisive blow with a multi-pronged night attack across mountainous terrain. It was a disaster. They were overwhelmed and routed. News of the defeat caused widespread rioting in Italy and the prime minister was forced to resign. A treaty was signed that recognised Ethiopia's independence. The agreement was adhered to until Mussolini broke it by attacking Abyssinia in October 1935. His determination to topple the regime of the Emperor Haile Selassie would turn him into a diplomatic outcast, push him into Hitler's arms and leave Austria swinging in the wind.

CHAPTER SEVEN

Showbusiness

Albert had lived through the lawless turmoil that engulfed Munich during 1919 and beyond. The violence that rocked Austria in 1934 did not dent his resolve to live there, particularly as he was about to take a job in the Viennese film business: 'The name of the company was the Tobis-Sascha Film Industry Ltd. I was the technical director of the studio.'[1]

Professor Hugo Junkers had been forced to sell the Kaloriferwerke in 1932 to the electronics magnate Robert Bosch. Courted by Hermann, Bosch was prepared to do business with the Nazis. Albert was ready to move on. The diverse range of Kaloriferwerke products that he was selling had brought him to the attention of Tobis-Sascha: 'Since the film industry needed our services in order to keep their film, I came into contact with this film company and got the job.'[2] Tobis-Sascha was the biggest studio in Austria, having recently swallowed up its main rival and begun to upgrade its facilities. Albert's social milieu already included movie people and his anti-Nazism was an advantage: the Sascha management were Jewish.

Film took root in Vienna at the turn of the century. In 1903 there were three cinemas. By 1915 there were 150. Alexander Graf Kolorat-Krakowsky formed the Sascha company in 1910, opened its first studio in 1916 and made big-budget epics like *Sodom und Gomorrha* (1922). The company sold its movies throughout central and eastern Europe and became Paramount's distributors in Austria. By the mid-1920s, the company was in trouble. Inflation had hit profits and foreign, mostly

American, films were dominating the box office, forcing the government to introduce quotas. The domestic market was simply not big enough. German audiences were vital if Austrian cinema was going to survive.

UFA, Germany's largest studio, was being run by the visionary Erich Pommer, whose work with the Austrian émigré director, Fritz Lang, produced outstanding cinema. Unfortunately the public stayed at home. *Metropolis* (1926), Lang's moody, dystopian sci-fi classic, nearly bankrupted the studio. Competition from Hollywood was intense. The right-wing German press baron, Alfred Hugenberg, raised the finance and bought UFA outright. Pommer, back from a spell in Los Angeles, started replicating American genres. Though the advent of 'talkies' in 1928/29 pushed up budgets, sound was eagerly embraced by UFA. It brought plenty of work for budding screenwriters like the legendary Billy Wilder, another Austrian émigré, and boosted the whole industry. Though the depression pushed UFA to the brink, it did not affect the public appetite for movies. In 1932–3, 238.4 million cinema tickets were sold.

The cost of sound threatened to cripple Austrian film. To survive, Sascha merged with a German company, Tobis AG. Tobis had established itself by patenting film sound technology and quickly grew to be nearly as big as UFA. In 1933, a year before Albert joined, the alliance was formalised. Tobis bought a 50 per cent share and the company became Tobis-Sascha Filmindustrie AG.

Oskar and Kurt Pilzer owned the other 50 per cent. Oskar, a corporate lawyer, was head of the Sascha board and got involved in production, directing three movies. Kurt watched the financial side while Severin Pilzer ran the film laboratories. Albert had a good relationship with Oskar and Kurt but was closest to Severin: 'They were very good friends and stayed in correspondence both during and after the war.'[3]

The company got a shot in the arm in 1933 with the release of *Leise Flehen Meine Leider*, based on the life of Schubert, the first of a series of hit musicals exploiting Vienna's cultural history. It was followed a year later by another smash, *Maskerade*. Things were looking up for Albert's employers. What they could not predict was the effect the new rulers of Germany would have on their biggest market.

* * *

The Nazi leaders were fully aware of the propaganda potential of film. They were also avid fans. Hitler watched at least two movies a night in his private screening room until war cut into his leisure time. He was fond of home-grown romantic comedies, musicals, and period epics. Watching Hollywood movies was a guilty pleasure. *King Kong* was one of his favourites. The man he chose to oversee the film industry was Joseph Goebbels, who believed that, 'Film will conquer the world as a new artistic manifestation. It will then be the strongest pioneer and the most modern spokesman of our age.'[4]

The son of a clerk, Goebbels had a formidable intellect that got him to university. In 1921, he received his doctorate in romantic literature. Wilfully unemployable, he wrote a rambling, angst-ridden autobiographical novel, and began a daily record of his thoughts, the infamous diary, which he religiously kept until his suicide in 1945 and intended for posthumous publication.

On 13 March 1933 Hitler made him head of the Reich Ministry for Popular Enlightenment and Propaganda. In June the Reich Film Chamber was set up as one of seven departments (along with those for literature, theatre, music, fine arts, press and radio), all under Goebbels. His aim was clear: 'It is not enough to reconcile people more or less to our regime ... we want rather to work on people until they have become addicted to us.'[5] He was interested in subliminal messages – 'Those whom the propaganda is aimed at must become completely saturated with the ideas it contains, without ever realising they are being saturated' – because 'The moment a person is conscious of propaganda, propaganda becomes ineffective.'[6]

He asked directors to resist churning out party political broadcasts: 'If I see a film made with artistic conviction then I will reward its maker. What I do not want to see are films that begin and end with National Socialist parades.'[7] His influence meant that of the 1,097 films produced in the Third Reich over 50 per cent were comedies. A mere 20 per cent were classed as political, mostly 'educational' films and documentaries. The other 30 per cent were dramas, often biopics of Germanic heroes. Audiences responded well to Goebbels's creative choices. In 1933–4, 244.9 million cinema tickets were sold; four years later the box offices registered 396.4 million.

Production figures remained stable throughout the Nazi era, if less than during the 1920s, only tapering off drastically in the last few months of the war. Nevertheless the industry managed to make sixty movies in 1944, including the monumental *Kolberg* (1945), about the brave defence of Kolberg by its citizens, besieged by a French army during the Napoleonic Wars. Goebbels wanted no expense spared to show that 'A people united at home and at the front will overcome any foe.'[8] The film took nearly a year to shoot. Some 187,000 soldiers, 4,000 sailors and 6,000 horses were removed from active duty to be extras in the battle scenes. Goebbels worked on the script and sat in the editing suite to finish his 'artistic hymn of praise to courage', convinced that 'such a film would be more useful than a military victory.'[9] It premiered in Berlin, among the rubble, on 30 January 1945. Soviet armies were poised to invade Germany and Stalin's soldiers captured Kolberg two months later. Goebbels wrote, 'In view of the severe repercussions on the Kolberg film, we could do without this at the moment.'[10] He was more concerned about his masterpiece flopping than the imminent Nazi defeat.

His obsession with movies spilled over into his private life. A self-confessed randy goat, ruled by 'the voice of Eros', Goebbels made ruthless use of the casting couch: 'In those days Berlin was a city of rumours . . . but one thing was easy to get a handle on . . . Goebbels the ladykiller.'[11] In 1936 he embarked on an affair with a Czech starlet, Lida Baarova, who was contracted to UFA. He made her dump her fiancé, showered her with expensive gifts and showed her off in public. After two years of this, his dutiful wife, Magda, stopped complaining to her husband – 'last night another long talk with Magda, which was nothing but humiliation'[12] – and complained directly to Hitler. The Führer banned Goebbels from seeing Lida. Her career over, she returned to Prague in 1938. Goebbels renewed his vows to his wife. It took nearly three years for him to regain the influence he had lost by playing the Hollywood mogul.

* * *

As the Nazis took power in the early months of 1933, many of the most gifted directors, producers, writers, actors, and technicians in German cinema, who were either Jewish, had left-wing sympathies, or both, left the country. This exodus of talent, that would soon make a huge contribution to American film, included Billy Wilder, Max Reinhardt, Peter Lorre, Erich von Stroheim, Otto Preminger, Fred Zinneman, Bertolt Brecht and Fritz Lang.

Though Lang was Jewish, his films were admired by Goebbels. After seeing *M* (1931), Goebbels wrote, 'fantastic . . . well made. Lang will be our director one day.'[13] He cited Lang's gothic *Die Nibelungen* as one of four films that the industry should seek to emulate. However, he did not appreciate Lang's latest offering, *The Testament of Doctor Mabuse* (1933), and had it banned by the censors on 29 March, the same day UFA fired all its Jewish staff: 'Each member of the committee must decide which colleagues and employees in his section can be dismissed immediately and which ones must be slowly deprived of office.'[14] Lang headed for Paris. His wife and creative partner, Thea von Harbou, stayed and wrote twenty-six movies for Goebbels.

Once UFA was compliant, Goebbels set about controlling which films got made and which did not. Scripts had to be approved before production. Finance was administered by the state-run FilmKreditbank. By 1936, it funded 73 per cent of all films made. The speed with which Goebbels acted sent shock-waves through the Austrian industry – 90 per cent of its audience was German. Economic necessity demanded some form of accommodation with the new regime. The Nazis were determined to prevent the recently sacked film people who had descended on Vienna from working again. During annual negotiations between the two industries, the Austrians agreed that no 'German nationals and German firms banned from participating in Germany'[15] would find employment in Austria.

The 1935 German–Austrian Film Trade Agreement tightened the screws. A Nazified agency responsible for classifying films ruled that any production involving Jews was 'foreign' and would have to pay huge fees to get shown in Germany. The costs were so prohibitive that the Austrians conceded. The cull began. Only extras and technicians were spared.

Somehow the Pilzer brothers, who were Jewish, managed to ride the storm and keep their share of Tobis-Sascha – not that the Nazis did not try to take it away. In August 1934 they leant on the Austrian Creditanstalt bank to call in its loans to Tobis-Sascha, hoping to force Oskar Pilzer to sell his 50 per cent. But the bank would not play ball, insisting on abiding by Pilzer's managerial contract, which did not run out until June 1936. The boss clung on. Albert focussed on doing his job to the best of his ability, confident 'that what was right would survive'.[16]

* * *

Hermann was a regular at glitzy film premieres. He had a home cinema where he watched comedies and hunting movies. He became the patron of a sub-genre of films celebrating the achievements of German airmen, such as *Pour le Mérite* (1938), which followed the heroic pilots of 1918, their subsequent abuse by the Weimar Republic, and their rise again after the Nazi take-over.

He invested his own money into *DIII 38* (1939), an action movie about high-speed fighter planes, and appeared in the drama documentary *Feuertaufe* (1940), about the bombing of Poland. Hermann delivered a monologue straight to camera, the Luftwaffe in action behind him: 'The air force and its exploits will go down in history. It is mainly due to the Luftwaffe's contribution that we owe the defeat and annihilation of the enemy.'[17] This was followed by *Stukas* (1941), dedicated to the feared dive bombers. All these films performed well at the box office and made healthy profits.

Hermann also had close social links to the movie business through his second wife, the actress Emmy Sonnemann. She persuaded Hermann to try and aid Henny Porten, one of UFA's biggest stars, whose husband, Doctor Wilhelm von Kaufmann, was Jewish. Porten had found fame in the silent era as Germany's First World War sweetheart. She had an international hit with *Anna Boleyn* (1920), and visited Hollywood. She comfortably made the transition to 'talkies', but 'because she refused to get a divorce, the former darling of the audience had been cut dead by the media and was not allowed to appear on stage or film'.[18]

Porten turned to Emmy, who turned to Hermann: 'He had no idea how he could help . . . therefore he called his brother Albert.'[19] Hermann asked Albert if he would 'work something out for Porten', using his influence at Tobis-Sascha. This was one of the few favours Hermann ever asked of Albert. The differences between them had precluded much contact for years. But the family links endured, the relationship remained civil, the channels of communication open. Hermann did not hesitate to pick up the phone and call his little brother.

'Albert helped. He provided Henny Porten with a big film contract. Naturally the film never got made but the actress had no more financial worries.'[20] Porten appears as the twenty-sixth name on Albert's Nuremberg list. Between 1938 and 1941 she got a few small roles before landing a decent part in a costume drama. In 1943 she got the lead in *Familie Buchholz*, another period piece. However, by then nobody was safe, especially those with a mark against their name. At the premiere of *Familie Buchholz* on 3 March 1944, only weeks after Porten's home had been flattened by Allied bombs, Hermann pulled her aside and begged her either to jettison her husband or run for her life. She did neither and still survived. She died in 1960, penniless and all but forgotten.

* * *

Hermann first saw Emmy Sonnemann on stage at the beginning of 1931. The thirty-eight-year-old, full-figured, pure blonde actress had been with the Weimar National Theatre repertory company for eight seasons, playing mostly romantic roles. She started dating Hermann during the summer of 1932. Things moved slowly. The memory of Karin loomed large. As a present Hermann gave Emmy a photograph of his dead wife.

By January 1933 Emmy was his live-in mistress, though a room in their Berlin apartment was set aside for Karin's possessions. Emmy was patient and eventually got her man. Hermann proposed and their engagement was announced in mid-March 1935. Their wedding date was set for 10 April. On the 9th a reception was held in the couple's honour at the State Opera House followed by a performance of Strauss. The next day, after a short ceremony at the town hall, a motorcade took them to the cathedral. As Eric Phipps, the British ambassador, caustically observed, 'A visitor to Berlin might well have thought the monarchy had been restored . . . The streets were decorated, all traffic in the interior of the city was suspended . . . Two hundred military aircraft circled in the sky.'[21] That evening there was a banquet at the Kaiserhof Hotel for 320 guests. Hitler gave a speech, and a portrait of Bismarck to Hermann. The groom gave his rosy-cheeked bride a diamond tiara and took her to a villa on the Adriatic for their honeymoon.

The opulent extravagance of their wedding was symptomatic of Hermann's lifestyle at the time: 'Besides his greed Goering developed an ostentatiousness which frequently verged on the ridiculous.'[22] He had become very wealthy, thanks to the state funds flowing into his coffers, topped up by bribes, donations and gifts from foreign diplomats, aristocrats, ministers, municipal assemblies, and major corporations like Lufthansa, IG Farben, UFA, Fox and Electrolux.

Typical of these arrangements was Hermann's relationship with Philip Reemstama, a former First World War flyer and now Germany's largest cigarette manufacturer. Hermann secured him tax breaks, got a court case against him dropped, and generally plugged his product at the expense of his rivals. During the occupation of the Ukraine during 1942, Hermann suggested Reemstama's cigarettes be used instead of money to buy food from the local population. Hermann's pay-off for his various favours was a million Reichsmarks a year for over a decade. He put the money into a special art fund to pay for his collection.

His wardrobe was an exotic, eclectic mix of imperial luxuries and military fashions. He collected daggers, the older and rarer the better. He had a fixation with precious stones, acquiring them by 'the pot'. 'He changed costume often during the day and appeared at the dinner table in a blue and violet kimono with fur-trimmed bedroom slippers . . . He wore at his side a gold dagger . . . not to mention the splendour and number of his rings.'[23] He took his favourite jewels with him everywhere, even to his Nuremberg cell: 'He had brought . . . a ruby, an emerald, and a blue diamond, each set in a heavy platinum mount. He told me that he always carried these rings so as to be able to select each day the colour which best suited his mood.'[24]

Hermann was also extremely fond of his pet lions. When they were not on loan to Berlin Zoo, he let them roam round his various homes, delighting him and unnerving his guests: 'These lions were not just cubs – the kind that society ladies might like to be photographed with . . . They were great hulking brutes. Many a voice was raised at his temerity in trifling with being slashed by tooth or claw.'[25]

He was fiercely proud of his reputation as a convivial and generous host. The British politician Sir Henry 'Chips' Channon noted in his diary that, 'The new regime, particularly Goering, are masters of the art of party giving.'[26] The one Hermann threw during the 1936 Olympics outdid his competitors, Goebbels and Ribbentrop, and left his 800 guests 'gaping at the display' laid on in the Air Ministry gardens: 'A corps de ballet danced in the moonlight . . . a procession of white horses, donkeys and peasants appeared from nowhere and we were led into an especially built luna park. It was fantastic – roundabouts, cafes with beer and champagne . . . the music roared.'[27]

The majority of his entertaining occurred at Karinhall. The log cabin had become a mansion at a cost of 15 million Reichsmarks, siphoned from the Air Ministry and Prussian state budgets. Visitors drove through an avenue of trees, then entered an extensive courtyard with a pond, a fountain, sculptures and flower beds. Once in the building proper, guests traversed a 50-metre-wide hallway that resembled an art gallery. There was a medieval-themed council chamber, a beamed office with a granite fireplace, and a huge map room, decorated with portraits of Napoleon and Frederick the Great.

The banqueting hall was lined with columns of red Veronese marble and curtains adorned with the letter H stitched in gold, and serviced by footmen in hunting uniform. Electronically controlled windows opened up onto a paved terrace with views over the lake. Fun and games could be had in the basement which was furnished with a swimming pool, a gym, a shooting gallery and a cinema. In the attic was a model railway that 'won the enthusiastic admiration of Benito Mussolini, the Duke of Windsor and many other well-known people'.[28] No wonder; there were 600 metres of track, eight locomotives, forty signal boxes, express trains, goods trains, armed transports, model planes, 'fire-spitting tanks' and infantry fighting over rivers, towns, and woods, all coordinated from a main control panel.

The line between official business and social activity at Karinhall was deliberately blurred. A debate about rearmament and Versailles might lead to a go on Hermann's train set or a midnight dip. The most privileged would get the chance to chase stag on his vast estate. Whenever possible, he got up at four in the morning and stayed out for six or seven hours on the hunt: '27 September 1936, very fine weather . . . guests arrive . . . stalking a royal stag . . . I felled it with a bullet in the liver . . . the stag collapsed . . . 30 September 1936 . . . stag was crying well . . . dropped it a range of about 100 metres, shot clean through his heart.'[29]

The sport was far more than a hobby to him. He took his responsibilities as Master of the Hunt and Master of the Forests extremely seriously. On 3 November 1935, a year after his Prussian Game Law had been extended throughout the Reich, Hermann gave a speech to mark the Festival of St Hubert, the patron saint of hunting: 'Forests and heaths and the things that live in them are put there by God and do not belong to the individual but to the whole nation . . . Remember, our ancestors demanded of the hunter that he should possess spirit and character . . . courage, care, bodily ability, ideals in thinking and love for his neighbour.'[30]

Threatening his vision, alongside 'Communism and Marxism . . . enemies of the hunt and of nature',[31] were unscrupulous marksmen motivated by 'the lust for profit . . . hunters who only shoot for gain and count the bag in hundredweights'.[32] Permits were reserved for hunters with their own pack of dogs. Quotas were imposed on kills. Penalties were increased for poaching. The use of horses, vehicles, poisons, nightlights, wire and steel traps was forbidden. Vivisection was made illegal; its practitioners risked 'being thrown into a concentration camp'.[33] The President of the International Council of the Chase praised Hermann for making 'a new law regarding hunting which has inspired the admiration of the whole world . . . founded above all things on the sublime traditions of the past.'[34]

He established three nature reserves, one near Karinhall, one in East Prussia, and one on the Baltic coast. He had a bison sanctuary where he reared rare bulls, cows and elk, with some success: 'By a system of careful breeding he has secured types of nearly extinct animals.'[35] He re-introduced the night owl, the wood goose, the heathcock, the raven, the beaver, and the otter. During 1936, 140,000 people paid 20 pfennigs each to visit Hermann's nature reserve at Schorf Heath, 'to find peace and relaxation . . . from the nerve-racking strain of town life'.[36]

* * *

Hunting gave Hermann the opportunity to mingle with the cream of European society, which dovetailed neatly with his ambitions to be a roving ambassador for Hitler's Germany. He made his first of many visits to Poland in January 1935, to meet the premier, and was invited hunting in the Bialowieza forest. The Polish ambassador joined Hermann at Karinhall in April. More Polish representatives went hunting there five months later. Hermann returned to Bialowieza as a guest of the Polish Army in February 1936. Trips through central Europe on state business and on his honeymoon, during which he met the Yugoslavian, Hungarian, Romanian and Bulgarian elite, resulted in similar reciprocal arrangements.

Hermann conducted diplomacy in a manner similar to Hitler, which, whether intentional or not, proved highly successful, enabling them to tear up Versailles and a host of other treaties that Hermann would later describe as 'toilet paper', redrawing the map of central Europe without a shot being fired in opposition. Their unconventional approach simultaneously impressed, embarrassed, baffled and alarmed the traditional diplomatic corps, with its classical education, civil service training and rules of engagement developed over the previous century.

Paul Schmidt was Hitler's interpreter during these crucial years, and as such privy to the highest-level discussions. A supremely gifted linguist, Schmidt was used by the Allies to translate court documents at Nuremberg. He accompanied Hermann to Poland and on other foreign trips. He was a regular at Karinhall. His muddled conclusions reflect the problems many intelligent, cosmopolitan men had unravelling their true intentions.

Signals were invariably mixed: 'Goering ... showed little of the considered tactics of Hitler. He went in for forthright utterance, no beating about the bush or diplomatic niceties.'[37] However, at the same time, Hermann, 'in contrast to Hitler ... was amenable to suggestion'.[38] Neither 'liked precision', but Schmidt conceded that Hermann was capable of 'adroitness', and handling 'very delicate situations ... with finesse which the German public would not have believed in this swashbuckling heavyweight'.[39] In short, Schmidt did not know what to think. Fanatical bullies or reasonable statesmen? Hitler and Hermann could alternate between these seeming polarities at will, sometimes shifting in the same sentence, friend then foe, then friend again. Foreign dignitaries left meetings with their heads spinning.

Hitler's main focus was on expansion in the east. As long as France could be neutralised as a European force he saw no need to pick a fight with Britain. Its blockade of German ports during the First World War had proved more effective than its army, while its merchant navy kept the home front supplied throughout. Attempts by German submarines to halt the flow of traffic merely brought the US in on the Allied side. Hermann was as keen as Hitler to prevent this nightmare scenario unfolding again – 'I tried to keep on best terms with England'[40] – and shared the Anglophile tendencies of his colleagues: 'Next to my own people, I feel closest sympathy with the English.'[41]

He was quick to exploit the British aristocracy's fondness for blood sports. Lord Lothian, a Liberal Party grandee, went hunting with Hermann. Lord Londonderry, who was Air Minister in 1931–5, was his guest on several occasions. After their first visit to Karinhall, Lord Londonderry and his wife both wrote to thank their host and began a correspondence that lasted until 1939. Lady Londonderry compared Hermann to the legendary hero Siegfried and said that she believed Hitler was 'a man of arresting personality – a man with wonderful far-seeing eyes'.[42] In May 1936, Hermann wrote to her expressing his wish that 'the two great Germanic nations, England and Germany, may come together to guarantee world peace, or at least peace for our own countries'.[43]

Lord Halifax, a Tory cabinet minister and master of the Middleton hounds, met Hermann during November 1937 at the International Hunting Exhibition, an event Hermann organised, which ran for three weeks and had up to 40,000 visitors a day. Hermann hosted the inaugural banquet on the 5th, wearing baroque hunting costume, having entertained the best shots in the world the night before. Halifax got the full treatment. Hermann was 'like a great schoolboy . . . showing off his forest and animals and then talking high politics'.[44] He described Hermann as 'a modern Robin Hood . . . a film star, gangster, great landowner interested in his property, Prime Minister, party-manager, head game-keeper'.[45] On the whole Hermann's British guests indulged his outlandish behaviour: 'They regarded him with the sympathetic understanding which Englishmen usually feel for anyone who is original or eccentric.'[46]

Sir Nevile Henderson replaced Sir Eric Phipps as ambassador to Germany in May 1937. Phipps had accepted Hermann's social invitations but had remained aloof and sceptical. Henderson positively warmed to him: 'Of all the big Nazi leaders, Hermann Goering was for me by far the most sympathetic.'[47] Hermann invited Henderson, who regularly stalked deer in Scotland, to Karinhall. After a couple of days' hunting, during which Henderson impressed by crawling on his belly to kill a stag, there was an evocative nocturnal ritual that clearly seduced the British ambassador: 'A bonfire of pine branches was lit . . . the hallali, or death of the stag, was sounded. In the starlit night, in the depths of the great forest, with the notes of the horns echoing back from the tall fir-trees, the effect was extremely beautiful.'[48]

Hermann demanded that, 'Great Britain . . . recognise the pre-dominant commercial position of Germany in Europe, and undertake to do nothing to hinder her legitimate expansion.'[49] Henderson accepted these terms: 'We are an island people and Germany a continental one. On that basis we can be friends and both go along the road to its own destiny without the clash of vital interests.'[50] Their understanding held until the Nazis invaded Poland. The result was war. This was a source of much regret for Henderson, given his fond memories of hunting with Hermann: 'From my host downwards everyone was simple, unaffected and extremely friendly. The weather was perfect and I enjoyed it immensely.'[51]

* * *

Hermann's efforts to build a special understanding with the British were undermined, not only by the reality of Nazi foreign policy, but by his erstwhile rival for their affections, Joachim von Ribbentrop. A successful wine merchant, Ribbentrop claimed unique insight into the British character, based on a year he spent in London as a teenager, a sojourn in Canada soon after, and his business dealings importing whisky from Scotland.

After distinguishing himself in the First World War, Ribbentrop married Anna Henkell, the daughter of a wine baron. 'A true evil genius',[52] she dominated her husband and got him close to Hitler during the early 1930s. Almost immediately Ribbentrop became slavishly dependent on the Führer, 'spellbound by this great and ... historic personality'.[53]

Hitler appointed him Ambassador Extraordinary and Plenipotentiary on a Special Mission to London in June 1936, then ambassador proper a year later. Ribbentrop marked his arrival at Victoria Station with a press conference, announcing that, 'A closer collaboration between our two countries is not only important but a vital necessity.'[54] Hermann had a low opinion of Ribbentrop, finding him 'weak and indecisive' with 'neither the background nor the tact for diplomacy'. He opposed Ribbentrop's appointment – 'I tried to advise Hitler to remove him' – because he was 'persona non grata with the British'.[55]

Though Ribbentrop had a few friends in high places, including the owner of the *Daily Mail*, Lord Rothermere, his arrogant, insensitive behaviour alienated many, earning him the nickname 'Brickendrop'. He had an unfortunate habit of giving the 'Heil Hitler' salute, like when he met the new King George VI on 4 February 1937. At Nuremberg, Hermann remembered this 'insult to the crown', and how he made Hitler understand the magnitude of the offence: 'Suppose Russia sent a good-will ambassador to you ... and he came and greeted you with "Long Live the Communist Revolution!"'[56]

Ribbentrop skulked back to Germany, licking his wounded ego. He put his dismal performance down to the intransigence and hostility of the British. On 2 January 1938 he wrote, 'Every day on which our political considerations are not basically determined by the thought that England is our most dangerous enemy would be a gain to our enemies'.[57]

* * *

However sincere Hitler might have been about peace with Britain, his main preoccupation was preparing for war. At a cabinet meeting on 9 February 1933, only a week after becoming chancellor, Hitler stated that, 'Germany's future depended exclusively and solely on rebuilding the armed forces.'[58] Hermann's Luftwaffe, officially revealed to the world on 10 March 1936, benefited hugely from this commitment. The air force got, on average, 35 per cent of overall military expenditure, which leapt from 746 million Reichsmarks per annum in 1933 to 5,821 million during 1936, and up to 17,247 million in 1938–9.

This compared favourably with his potential antagonists. French investment in their air force was low until 1939, when an increased effort was made. Even then, the total spent was scarcely a twenty-fifth of Germany's. The RAF got a 40 per cent share of Britain's defence budget in 1939, which amounted to just a quarter of what Hermann was spending. Only the Soviets were giving armaments the same priority and such an inflated slice of state budgets.

The aircraft industry expanded to meet demand. The workforce swelled. On 21 January 1933, the total employed was 3,998. Two years later, it was nearly 70,000. By 1938, 146,263 worked in air-frame manufacture, and 57,749 in engine production. Many of these were at the Junkerswerke in Dessau. After Professor Junkers had been unceremoniously removed, Heinrich Koppenberg, a steel man, was put in his place to meet Hermann's exorbitant requirements.

Ever the publicist, Hermann could not resist inflating Luftwaffe numbers for foreign journalists and statesmen, often doubling figures. He never missed the chance to impress a visiting celebrity. Charles Lindbergh, the American aviation hero, was his guest during the 1936 Olympics. Hermann showed him the sights, wined and dined him at Karinhall, and wowed him with a carefully stage-managed visit to the Junkerswerke at Dessau. Lindbergh went back to the States something of a fan. Two years later Hermann awarded him the Service Cross of the German Eagle.

As the number of available planes increased rapidly, Hermann had to decide what to do with them. He made clear what he expected from his pilots in a speech to a thousand lieutenants on 20 May 1936, stressing 'three qualities which count and are age-old virtues of the soldier ... comradeship, the fulfilment of duty and readiness to make sacrifices'.[59]

He began by putting his own men in key command positions. Milch, the ex-Lufthansa man, remained the lynchpin. He created an administrative framework and an infrastructure of integrated facilities. By 1936 the Luftwaffe had thirty-six fully equipped air bases with up-to-date communication systems. Nevertheless, Milch was far from secure. As ever Hermann's competitive instincts, and the towering edifice of his ego, made him wary of anybody who might steal his thunder. He did have an ace up his sleeve. Milch's father was Jewish. When this was brought to Hermann's attention he had a fake birth certificate drawn up which gave Milch an Aryan father, and made his mother invent an affair to confirm the story.

Milch went in and out of Hermann's favour over the years, but Hermann never used the truth about Milch's ancestry to end his career. Milch's knowledge and expertise were simply too valuable to dispense with, even though he was not shy about criticising Hermann's performance.

To off-set Milch, Hermann drafted in some old war buddies and flying heroes, men he could feel comfortable with. His former sparring partner Bruno Lörzer was made president of the Air Sports Club, which quickly absorbed all civilian aircraft organisations. Bruno, who first introduced Hermann to the skies and ended the war with forty-four kills, had flown with the Freikorps and been active in the glider clubs which served as cover for training pilots during the 1920s. Karl Bodenschatz, who had been Hermann's personal adjutant when he was commander of the Richthofen Squadron, gladly resumed these duties again.

Ernst Udet exemplified both the bravery and the self-indulgent narcissism common to German aces: 'For the sake of flying you sometimes have to make a pact with the devil. But you must not let yourself be devoured by him.'[60] Second-highest German scorer during the First World War with sixty-two kills, he was a poet, a drunk, a womaniser, an acrobatic pilot and a movie stuntman. In 1933 he became a supporter of a prototype dive bomber, the Sturzkampfflugzeug, better known as the Stuka, constructed at the Junkers factory in Sweden. Hermann and Milch were similarly impressed. Udet was made Inspector of Stuka Pilots and entered the circle of power.

In 1936, despite the fact that Udet had no relevant training or expertise, Hermann appointed him Director of the Technische Amt, the Technical Department of the Air Ministry, an organisation set up three years earlier to oversee aircraft development, research, design and production. By 1939 Udet was in charge of twenty-six departments and 4,000 staff.

* * *

Strategic bombing had been a key component of military thinking since the First World War. A German bomber, the Gotha, began raids on British coastal towns during the spring of 1917. On 25 May, 21 bombers attacked Folkestone, leaving 95 dead and 195 injured. On 15 June, 18 Gothas attacked London; 162 people were killed at Liverpool Street Station. The raids continued through June and July, sometimes at night. The Allied response a year later was unequivocal. Hugh Trenchard, head of the recently formed Royal Air Force, launched 675 raids over southern Germany, hitting cities like Bonn, Cologne, Frankfurt, and Stuttgart.

Despite the high casualty rates of these operations, Trenchard considered them the key to 'ultimate victory' in the future. Bombing could achieve 'the destruction of enemy industry' and 'the lowering of morale',[61] if carried out 'without scruple . . . whatever the . . . legality . . . humanity . . . or the military wisdom'.[62] German commanders disagreed. They believed air power was best employed supporting the land forces. Hermann had other priorities: 'The Führer does not ask me how big my bombers are but how many there are.'[63] An attempt was made to build a long-range heavy bomber at the Dessau Junkerswerke which could reach targets as far away as Highland Scotland or the heart of the Soviet Union. When its chief proponent was killed in an accident on 3 June 1936, the so called 'Ural bomber' programme petered to a halt.

Instead, companies like Messerschmitt concentrated on building faster fighters with heavier guns, Heinkel and Dornier built medium-range heavy bombers, and Junkers worked on a fast, twin-engined bomber, which was Hermann's particular hobby horse. The Ju 88 fitted the bill, with a speed of 500 km/hr and a 2-tonne bomb load.

Many of the new models and designs were tried and tested in Spain. Nazi intervention proceeded swiftly after the civil war between the socialist leaning Republican government and the Army-backed

Nationalists began in the spring of 1936. Hitler's reasons were clear: 'If Spain really goes Communist, France . . . will also be Bolshevised . . . and then Germany is finished.'[64] Luftwaffe 'volunteers' travelled to Spain carrying fake papers. Their secret mission did not stay secret long. The Spanish right, led by General Franco, had an entire army stationed in the colony of Morocco but not enough planes to transport them. Between August and October 1935 the Luftwaffe flew hundreds of missions and carried the entire force of 13,900 men, and 270 tonnes of equipment, to Spain.

Once part of the conflict, they augmented ground operations, softening up Republican troops or cities under their control, like Madrid or the valuable port of Alicante, which German bombers hit during November 1936. Their control of the skies was challenged by Soviet fighters, which initially proved superior in dog-fights. Fighting then moved to the Bilbao region. It was during this offensive that the Luftwaffe attacked the market town of Guernica, under the mistaken belief that Republican troops were stationed there. On 26 April 1937, sixteen fighters escorted twenty-six bombers in waves of attacks lasting three hours, starting at 4.30 in the afternoon. When they had finished the town was in ruins and 1,000 civilians lay dead.

International outrage and condemnation followed, the atrocity captured by Picasso's savage work, 'Guernica'. At Nuremberg, Hermann showed little remorse, not surprising from a man who had ordered the aerial destruction of some of the oldest, finest and most famous cities in the world: 'Guernica had been a testing ground for the Luftwaffe. It was a pity; but we could not do otherwise, as we had nowhere else to try out our machines.'[65] The Spanish campaign, which ran until March 1939, was a valuable exercise for the Luftwaffe, resulting in a total of 313 enemy planes downed for a loss of 72 aircraft in action and roughly the same again through accidents. Hermann's Luftwaffe had performed well. The real test of his leadership, and the industry he managed, was yet to come.

* * *

During August 1936 Hitler signed a confidential decree which read, '(1) The German Army must be ready for action in four years; (2) The German economy must be ready for war in four years.'[66] To achieve this Hermann was put in charge of the Four Year Plan. According to him, rearmament was 'the primary necessity',[67] to be carried out 'according to schedule and the planned scale'.[68] This was 'the task of German politics'. On 4 September 1936, he told the council of ministers that Germany had to be ready 'just as if we were actually in the stage of imminent danger of war'.[69]

The result was to distort the peacetime economy. Hermann's Four Year Plan office sucked up a third of all German industrial investment during 1936, and over half the total for 1938. His air force got another 20 per cent. Though imports kept roughly level with exports, the national debt doubled between 1935 and 1938 and exceeded government expenditure, which also doubled. Agriculture was under strain, and labour shortages were becoming chronic. Hermann opened the first meeting of the Reich Defence Council on 18 November 1938 with this dire pronouncement: 'Gentlemen, the financial situation looks very critical.'[70]

Despite his ignorance – 'I have never been a businessman ... this was something completely new to me'[71] – Hitler considered Goering the right man for the job. This was partly due to the connections Hermann had nurtured which overlapped with his involvement in aircraft manufacture. On 14 December 1933, he signed a deal with Doctor Carl Krauch of IG Farben to make synthetic gasoline. In the spring of 1935 Hitler put Hermann in charge of similar experiments with rubber. By mid-April foreign currency exchange had been added to his remit.

Hjalmar Schacht was instrumental in smoothing Hermann's progress. As economics minister he had dramatically reduced unemployment by investment in motorway building, the auto industry and construction. He was against massive rearmament, while keen to encourage growth through exports and expanded consumer demand. As 1936 approached there were concerns about possible food shortages after a poor harvest and a 50 per cent fall in oil imports after tricky negotiations with Romania, by far the biggest supplier to Germany, and the Soviet Union. These worries were more of a political headache for Schacht than an economic one. He was caught between demands from the Army, which wanted more investment in weapons, and from Agriculture Minister Walter Darre, who wanted more of Germany's dwindling foreign currency reserves to pay for increased food imports.

Schacht had a low opinion of Hermann's competence – 'Control was now in amateur hands'[72] – but he acted in the belief that Hermann would be a counterweight to the extremists: 'For a long while many had hoped that Goering would find and pursue the path of political moderation. At the beginning ... I too shared that hope.'[73] Of course he was wrong. Schacht was increasingly ignored. In the wake of the Blomberg–Fritsch affair he was ousted from government. Not long after he was ejected from the board of the Reichsbank. His name later appeared on a list that connected him to the 1944 bomb plot against Hitler. He was arrested and detained until the Americans arrived. He stood trial at Nuremberg and was acquitted.

Hermann seized the chance which Schacht engineered and Hitler endorsed, realising that these 'special powers ... were vastly more important than those that the Führer has entrusted me with before'.[74] Hitler's support was partly tactical, but it was also emotional. The two men shared the same basic vision of the world, the same fundamental instincts about human nature, that ultimately everything could be reduced to a question of will.

During Hermann's speech at the Berlin Sportsplatz to launch the Four Year Plan he admitted his lack of expertise – 'economy is not my territory'[75] – but dismissed this handicap because he possessed 'limitless will ... from which alone great things can be done ... As long as the will remains unbreakable, all is unbreakable.'[76] Hitler considered Hermann 'the best man I possess, a man of the greatest will-power, a man of decision who knows what is wanted and will get it done'.[77]

To preserve the foreign currency needed to import the essentials for rearmament, he put tight restrictions on currency exchange, and ring-fenced the state reserves. In 1936 he began hauling in foreign currency held by German nationals living abroad, offering Reichsmarks in exchange. Soon he went after all money banked abroad by Germans, wherever they lived. The Dresdner Bank was put in charge of all financial transactions involving the Four Year Plan. The bank had already helped Goebbels control film finance and dealt exclusively with Hermann's slush fund, the Aviation Bank, and had a Nazi board. It was the ideal conduit, allowing Hermann to monitor the flow of his money.

With the independence of the unions smashed, labour relations depended on keeping jobs secure and bellies reasonably full. However, delivering on rearmament meant freezing wage levels. Hermann sweetened the pill: 'When we demand fixed wages, we also pre-suppose fixed prices and their remaining fixed.'[78] A controller was put in place to 'compulsorily reduce prices which to us may seem too high'. Anyone bucking the system faced 'draconian methods ... so strict as to be thought barbaric'.[79]

There were tax incentives for coal production. Money poured into IG Farben's research into synthetic materials from fuel to fertiliser. The textile and automobile industries received special attention; an army needed transport and it needed clothes. Hermann set up pleni-potentiaries to meet targets across the board. Bilateral agreements were made with Romania, Yugoslavia, Spain, Turkey, and Finland, trading German weapons for food and raw materials.

It was calculated that Germany would suffer shortages of iron ore, rubber, oil, flax, jute, and copper in the event of war. Iron ore, the main ingredient of steel, was especially important. In 1933–5 Germany produced a mere 25 per cent of the ore it consumed. 35 per cent was imported from Sweden, a trade route vulnerable to the British Navy, and 21 per cent from the old enemy France. Hermann's solution was simple: 'We are going to build the biggest steel works in the world at Salzgitter.'[80] In 1937, he beat off opposition from a cabal of Ruhr industrialists, who, convinced German iron ore was of inferior quality and egged on by Schacht, challenged Hermann's authority with their Düsseldorf memo. Hermann, who had all their phones tapped, threatened them with a charge of sabotage. They quickly backed off.

His aim was to mine 21 million tonnes of ore a year, and convert it into steel. Ancillary industries for finished products were incorporated with the Salzgitter factory into the HermannGoeringWerke, a state owned conglomerate which bought up 53 per cent of arms manufac-turers in the Ruhr and invested in transport and construction. By 1939 it was the largest enterprise in Europe.

Hermann went into the oil business with an aspiring American tycoon, William Rhodes Davis. Hermann got the Reichsbank to lend Davis the capital to start drilling fields in Texas and Mexico which would then supply a refinery they would build together near Hamburg. Along with Davis's German partners, the Clemm brothers, they formed EuroTank. By 1935 Davis was shipping thousands of barrels to Hermann, who provided the cash for bribes to help secure Davis's access to Mexican oil. At the same time Hermann rewarded the Clemm brothers with the franchise for German hops. By 1940 Davis was under investigation by the Roosevelt administration. In 1941 he died of a heart attack. EuroTank disappeared into the HermannGoeringWerke. The Clemm brothers diversified into diamond smuggling, much to Hermann's delight.

Hermann also had a relationship with another American oil baron, Walter C. Teagle. He was chairman of Standard Oil, which in 1941 was the largest petroleum company in the world with $120 million invested in the Reich. Teagle was a keen game hunter and Hermann admired his skill. Standard Oil had a major share of the vital Ploesti oilfields in Romania. During the spring of 1941, with the Romanian leader, Marshal Antonescu, acting as a go-between, Hermann struck a deal with Teagle that ensured Standard Oil kept the black gold pumping out of Ploesti throughout the war.

* * *

Hermann's fiscal policies had a catastrophic effect on the teetering Austrian film industry. Due to 'the more restrictive foreign exchange policy which Germany is operating',[81] half of what the Austrians were owed for their box-office takings in Germany during 1936, around 2½ million schillings, remained unpaid, frozen in German banks. The shortfall caused production to grind to a virtual halt. The Austrian film minister did his best to persuade the Germans to release the money; however, as he confided in a memo, 'There can be no solution to the transfer problem for the Austrian film industry, especially for Tobis-Sascha, whilst the Pilzer Group remains essentially in control.'[82]

Fresh moves were made to oust Oskar Pilzer from Tobis-Sascha, which was facing bankruptcy thanks to Hermann's measures. This time Oskar saw no alternative but to step down. But he was reluctant to sell his shares. Various attempts were made by Goebbels's trust company, Cautio, to purchase them. Finally, in late 1936, the Austrian Credit-anstalt bank, which had delayed Pilzer's downfall two year earlier, acted as Goebbels's agent and bought him out. This marked the end of Pilzer's involvement in Austrian film and the beginning of the end for all other Jews in the business, no matter how lowly their station.

Albert soldiered on as studio manager, balancing the books and trying to keep the wheels in motion. An insight into his working life is provided by the reminiscences of Ernst Neubach, a veteran Jewish director, producer and screenwriter, with credits on 150 movies: 'Once again I had got into deep debt with my film . . . and was unable to pay the studio costs.'[83] This resulted in a phone call from Albert: 'Goering here, I am calling about the bills. I will be forced to cut off your electricity.'[84] On his way to meet Albert, Neubach reflected on what he knew about the man: 'Nobody could quite understand why the brother of the powerful Hermann Goering had taken up a position . . . for 800 schillings a month when without doubt he could have gone for a great career in German industry.' He arrived at the office where 'Studio manager Albert Goering sat behind his desk and proceeded to elaborate about figures . . . Finally he lifted his oval face with the long sideburns, the thin moustache and the bald head and looked at me . . . The warmth of glance swept away his rather stern manner of speaking.' Albert gave him three days to sort the problem. Then Neubach 'invited him out for a cup of coffee . . . because he practically lived on coffee . . . Over the third cup in the Café Seibenstern Albert became very talkative and told me about his pretty little house in Grinzing and his immigration to Vienna.'[85]

During the short-lived crisis that preceded Hitler's occupation of Austria, Neubach was 'called up' as an Army reservist and was not at home when 'the Gestapo came looking' on the morning of 14 March 1937. His wife, Christina, 'who had stayed in Vienna', managed to meet him in Paris. She told her husband that, 'Albert Goering had immediately offered his assistance should she need any help.'[86]

Oskar Pilzer and his family were at home when the Gestapo turned up on their doorstep. George Pilzer, Oskar's son, sixteen at the time, vividly remembered the scene: 'The Nazis broke into our house . . . we were very frightened . . . they were very menacing. They took my father, put him in a corner, put a gun behind his back and stole a number of things . . . Then they took off with my father.'[87] Albert intervened straight away: 'Mr Goering was informed and he . . . exerted all influence and I underline ALL influence to find where they kept my father and to obtain his immediate release. This our family owes to Albert.'[88] Albert did not stop there and 'personally accompanied Oskar to the border'.[89] Pilzer was number twenty-four on Albert's Nuremberg list.

The Pilzer family stayed in Paris until 1939. When Oskar died after an operation the others went on to Spain and then America, where Kurt and George got work in the film industry. They did not forget what Albert had done for them. When they heard he had been incarcerated by the Allies after the war, Kurt wrote demanding his release.

'21 December 1945. Memo for record: Personal letter from Kurt Pilzer, NYC, requests that in connection with Albert Goering's arrest, consideration be given to Goering's kind favours to Pilzer when latter was subject to Nazi tyranny.' The response of the War Crimes Branch was predictably dismissive: 'It is recommended that no action be taken in regard to this matter.'[90]

CHAPTER EIGHT

Death March

Though the rise of Ribbentrop forced Hermann to relinquish his grip on foreign affairs, he continued to take a 'special interest' in resolving the Austrian question. He was so confident of the outcome that he had an artist paint a huge map of Europe in a prominent spot at Karinhall during the summer of 1937, done in the style of a medieval fresco, showing no border line between Austria and Germany.

The two countries signed a semblance of an agreement on 11 July 1936. Hitler recognised Austria's 'full sovereignty' in exchange for the release of up to 17,000 Austrian Nazis and the lifting of the ban on the party. Schuschnigg also promised to give at least two cabinet posts to pro-unionists. This conformed to Hitler's strategy of slow absorption while maintaining the threat of military intervention. Simultaneously, and often without any prompting, Austrian Nazis continued to foment plans for a coup.

Hermann made several trips to see Mussolini in 1937, hoping to convince him to give up his stubborn defence of Austrian independence: 'Goering was very outspoken on this matter, frankly telling Mussolini that the *Anschluss* would and must come and that the event would not be delayed.'[1] Mussolini refused to be bullied and 'shook his head vehemently . . . It was the only sign of opposition he gave that day.'[2]

Mussolini's reluctance to concede was nothing more than macho posturing. His assault on the regime of Emperor Haile Selassie in Ethiopia had deprived him of the international goodwill he would have needed to take a principled stand, as had his support for Franco – Italy openly supplied ground troops as well as planes throughout the Spanish Civil War. His African campaign, which saw the frequent use of poison gas, began on 3 October 1935, with aircraft bombing the Ethiopian capital, Addis Ababa. By 5 May 1936, it had fallen to the Italians. However, this huge country had to be occupied and fighting went on. Mussolini decreed 'a systematic policy of terror and extermination against rebels and any in the population in favour of them'.[3] Fascist commanders acted with extreme brutality, committing racial atrocities and using 'pacification' techniques perfected in Libya a few years earlier.

Mussolini's imperial ambitions brought him ever closer to Hitler. Pacts were signed which underlined their opposition to both Communism and liberal democracy, and acknowledged that Europe could do with a little re-designing. Mussolini's first visit to Germany in September 1937, when the Nazis pulled out all the stops to show him that the future did indeed belong to them, was enough to convince him of the inevitability of Austria's fate.

* * *

The run in to the *Anschluss* began in February 1938 with a meeting between Hitler and Schuschnigg, during which the Führer, flanked by his generals, subjected the Austrian chancellor to one of his hysterical tirades. On a calmer but no less threatening note, Hitler quipped that he might 'turn up in Vienna overnight, like a spring storm'.[4] Nevertheless Schuschnigg went home with a ten-point programme which he immediately called 'an honourable peace . . . which will put a definite stop to the struggle'[5] – which made it even harder to comprehend what he did next. On 9 March he announced that a plebiscite would be held four days later to decide the country's future, and asked 'for a free and German, independent and social, a Christian and united Austria'.[6] Nobody was more surprised than Hitler, who prepared for invasion.

Hoping to avoid armed confrontation, Hermann berated the Austrian leaders into submission over the phone: 'I, myself, set the pace and . . . brought everything to its final development.'[7] He was 'in his element'.[8] Over the course of the afternoon and evening of 11 March, Hermann had twenty-seven separate phone conversations with Vienna, escalating the threats as he went. At 6.34 p.m., he bellowed down the line, 'In five minutes the troops will march in by my order.' Around 8.00, Schuschnigg got on the radio and announced the surrender of his government: 'We are not prepared . . . to shed blood, and we decided to order the troops to offer no serious resistance.'[9]

Job done, Hermann left his office in Berlin and hurried to the Winter Ball, which he hosted every year at the Aviation Building. The US chargé d'affaires observed that the lavish party 'would strike envy in the hearts of any one of our Hollywood directors'.[10] Sir Nevile Henderson was there. Hermann told him that the *Anschluss* was under way but not to worry. Lord Halifax, now Foreign Secretary, explained the British position in a telegram sent to Vienna the following day: 'His Majesty's government is unable to guarantee protection.'[11] Hermann also reassured the Czech government that the *Anschluss* was not a prelude to an attack on their country. Mussolini gave his response by not reacting at all, earning Hitler's sincere gratitude and the promise that he would 'never forget this'.

German troops moved in at dawn on the 12th. Hitler followed soon after, crossing the border at tea-time, near his birthplace. He headed for Linz, where he spent a triumphant forty-eight hours before moving on to Vienna. On 15 March, he spoke in front a crowd of 250,000: 'I can in this hour report before history the fulfilment of my greatest aim in life – the entry of my homeland into the German Reich.'[12]

That day, Hermann's sister Paula, no doubt pleased that her Austrian husband had been offered the post of minister for justice, wrote a thank-you letter to Hermann which conveyed her giddy mood: 'For three days I have been going about in a dream, I just can't believe this gigantic and wonderful event! I'm so deeply moved.'[13]

Albert's reaction was far less enthusiastic. To ensure a big enough audience for the Führer's speech, thousands of Viennese were drafted in to bulk out the crowd: 'The staff of all the companies were ordered to march up. When the Tobis staff asked him [Albert], whether he would come . . . he replied, "Whoever feels like joining this nonsense, may go. I am staying in the office."'[14]

* * *

Himmler did not hesitate to crash the party. As soon as Schuschnigg resigned, he flew from Berlin to Vienna, arriving at 5.00 a.m. on the 12th. He quickly took over the Hotel Regina for himself and his staff, while Gestapo HQ was located at the Hotel Metropole. He replaced the chief of the Vienna Police with a prominent Austrian Nazi and

Ernst Kaltenbrunner, an SS thug, was appointed as State Secretary for Security.

Himmler was well-prepared for the *Anschluss*. Prior to 1938, the SD Department III had run covert operations and hit squads across the border, while intelligence agents and analysts gathered statistics and information. From January 1938, all staff at SD headquarters were taken off normal duties to work round the clock compiling and collating data on those earmarked for arrest, which was then transferred onto index cards, fed through a tabulating machine, the Hollerith, and sorted by category.

The Hollerith machine, a sophisticated forerunner of the computer invented in the United States by a German, Hermann Hollerith, was the exclusive property of the giant IBM corporation. A German subsidiary, Deutsche Hollerith Maschinen Gesellschaft, or Dehomag, was formed in 1910 by Willy Heidinger, who would later become an enthusiastic Nazi, and was granted a licence to market the machines. Faced by financial ruin in the early 1920s, Dehomag was kept in business by IBM New York, which bought a 90 per cent share in the company.

By 1933 Dehomag was IBM's highest grossing outlet in Europe. The Nazis offered even greater profits. Dehomag's Hollerith machines counted the Jews, organised the rail network, coordinated the Luftwaffe, and administered the business of government and the private sector. In 1937 the chief executive of IBM, Thomas Watson, visited Germany, met Hitler and was fêted by Hermann at a banquet held in his honour. During the war Dchomag thrived. The Hollerith was essential to the smooth running of the military effort and the Holocaust. The machines found their way to the concentration camps and were housed in especially erected and reinforced buildings.

On his way home after the *Anschluss* celebrations, Himmler stopped off at Mauthausen, near the Danube. He was looking for a site to build a camp similar to Dachau which had a working quarry nearby that could supply the SS German Earth and Stone-Work Company. The area around Mauthausen had exactly what he wanted. Himmler gave orders for construction to begin right away. Meanwhile his men were hunting down potential inmates. Anything from 20,000 up to 70,000 people were seized in the first few days of the *Anschluss*, the majority released after a taste of Nazi hospitality. The more important citizens were locked in the attic of the Hotel Metropole.

Albert responded to this unfolding persecution with energy, determination and courage. Without a second thought he set about helping his friends and work colleagues. Doctor William Szekely, an American-Jewish film director, working on a movie with the German heart-throb Zarah Leander, recalled the scene: 'We were stuck in Vienna. All ways of obtaining the necessary papers ... had been exhausted. Every day friends were arrested and bank accounts confiscated ... Albert Goering, a friend of mine, helped us out. He organised exit visas ... went to the bank for me in Vienna and brought the contents of my account to Zurich to make sure I would not be without funds.'[15] Szekely made it to Paris and later Hollywood. He was number thirty-three on Albert's Nuremberg list.

Greta Wolfe, the wife of Albert's Jewish doctor, Max, remembered how her family benefited from his assistance – 'Just to mention his name was protection ... We ought to have been stranded in Vienna' – but Albert got Max's brothers released from prison and 'organised an exit visa for him too'.[16] All three made it to the USA. Albert did not consider them prominent enough to include on his list, like many others he would liberate over the years.

Those who did make it on were: Doctor Alsegg, a Jewish film director at the Vienna based InterGloria, who reached either the UK or Los Angeles; Alfred Barbash, a Jewish producer at Tobis-Sascha, who landed in the UK; a Jewish professor, Doctor Bauer, who got to America; a Jewish director at Tobis-Sascha, Doctor W. Gruss, who also ended up in Britain; and another Jewish medical man, Doctor Medvey, who sought refuge in the States.

Albert met Szekely in Paris later that year, where the director was shooting a movie with Maurice Chevalier and Erich von Stroheim. Over dinner, once 'the good French wine made Albert more talkative',[17] he opened up to Szekely.

'From a policeman I found how they were treating Chancellor Schuschnigg. The Gestapo had locked him in an attic room in the Metropole Hotel in Vienna and treated him like a criminal. Day and night the loudspeaker opposite his window blasted SA marches. The light was on non-stop, the storm-troopers treated him roughly, insulted him. He was not even allowed to go for a walk or read a newspaper and his wife was not allowed to see him ... When I was in Berlin I talked to Hermann, "Is it German to treat a beaten enemy as roughly as that?"

Hermann got on the phone . . . and Schuschnigg was finally interned outside Vienna in a villa together with his family.'[18]

Albert was not the only one pleading for Schuschnigg's release. Sir Nevile Henderson pitched up at Karinhall on 26 April to find Hermann 'mad with rage', and distinctly disinterested in granting his wish. Hermann's comradely feelings towards Henderson were insignificant compared to his sense of obligation towards his family.

That his family exercised some emotional purchase over him was equally well demonstrated by the case of an ageing Habsburg prince. According to Albert, 'At Mondsee lived the old Archduke Joseph Ferdinand, a totally apolitical, peaceful gentleman. This did not stop the storm-troopers from arresting him early one morning, shaving his head and transporting him to Dachau. My sister, Frau Rigele, told me about it, one day before Hermann arrived in Vienna for his triumphant parade. The evening after, the whole family sat together in my house in Grinzing and Hermann allowed everyone a wish. My sister and I asked for the immediate release of the old archduke. Hermann was very embarrassed. But the next day the arrested Habsburger was free again.'[19]

The first few weeks of the *Anschluss* established a pattern of cooperation between the brothers. Albert had enough power to act independently of Hermann, but, as he admitted at Nuremberg, 'I required his help in . . . the most important cases.'[20] This was confirmed years later by Hermann's daughter, Edda Goering: 'At that moment where higher authority or officials were involved, it was certainly not possible except with the support of my father, which he did get.'[21]

* * *

Albert's efforts were of little consequence when set against the tide of events during that spring. The abject capitulation of the Austrian state and its citizens was given 'democratic expression' by a plebiscite, held on Sunday 10 April, which offered the voter the choice of saying 'Yes' or 'No' to the *Anschluss*.

At Nuremberg Albert described the electoral process: 'The whole thing took place in a rather large hall', where the voter was met by several officials who 'would hand you an envelope which had a sheet of paper in it, and there were two circles . . . the larger . . . meaning Yes, the smaller . . . meaning No . . . At the other end of this hall was a telephone booth, and you were supposed to go in there, make your cross, put the ballot in the envelope . . . and drop it in the box.'[22]

However, conditions were hardly free or fair. As people entered, 'The officials would greet them with a Heil Hitler.' Then the hapless voter was told, 'You are voting Yes, there is no reason to go into the booth.' The intimidation worked: 'Everybody would make the cross in the larger circle . . . nobody dared to . . . vote secretly . . . I was the only one among hundreds . . . I proceeded to the booth . . . made my cross in the No . . . sealed the envelope and put it in the box.'[23]

Albert's experience was reflected in the results. 4,484,000 voted Yes, only 11,929 voted No; there were 5,776 spoilt ballots and 350,000 Austrians were not permitted to vote. This category included Jews, political prisoners and common criminals.

* * *

The arrival of the Nazis released the pent-up anti-semitism of large sections of Viennese society that had festered like a boil on the city's body politic since its Jewish population had begun to mushroom in size from the end of the nineteenth century. The result was an instantaneous pogrom. Mobs roamed the streets, flanked by Nazi storm-troopers, smashing up shops, beating and humiliating Jews at random. The grotesque atmosphere was captured by a *Daily Telegraph* correspondent: 'It was an indescribable witches' sabbath . . . The air filled with a pandemonium of sound in which intermingled screams of "Down with the Jews . . . perish the Jews."'[24]

Albert did not hesitate to get involved: 'All day he was out and about saving Jews he knew or didn't know.'[25] He happened to walk past a baying crowd outside a looted shop and saw that, 'There was an old Jewish woman . . . and they had fastened a sign on her which read, "I am a sow Jew", and she was forced to scrub the floor with hydrochloric acid. I went in at once and liberated her, and whilst I did so, I got into trouble with two SA men and was arrested immediately . . . They saw my name and they realised that my brother was Hermann Goering . . . and I was released and warned that such a thing must not happen again.'[26]

This apparently uncoordinated anti-semitism was given sharper focus by Hermann during a speech on 23 March. His message was blunt: 'The Jew must clearly understand one thing at once. He must get out.'²⁷ The next day 3,000 applications for visas were made at the US Embassy. If those who stayed needed an even bigger hint to leave, they got it on Kristallnacht.

* * *

On 7 November 1938, Herschel Grynszpan, a seventeen-year-old Polish Jew living rough in Paris, whose whole family had been physically deported from Germany over the border into Poland and left stranded in no-man's-land, walked into the German Embassy with a gun and fatally wounded Ernst vom Rath, a minor civil servant. Rath died on the 9th, the same day as the Nazi putsch remembrance which brought Hitler and his cronies to Munich every year. During the evening temperatures rose, inflamed by Goebbels's rhetoric, and the plans for revenge were put into action. Hitler authorised the arrest of 20,000–30,000 Jews. They were to be thrown into camps, given a short, sharp, shock, then released. Kristallnacht was under way.

The organised anarchy naturally extended to Austria: 'The air was full of ... mindless hatred.'²⁸ Across the Reich, approximately 8,000 homes and business premises were destroyed; a hundred synagogues were wrecked, 200 burnt to the ground. Overall 91 Jews were killed as the punishment rumbled on until the 13th. The blood-lust was so terrifying that 680 Jews in Vienna committed suicide.

Hermann, who slept through the carnage that night while travelling on his private train from Munich to Berlin, did not react kindly to news of the widespread destruction. On the morning of the 10th, he held a bad-tempered meeting at the Air Ministry where he called the pogrom 'a bloody outrage'.²⁹ His immediate concern was the potential drain on state finances, the sheer cost of it all, estimated at 225 million Reichsmarks.

The pogrom gained its name from the vast amount of glass broken. Every Jewish window that could be smashed was. Germany imported much of its glass from Belgium. At a four-hour summit which Hermann chaired that afternoon, attended by a hundred Nazi officials including Goebbels, he blustered angrily, 'It's all foreign plate glass and it's going to cost a fortune in hard currency.'³⁰ In addition the Jewish properties vandalised were insured by German firms. The pay-out for glass damage alone was estimated at 6 million Reichsmarks. Hermann fumed, 'I wish you had killed 200 Jews and not destroyed so much property.'³¹

Faced with such a crippling bill, he favoured a typically corrupt and extortionate solution. The victims would be made liable for the damage. A Decree for the Restoration of the Street Scene was drawn up, which ordered the Jewish community 'to pay a fine of one billion'.

The meeting moved on to larger issues. Hermann pushed for greater powers to speed the economic rape of the Jews. He got a Decree for the Expulsion of Jews from German Economic Life, and a Law on the Use of Jewish Assets. Efforts to expropriate German Jews had intensified in the first half of 1938. By April 60 per cent of Jewish companies, small businesses, and artisan workshops had been 'Aryanised'. Tactics used ranged from boycotts, the removal of credit, penetration of boards, share manipulation, tax penalties, health and hygiene checks, and strict application of biased labour laws.

Austrian Jews suffered a similar fate. By late 1938, 40,000 of their homes had been 'Aryanised'. Hermann's economic advisor, Helmut Wohlthat, was put in charge of asset-stripping Jewish corporations. The total estimated value of confiscations in the year following *Anschluss* was 2,295,085,000 Reichsmarks.

This daylight robbery went hand in hand with increased emigration, coordinated by Adolf Eichmann from his Central Office of Jewish Emigration in Vienna, which opened for business on 22 August 1938. Not old enough to fight in the First World War, Eichmann became a member of the right-wing German–Austrian Young Veterans' Association. During 1932 he joined the Austrian Nazi Party and enrolled in the SS unit Standarte 37. When he lost his job at an oil company in June 1933 Eichmann headed for Bavaria, where he trained with the Austrian Legion until it was disbanded after the July 1934 coup attempt. A few months later he transferred to the SD in Berlin and made a name for himself as a diligent, thorough administrator. He did a spell studying Freemasons before moving to the SD Jewish Department IVb, where he became regarded as an expert on Zionism and the viability of Palestine as a Jewish homeland.

Eichmann created a fund out of the pockets of wealthy Jews to pay for their own emigration. By 21 November, only two months after he had begun, Eichmann claimed 350 Jews were leaving Austria per day. His Central Office in Vienna was the model for the one set up by Hermann on 24 January 1939 to cover the whole Reich, which he immediately handed over to Himmler's chief accomplice, SD chief Reinhard Heydrich.

According to the census of 17 May 1939, 121,138 Jews remained in Austria. By October 1941, when the Nazis stopped any further emigration, there were 85,000. Just over a year later, there were just 8,102 left. At the end of the war the estimated death toll of Austrian Jews was 65,000.

* * *

Of the four charges levelled against Hermann at the Nuremberg trials, Counts Three and Four, for 'War Crimes' and 'Crimes Against Humanity', related specifically to the Final Solution. The Allies' final judgement on Hermann was unequivocal: 'There is nothing to be said in mitigation . . . His guilt is unique in its enormity. The record discloses no excuses for this man.'[32]

Hermann disagreed: 'I never gave any commands for the execution of those atrocities.'[33] He had found the rumours of their existence hard to believe: 'I just shrugged it off as enemy propaganda.'[34] Faced at Nuremberg with grisly cinematic evidence of the killing fields, he challenged its veracity: 'Anybody can make an atrocity film if they take the corpses out of their graves and then show a tractor shoving them back again.'[35] He consistently rejected the heart-rending and deeply shocking testimony from survivors. When presented with statistics concerning the death toll at Auschwitz he commented, 'I've thought it over, it's technically impossible.'[36] Even if it was true, he denied any part in such cowardly behaviour: 'I'll admit I've been hard . . . I haven't been bashful about shooting a thousand men for reprisal, or hostages, or whatever you please . . . but cruel . . . that is so far removed from my nature.'[37]

Hermann had developed a rather nebulous, if not downright perverse distinction between an act of war and an act of cruelty, such as the order he issued on 16 October 1942 concerning the sabotage of railway lines by Soviet partisans. Any unauthorised 'Russian' caught within a thousand metres of the track was to be shot. If they succeeded in doing any damage then they were to be hung from the nearest pole, the villages close by destroyed, the men shot, and the women and children sent to camps.

Hermann could somehow live with this but not accusations that he sanctioned the slaughter of helpless Jews. He liked to think he was not capable, citing his love for animals: 'In 1934 I promulgated a law against vivisection . . . how could I possibly be in favour of torturing humans?'[38] In his defence he categorically stated, 'Whenever Jews applied to me for help, I did so. Of course, these were people whom I knew before, and their friends and relatives.'[39]

Support for Hermann's claims comes primarily from Emmy, his second wife, and from Albert. Emmy was never interested in politics, and had no taste for Nazism. At the end of the war her assessment of Hitler was that, 'He must have gone insane.'[40] Hitler did not trust her, niggling Hermann about 'her sentimental weakness'.[41] As a theatre person, she had many Jewish connections. She did her utmost to badger Hermann into helping them. According to her he did so whenever he could.

Though there is no reason to doubt her sincerity, Emmy's judgement was clouded by her idealised image of Hermann. She saw only the good in him. Even when Hermann stood accused of ordering the death of millions, Emmy refused to countenance his guilt: 'You know my husband. He is not a man obsessed by hatred. He only wanted to enjoy life and let other people enjoy it.'[42]

As a result her recollections need to be viewed with caution. Nevertheless, there are several examples of Hermann exhibiting the merciful spirit Emmy repeatedly credited him with. The Jewish art dealer, Kurt Walter Baschitz, one of Hermann's team hunting down masterpieces, was arrested in 1943. Hermann got him released. In the summer of 1944 Hermann instructed his private detective to escort Baschitz to the Swiss border and make sure he got safely across.

Hermann did his best to keep Jewish scientists engaged in vital wartime research out of the camps. He protected the Jewish talent at the prominent Prussian state operas and theatres he ran, allowing them to perform regardless of any bans laid down by Goebbels. He made sure that the Jewish wife of Max Lorenz, star performer at the Wagner festivals in Bayreuth, got an honorary Aryan certificate. Hermann's personal attaché rescued the old Jewish couple who had tended Hermann's bullet wounds in the confused hours after the Munich putsch debacle, and got them to safety.

Further evidence that Hermann might indeed have possessed a conscience comes from Albert's interrogation testimony at Nuremberg. On 3 September 1945, he said Hermann 'always had a warm heart and when he heard something that was unjust and I called it vehemently to his attention, he always tried to right things'.[43] On the 25th, Albert was asked about a report he had written, 'as a humanitarian act in accordance with my religion'.[44]

Albert: 'I met one day a Doctor Max Winkler ... He had just come back from Poland, and he told me what terrible things he had heard there about what was happening ... Whole train loads of Jews, men, women and children, old and young, had been taken up into the mountains and they had been shot by machine guns ... At once I said I'm going to make a report on it.'

Interrogator: 'What is the date of the report?'

Albert: 'It may have been 1941 or 1942.'

Interrogator: 'Well, which year did you think it was?'

Albert: 'I know it was at the same time when the German Jews were collected from Berlin and other towns and deported.'[45]

The first trains intended for the death camps left Vienna between 15 October and 2 November 1941 carrying 20,000 Jews. Five trainloads of Austrian gypsies followed over the 8th and 9th. Between the 15th and the 23rd trains began rolling out of Munich, Frankfurt, Berlin and Breslau. Transports continued until 15 December, then began again on 21 January for another four weeks. Out of a total of thirty trains, eleven went from Vienna. Most of those aboard were murdered on arrival, dispatched with a single bullet.

At Nuremberg, the interrogator let Albert continue his story.

Albert: 'I filed the report with the Air Ministry, and requested that it be given to my brother. Then when I came back some time later, I asked what had happened ... I received the answer that it had been transferred to the competent department, which in my mind could only mean Himmler, and thus the vicious circle was completed ... The thing ended where the murder had started.'[46]

Albert then described a conversation he had with Hermann over dinner one night about 'the general subject of the Jews, Gestapo, and so on'. He remembered Hermann saying that, 'Personally he had a plan whereby a large area of Poland, with Warsaw as the capital, should be given to the Jews, who were to be collected there ... and that they would be autonomous in the area ... This was really a huge ghetto, but nevertheless it was a much more humanitarian idea.'[47]

Obviously intrigued, the interrogator pressed on.

Interrogator: 'What did your brother say when you told him about the terrible things happening to the Jews?'

Albert: 'Well, his reaction was always that those things were exaggerated, because he had exact reports on them. He said for me not to mix into affairs of state, and affairs of history.'

Interrogator: 'But he never denied knowledge that these things were going on?'

Albert: 'No, he never denied them. He only made them seem less strong.'[48]

As the questions continued, Albert became more defensive – 'In the earlier days he would help me, but later on he did not have enough interest' – talking openly, for the first time since his incarceration five months earlier, about the tensions between them.

Albert: 'He told me if I wanted to protect the Jews and wanted to help them, that was my affair, but I would have to be much more careful and more tactful, because I made endless difficulties for him in his position.'

Interrogator: 'But he never sympathised with your point of view on the Jews?'

Albert: 'No, we were the worst opponents in all those things, from A to Z . . . There was nothing between us.'[49]

The interrogator wanted an outright condemnation of Hermann but Albert shifted the blame onto Himmler. The SS leader had prevented Hermann from acting: 'At the beginning he had the power to do so; later he did not because Himmler was so powerful.'[50] Albert's statement of Hermann's 'weakness towards Himmler' regarding Jewish policy, does bear some truth, especially in the last years of the war when Hermann was increasingly yesterday's man. His wife's efforts to free a Jewish actress friend, Rose Korwan, during March 1943, give an indication of where power lay by this point.

Rose was arrested after her husband was picked up with false papers and no star of David. Emmy Goering called Himmler straight away: 'I begged and implored him to do me this one favour.'[51] Himmler promised to send them both to Theresienstadt, 'one of our best camps'. However, the next day Emmy heard that their train had gone in the opposite direction. She told Hermann, 'who called Himmler . . . during the evening he received a note informing him that Himmler had telephoned . . . and that Rose and her husband had arrived safely.'[52] Of course, their actual destination was the gas chamber.

* * *

'I was never anti-semitic. Anti-semitism played no part in my life.'[53] At Nuremberg, Hermann had the bare-faced audacity to utter these words. How was it possible that he thought the world would believe him? To deny exact knowledge of the day-to-day operations of the camps was one thing, but such a warped perspective almost defies analysis. After Hitler's appointment as chancellor in January 1933, measures against German Jews started almost immediately. Within twelve months they had been excluded from the civil service, the judiciary, the legal profession, the entertainment business, the arts, the universities, and all schools. Jewish doctors and dentists were forbidden to treat Aryans. Yet Hermann, the benign, still thought that, 'The Jewish question has not yet been completely solved.'[54]

The Nuremberg Laws followed, made public by Hitler on 15 September 1935, 'to establish tolerable relations with the Jewish people'. The Citizenship Law and the Law for the Protection of German Blood and Honour, meant that Jews were no longer German. Mixed marriages and inter-racial sex were now a crime. Supplementary decrees on how to define Jewishness were drawn up, using grandparents as a starting point. Then came Kristallnacht. As Hermann put it at Nuremberg, 'After that something had to happen.'[55]

This was the understatement of the century. The wheels of Armageddon picked up speed as the Nazis entered Poland. Five units of the Einsatzgruppen der Sicherheitspolizei (Special Task Force of the Security Police) and two Einsatzkommando were formed. Their mission was the 'combating of all anti-German elements in hostile country behind the troops in combat'.[56] They marched in with a list of 30,000 marked for detention, anybody who might conceivably offer resistance: politicians, academics, poets, priests, aristocrats, businessmen. They made over 10,000 arrests in the first few weeks of the war and killed an estimated 17,000 in under two months.

Attention turned to the Jews. Hermann set up a new agency, the HTO, Haupttreuhandstelle Ost, Main Trusteeship Office East, on 19 October 1939, to confiscate their assets. The HTO cooperated closely with the SS and SD. On 4 January 1940 Eichmann held a meeting about the proposed evacuation of Jews with SD experts and an HTO man present. On the 30th, the HTO attended a session chaired by Heydrich to discuss the deportation of Jews to the General Government, a rump state and designated dumping ground for undesirables that replaced what was left of Poland after its 'Germanic' areas had been re-incorporated into the Reich.

The future of non-Aryans in the newly occupied lands was being given serious thought by Himmler. During May 1940 he penned a memo on the subject. Having considered the fate of other inferior ethnic groups, he turned to the Jewish problem: 'I hope completely to erase the concept of Jews through the possibility of a great emigration . . . to a colony in Africa or elsewhere . . . This method is still the mildest and the best, if one rejects the Bolshevik method of physical extermination of a people out of inner conviction as un-German and impossible.'[57] His words mirror the line Hermann spun at Nuremberg: 'That the Jews should be evacuated from Germany was clear . . . but not that they should be exterminated. After the war the Jews were to be brought to Palestine or elsewhere.'[58]

A possibility for chucking them out of continental Europe reared its head after the fall of France in June 1940. The island of Madagascar was one of France's African colonies and the Nazis had already discussed it as a potential destination. The plan amounted to stranding millions of penniless and destitute Jews on an island too small to accommodate them and without enough resources to keep them alive. Hitler endorsed it. Everyone else followed. Heydrich set Eichmann to work studying feasibility. Hermann's Four Year Plan office tried to figure out how to seize the accumulated capital of European Jewry in one fell swoop.

By December 1940 the Madagascar project had been abandoned. Meanwhile the situation for Polish Jews progressively worsened. As early as 21 September 1939, Heydrich had instructed his Einsatzgruppen commanders to initiate ghettos within three to four weeks, 'for control and deportation'. Between January and March 1940, the population of the Warsaw ghetto rose to nearly half a million, with a density eight times the city average. Disease and malnutrition were rife. By 1941 thousands were dying every month: 'The corpses of those who have died of starvation lie in the streets.'[59]

The ghettos were of special interest to Hermann's HTO. They set about raiding Jewish businesses, removing all finished and unfinished products, all raw materials and equipment, and Aryanising firms they thought to be worth preserving. They ignored any gold or silver, which was earmarked for the SS. The goods seized were taken to collection points and sold. All proceeds went to the HTO.

During July 1941 Hermann officially granted Heydrich responsibility for Europe's Jews: 'I further instruct you to lay before me shortly a comprehensive draft of the organisational, logistical, and material advance preparations for carrying out the desired solution of the Jewish problem.'[60] By now the invasion of the Soviet Union, Operation Barbarossa, was under way. The total slain by Einsatzgruppen by the end of July, according to their own reports, was 63,000, 90 per cent of whom were Jews.

That summer, private meetings were held between the top Nazis. It seems likely that the Jewish question was high on the agenda. On 20 August Himmler had lunch and a long walk with Hermann followed by dinner with Hitler. No explicit orders were given yet, but through the autumn and winter the elements of the Final Solution were put into place.

The euthanasia technicians, who had masterminded the gassing of Germany's mentally ill, handicapped and educationally sub-normal, were brought in as advisors. Gas vans appeared on the Eastern Front which had been used to exterminate what was left of Serbia's Jews after the Nazis had shot almost all the adult males as part of a reprisal policy that saw 200 murdered for every German soldier killed. On Sunday 12 October 10,000 Jews were butchered in the Ukraine. The bloodshed was taking its toll on the morale and discipline of the executioners, often drunk on duty. A less intimate method of mass murder was required.

The scale of the barbarism was so great that it would have been impossible for Hermann not to know. Everybody around him did. On 1 November 1941, Ulrich von Hassel, the Nazis' ambassador to Rome, noted that Gritzbach, Hermann's biographer and faithful flunkey, 'was very shocked by the execution of the Jews'. However, 'Goering would not take action because the order had come from the Führer himself.'[61]

At home, demented anti-semitism prospered. In September 1939, German Jews had their radios confiscated. In 1940 they were banned from using a house phone, by 1941 they could not use public phones either, or libraries. 1942 saw them deprived of newspapers, magazines, fur coats, typewriters, bicycles, cameras, electrical appliances, and binoculars. Strict rationing of food, clothes and shoes was introduced. In Dresden, Jews were not allowed to buy or pick flowers.

* * *

Hermann was represented by Erich Neumann, a Prussian civil servant, at a notorious conference organised by Heydrich and held on 20 January 1942 in a villa by the Wansee in Berlin, an exclusive area where leading Nazis had summer homes. The result was the Wansee Protocol, of which thirty copies were made and circulated widely. It discussed, 'a) the expulsion of the Jews from every sphere of life of the German people,' and 'b) the expulsion of the Jews from the living space of the German people.'[62]

This was to be achieved by adopting a fresh approach: 'III) Instead of emigration, the new solution has emerged, after prior approval by the Führer, of evacuating Jews to the east', offering 'temporary relief' and 'the practical experience which is of great significance for the coming Final Solution'.[63] Extinction was the order of the day: 'Under appropriate leadership the Jews should be put to work in the east . . . Doubtless the large majority will be eliminated by natural causes. Any final remnant . . . will have to be dealt with appropriately.'[64] An exception was made for 'Jews employed in industries vital to the war effort',[65] but this would not hold for long.

In mid-March 1942, 75–80 per cent of all Holocaust victims were still alive. A year later, only 20–25 per cent remained. On 2 March 1943, Goebbels wrote in his diary, after visiting Hermann's cliff-side home at Obersalzberg, 'Goering realises perfectly what is in store for all of us if we show any weakness in this war. He has no illusions about that. On the Jewish question, especially, we have taken a position from which there is no escape.'[66]

If anybody was left in any doubt, Himmler spelt it out to the provincial leadership and party big-wigs in his speeches at Posen on 4 and 6 October 1943: 'The Jews must be exterminated.' Nazi Party members all shared 'the responsibility for a deed – not only an idea', and were obliged to take 'the secret with us to our grave.'[67]

* * *

Hermann was nobody's fool. Those who met him usually remarked on his intelligence. If this failed he had his network of stooges, agents and phone-taps to fall back on. However, he had a staggering capacity for only ever seeing what he wanted to see: 'Ach, those mass murders! It is a rotten shame, the whole thing. I'd rather not talk about it or even think about it.'[68] His refusal to accept his role in the massacre of the Jews was perhaps his most spectacular act of denial and self-deception.

The distinguished historian Christopher Browning has drawn attention to a distinction made by other eminent scholars in the field of Holocaust studies that highlights different strains of anti-semitism in Germany during the Nazi period, the 'xenophobic' and the 'chimeric'. The 'xenophobic' anti-semite believed a Jew could never be truly German; Jews were at best a disenfranchised, isolated minority, at worst, an alien threat to the nation's health. To the 'chimeric' anti-semite, Jews were not even human; they were another species altogether, creatures spliced together from medieval demonology and the biological determinism of post-Darwinist science, beings that wore both the face of Bolshevism and high finance, a transcendent, all-embracing hate figure.

On the eve of the First World War, chimeric anti-semitism was a minority interest on the far right of politics. The xenophobic idea, that Jews remained essentially outside the nation, was prevalent among conservatives, a form of 'cultural code', not dominant but not insignificant either. Certainly Hermann would have been exposed to it at the cadet schools he attended and as a fighter pilot. Defeat and the social catastrophe that followed gave the language of xenophobic anti-semitism a more extreme edge.

At this stage Hermann married Karin, who, to all intents and purposes, was a chimeric anti-semite. Her intensely emotional and irrational fear of Jews chimed exactly with Hitler's. It drew her to Nazism like a moth to the flame. How much her visceral hatred rubbed off on Hermann is hard to say. As it was Karin died and Hermann went on to marry Emmy, her polar opposite.

Hermann said that, 'If it were on the basis of anti-semitism I would never have been interested in the Nazi movement.'[69] He approved of the removal of Jews from the Reich but not their elimination: 'What he [Hitler] did was right from a nationalist point of view – except for the mass murders – which really made no sense even from a nationalist point of view.'[70]

Hermann's position was similar to that of Hitler's conservative allies. They 'favoured de-emancipation and segregation . . . They strove to end the allegedly "inordinate" Jewish influence on German life, though this was scarcely a priority.'[71] In the dock at Nuremberg Hermann spoke their language: 'After Germany's collapse in 1918 Jewry . . . became very powerful in all spheres of life, especially in the political, general intellectual and cultural, and, most particularly, the economic spheres . . . In addition was the fact that ... those parties which were avoided by nationally minded people also had Jewish leadership out of proportion to the total number of Jews.'[72] The remedy was straightforward: 'Germany should be led by Germans ... The main point was at first merely to exclude Jewry from politics, from the leadership of the state. Later on, the cultural field was also included.'[73]

However, Hermann was far more radical than the conservatives on almost everything else. His brand of nationalism was utterly merciless: 'When it is a question of the interests of the nation ... then morality stops.'[74] He wanted to sweep away the old order, not preserve it: 'I joined the party precisely because it was revolutionary.'[75] But Hitler was a chimeric anti-semite. For him, a showdown with the Jewish race was the cornerstone of that revolution, the heartbeat of his political philosophy.

This was not just a matter for private conversation or state conferences. Hitler never tired of letting the world know his intentions, from the mass publication of his racist doggerel *Mein Kampf*, to one of his last 'great' speeches, broadcast from the Reichstag on 30 January 1939, during which he warned 'international finance Jewry' that another world war would lead to 'the annihilation of the Jewish race in Europe'.[76] On 13 February 1945, while dictating his thoughts to his faithful private secretary and ever present shadow, Martin Bormann, who was compiling the Führer's final 'Testament', Hitler congratulated himself on a job well done: 'We have lanced the Jewish abscess; and the world of the future will be eternally grateful to us.'[77]

As the evidence of the Holocaust revealed at Nuremberg became impossible to ignore, even for Hermann, he still tried to downplay the centrality of anti-semitism to the Nazi project, calling it 'completely irrelevant and incidental. It only became basic or important because a faction of Nazis who were fanatic racial exponents became politically powerful ... National Socialism could also have taken a much different course.'[78]

What Hermann failed to acknowledge was that this 'faction' became so influential precisely because they wholeheartedly embraced Hitler's homicidal racism. Moreover, Hermann aided and abetted them, granting fanatics like Himmler room to manoeuvre, even though the SS leader was a chimeric anti-semite of the highest order, with his own peculiar blend of occultism and racial science: 'We are joined in battle with the oldest enemy our Volk has had for centuries – with Jews, Freemasons and

Jesuits. We did not seek this battle . . . It is there according to historical law', and resembled 'the struggle of the plague bacillus against the healthy body'.[79]

Hermann accepted without hesitation that power in the Third Reich required allegiance to Hitler's anti-semitic agenda. If it meant turning a blind eye to the Final Solution, then so be it; this was a price worth paying to achieve victory on his terms. This commitment made a nonsense of his pious statements about honour. He was as drenched in blood as any of them. Hermann's defence of his noble character often verged on the ludicrous: 'I revere women and I think it's unsportsmanlike to kill children. That is the main thing that bothers me about the extermination of the Jews.'[80]

* * *

By early 1945, as the Allies closed in on Germany, one of the largest camps still working was at Mauthausen in Austria. The war may have been lost but the killing continued. Between January and May 15,000 gypsies, mostly from the Soviet Union, were murdered. Around 10,000 assorted Jews from all over the shrinking Nazi empire, 3,777 Poles, 3,214 Hungarians, 3,214 Yugoslavians, 25 Soviets, 248 French, and 169 Greeks met the same fate, along with 64 German, 2 Polish and 3 Czech homosexuals, 43 Jehovah's Witnesses, 4,529 prisoners of war from the Soviet Union, and 2,163 Spanish Republicans who had been shipped there from France.

Methods of execution were not sophisticated. That SS image of ice-cold efficiency was always mere camouflage for their awesome, degenerate sadism. Lurking behind all the euphemisms, the coded, bureaucratic language, the vulgar jokes and the deranged fantasies, was the naked violence of a savage street assault. An eyewitness account by a Belgian resistance worker of the beating of a fellow prisoner in the dying weeks of the war, bears this out: 'The SS man . . . alternately . . . slogged his jaw and kicked his stomach . . . until one tremendous kick . . . brought blood gushing from the man's mouth . . . the guard continued kicking him in the face, head, groin and legs. The twitching form at last lay quite inert and the pavement was quickly thick with blood.'[81]

American troops reached Mauthausen in early May 1945 and discovered 10,000 bodies heaped in piles, and nearly four times as many survivors, of whom another 3,000 died soon after. It was the last concentration camp to be liberated by the Allies. The Nazi search for an answer to the Jewish question ended in Austria, where, seven years earlier, it had begun to gain its deadly momentum.

PART THREE

Don't forget that the great conquerors of history are not seen as murderers – Genghis Khan, Peter the Great, Frederick the Great – Don't worry, the time will come when the world will think differently about all this.

Hermann Goering, in G. Gilbert, *Nuremberg Diary*

The essence of war is violence; moderation in war is an imbecility.

Lord Macaulay, 1831

I have helped people from Romania, Bulgaria, Hungary, Czechoslovakia, and Germany, whenever I could, whether they were poor or whether they wanted to emigrate ... and I never expected or received any compensation for it ... because I did this for religious reasons.

Albert Goering, 25 September 1945

death is a master from Germany/his eyes are blue he strikes you with leaden bullets/his aim is true.

Paul Celan, *Death Fugue*

CHAPTER NINE

Resistance

A few days after the Allies entered Rome on 4 June 1944, British intelligence officers interviewed four members of the Free Hungarian Association, formed to facilitate connections between the Allies and the Hungarian underground. One of these men, Doctor Kovacs, had strong links to 'the internal subversive movement in Hungary', and spoke of his 'dealings'[1] with Albert Goering.

Tired of working for 'party acrobats from Berlin who turn every waltzing melody into a Prussian march',[2] Albert left Vienna in late 1938 to take up a post at the Tobis-Italiano company in Rome. Though the film industry there was not as tightly censored, it was still run according to Fascist guidelines. Albert's wife and companion of seventeen years, Erna, was stricken by cancer. He wanted Dr Kovacs to treat her. The doctor was Jewish and understandably nervous. However, when they met, Albert 'burst into a tirade against his brother, Hitler and the Nazi regime'.[3] Kovacs agreed. He and his family became regular visitors to Albert's home.

Albert started donating money to Kovacs 'for the assistance of Jews and other refugees from Nazi tyranny' out of the surplus from his wage packet: 'He required no receipt nor knowledge of who was helped.'[4] In the summer of 1939 Albert 'opened an account with the bank of Orelli in Berne'. He told Kovacs that, 'It was only necessary for him to write to the bank to obtain money for the assistance of refugees and for helping them to escape via Lisbon.'[5] As the war progressed he 'gave Kovacs a statement in writing to the effect that Kovacs was his personal physician'[6] and should not be 'molested'. The doctor appears as number fourteen on Albert's list.

* * *

After the *Anschluss* the Nazis turned their attention to Czechoslovakia, having already begun the process of fomenting separatist tendencies in this far from homogeneous republic. The Sudetenland, with its large German population and home-grown Nazi Party, experienced the familiar combination of political agitation and terrorism. Slovakian nationalists were also encouraged.

On 1 October 1938, the Sudetenland was ceded to Hitler after the Munich conference. On 15 March 1939, the Nazis marched into Prague, having harassed the Czech President Hacha into ordering his well-equipped and prepared army to offer no resistance. When Hermann threatened to bomb Prague into dust Hacha fainted. The same day, under pressure from Hitler, Slovakia declared independence.

On the 16th, what was left of the Czech nation became the Protectorate of Bohemia and Moravia. Hitler put the moderate ex-foreign minister Konstantin von Neurath in charge to mollify international opinion. An SS man, Hans Frank, was appointed state secretary. Himmler's preparations had begun during the summer of 1938 and followed the *Anschluss* blueprint. Index cards were sorted, courtesy of IBM, and lists of suspects drawn up. As the Wehrmacht moved in so did the Einsatzkommando. Gestapo headquarters were established in the main cities.

A month later, Hermann explained that the occupation had been carried out 'in order to increase German war potential by the exploitation of the industry there'.[7] He was hoping to repeat what he had done in Austria, where he brought eleven major companies and a host of smaller ones under the control of the HermannGoeringWerke. He was particularly interested in the world-famous Skoda armaments factory. Established by Emil Skoda in 1859, it was the largest supplier of weapons to the Austro-Hungarian Empire during the First World War.

Hermann pursued his favoured strategy of using the ever reliable Dresdner Bank to mount a takeover bid. It concentrated its efforts on acquiring the 56 per cent share of Skoda held by a French consortium, but Skoda management acted first, making an alliance with a banking syndicate which bought the shares before Hermann's agents could. He was temporarily frustrated but did not give up. By October 1940 he had acquired a 63 per cent share.

With the Nazis installed in Prague, the Skoda management heard of a plan to dismember and relocate their company. Something had to be done. Bruno Seletsky, Skoda's export director, had a brainwave. He was an old friend of Albert and had recently visited him in Rome. The two had first met in Argentina in 1930 when Albert was in South America doing business for the Kaloriferwerke. Bruno suggested they 'accept into Skoda's employment his friend Albert Goering who in his thinking is an anti-Nazi and an Austrian citizen and who, as brother of Hermann Goering, could provide us with valuable assistance.'[8]

Without hesitation the company offered Albert a job, hoping he might 'prevent the liquidation of Skoda enterprises and transfer of machinery and equipment to other German businesses', and 'avoid orders for arms for German military power by increasing exports'.[9] Dissatisfied with life at Tobis-Italiano, Albert accepted their offer, but only after he had gained Hermann's permission: 'I asked my brother as head of the family, and not in his official capacity . . . I thought I would ask him as a matter of courtesy.'[10] Hermann had no objections, even though 'He knew my aversion to National Socialism and must have expected that I would make all sorts of difficulties. However, he was very generous and when he heard that I could prove myself he said, "Well, by all means go and work there."'[11]

* * *

Albert's contract began on 1 June 1939. He replaced his friend Bruno Seletsky as export director and repaid him by getting him safely to Switzerland. He was number twenty-eight on Albert's list. Albert was to spend his first year at the factory in Pilsen, a medieval town whose main square was dominated by a Gothic cathedral. Out of a population of 130,000, 75,000 worked at Skoda.

October 28th was the National Holiday of the Czech Republic, an event marked by celebrations and patriotic demonstrations. In 1939 it was a chance for the Czech people to show their solidarity against the invader: 'Wherever possible work stopped in the republic. In factories under German supervision there was merely a pretence of work, otherwise none at all. In Pilsen the working class made a procession.'[12]

Nazi storm-troopers were deployed on the streets of Prague to intimidate the public. Later in the day the Einsatzkommandos arrived, beating passers-by with whips and steel cords. Hundreds of members of the intelligentsia and youth associations were taken to Pankras prison. Status and rank were no protection against torture. When the body of a senior diplomat was finally inspected by his wife, she saw he had been scalped and his sexual organs removed. The leaders of the Student Council were executed. All Czech universities were closed for three years.

One of the victims of the purge was an eminent surgeon, Doctor Josef Charvat, who was also leader of the Czech Boy Scouts, a large nationalist organisation that quickly became part of the resistance movement. He was snatched at dawn with no explanation, and sent to Dachau. Albert was one of his patients. Josef's desperate wife wrote to him. Albert improvised: 'On a sheet of headed notepaper which only bore the family name and a crest of arms, he wrote a message instructing the camp commander . . . to release the newly arrived Doctor Charvat instantly . . . this letter he signed quickly with "Goering". In Dachau, the letter made such an impression that nobody dared asked for further information. Since there were two Doctor Charvats from Prague in the camp, they released both of them to be on the safe side.'[13] The other Doctor Charvat was a Communist activist.

Frau Alexandra Otzoup also received Albert's help: 'In the autumn of 1939, my husband and his son from his first marriage were persecuted. Herr Goering managed to turn the imprisonment in a concentration camp into an expulsion from the country and organised their departure.'[14] She and her daughter were unable to leave but Albert guaranteed their safety. Professor Divas owed him a similar debt: 'Without Goering's intervention, his son would have been shot.'[15] Divas was number seven on Albert's list.

At the Pilsen factory he made it clear where his sympathies lay: 'In his office there was no picture of Adolf Hitler, which everybody else had to have . . . When conferences and business meetings were held, he expressed the opinion that the Nazi management were incompetent, and that Hitler . . . would surely lose the war, which was a major shock for all the other participants.'[16] Albert refused to 'greet the Nazi salute with a Nazi salute. He replied by lifting his hat or else saying "Gruss Gott".'[17]

When an order came through in April 1940 to remove all Czech notices in the administration buildings and replace them with German ones, 'Albert Goering . . . after a quite intense debate with the chief of the

SD, Doctor Bolschwing, managed to get the order withdrawn.'[18] This held for a while until the measure was adopted in Albert's absence.

* * *

From the mid-1930s Czech military intelligence had anticipated Nazi aggression and forged contacts with the British secret service and its station chief in Prague. When it became clear invasion was imminent, a British military vehicle arrived at the underground car park of the Czech War Ministry and removed the most important files. The next day, eleven top intelligence officers flew to London, having told their families nothing of where they were going. A group of Czech politicians arrived soon after and set up an exile government.

The Czech underground was organised into distinct groups running in parallel with little or no contact between them, each led by a three-man cell. This structure was replicated from top to bottom. During 1940 British intelligence began collaborating with the resistance. In two years they mounted thirteen missions, dropping in twenty-eight Czech agents by parachute, of whom twenty-one were killed. Three became Gestapo informants.

Disabling Czech industry was a high priority. British aircraft first tried to attack the Skoda factory in October 1940, then again in November, and again a year later, causing zero damage. A plan was hatched for another raid on 26 April 1942 that involved agents planting a radio beacon to direct the planes to Skoda. Three Czechs landed with a transmitter known as a Eureka set. They buried the Eureka and split up. Two made it to safe-houses; one was arrested a few days later. The radio was dug up by a local farmer and handed over to the Gestapo. Plan B was to light fires. This they managed to do, but only one plane found the factory and dropped its load five miles off target.

Skoda was a hive of anti-Nazi activity. Some members of staff were affiliated to the Defence of the Nation, DON, an Army-led organisation. However, they 'were not so well trained in clandestine work and so the Gestapo discovered that they were in DON and arrested them'.[19] On the shop-floor, 'Here were several resistance groups active ... connected to the scouts, physical training groups, youth groups. Each group had their own staff and leaders ... Some were non-political, some were Communists. The Communists had the best experience of clandestine work.'[20]

A scout leader acted as a liaison between different networks in the factory and helped smuggle out crucial information: 'We stole plans for German cannon and transported them to Slovakia, where they handed them to the Russians, who used them to manufacture.'[21] Other workers were 'personally involved in sabotaging the tooling for tanks and cannon . . . We would alter the gauges on machine tools and sabotaged the gun barrels.'[22]

Albert turned a blind eye to these activities. According to one source, 'Albert and a bunch of Skoda colleagues drove a truck to a local camp . . . He said . . . I need workers. He filled up the trucks with these workers. The head of the concentration camp agreed, because it was Albert Goering. He took them to the woods and let them out.'[23]

* * *

On 27 September 1941, Reinhard Heydrich, Himmler's right-hand man, replaced Neurath as Protector of Bohemia-Moravia, with the express purpose of destroying the resistance and boosting industrial productivity. Born in Bavaria, Heydrich was a gifted violinist whose 'unusual intellect was matched by the ever watchful instincts of a predatory animal'.[24] In 1919, aged fifteen, he joined a Freikorps unit as a messenger. Three years later he entered the Navy, becoming a wireless operator before moving to signals interception and code-breaking.

He was dismissed in 1931 because of a scandal involving the daughter of a well connected man. The next day he joined the Nazi Party. A devotee of spy novels, he was chosen by Himmler to form the SD, which he built up on the lines of the British secret service: 'The SS has adopted as its ideal this English view of intelligence work as a matter for gentlemen.'[25] Universally feared, he trawled whorehouses inflicting horrible cruelty and was a championship fencer. He briefly exercised his penchant for violence as a Luftwaffe fighter pilot, earning the Iron Cross First and Second Class before Himmler grounded him.

On arrival in Prague, Heydrich immediately imposed martial law and licensed special courts. Within two months around 5,000 people had been detained and hundreds condemned to death. He increased recruitment of informers, known as 'A-Persons'. The number of moles quickly grew too large for Gestapo HQ to handle. An alcohol importing business was established as a front and its warehouse used for debriefings.

Meanwhile Heydrich attempted to woo Czech workers. As compensation for twelve-hour shifts he increased fat and tobacco rations and distributed 200,000 free pairs of shoes. May Day was declared a national holiday. Some 3,000 armaments workers, the majority from Skoda, were given the chance to spend the day at luxury hotels in swanky resorts while thousands of others were given free football, cinema and theatre tickets.

At the same time he went after the Skoda management. Possession of guns by Czech citizens was punishable by death. Anticipating trouble, Vambersky, the general director of the Skoda board, handed in a crate of guns and ammo that was being held in a safe at Skoda to the local police, making sure he got a receipt. The Gestapo found out, raided Vambersky's apartment and stole some valuable antiques. Next they accused him of not having a valid gun licence. Vambersky asked for Albert's help. Albert visited Hermann in Berlin and 'persuaded him to give him a letter addressed to Heydrich concerning the case of Vambersky, asking Heydrich to help in the matter'.[26] The investigation was dropped.

Soon after, Albert found himself going back to Berlin to remonstrate with Hermann after Hromadko, the chairman of the board, was arrested: 'I went up there and told him that he would have to get him out at once, otherwise there would be a rebellion in the Skoda Works.'[27] Hromadko was released. He is number eleven on Albert's list.

Skoda's subsidiary, Omnipol, also came under attack. Founded on 22 October 1934, Omnipol imported goods from countries suffering currency problems because of the depression, which were then re-sold in Prague to settle their debts with Skoda. For example: 'When the Romanian government would not release money due for payments, Omnipol would obtain food in Romania, bring it to Prague, and convert it into money there.'[28] By 1938 the company had branches in twenty countries world-wide.

In October 1941, Skoda's head of administration, Hans Modry, wrote a damning report about Omnipol's poor financial performance which blamed Febrans, a Nazi who had increased costs immeasurably by adding 'forty German administrators each of whom had a salary twice that which a Czech administrator made'.[29] Febrans saw the report and threatened Frantisek Zrno, a company director, with photographs that showed him, 'at the Prague Fair in March 1938 in the company of the two directors of the London subsidiary of Omnipol',[30] a German Jew and a British general.

Zrno and four other managers were taken in for questioning. Albert informed Hermann, but nothing happened. On 5 January 1942 he wrote to General Bodenschatz, previously Hermann's personal adjutant, now head of his cabinet, and pointed out that Heydrich was determined to hang on to Zrno and delay the release of the others. He reminded Bodenschatz that, 'I also asked you at the time . . . that you deal with the problem. But unfortunately, there was no reaction from any side . . . Meanwhile we can see that nearly 2½ months has passed and nothing has happened.'[31]

To press home his point Albert dragged Bodenschatz with him to see Heydrich. Face to face with the Nazi executioner, Albert insisted he 'pay attention to Hermann Goering's order that the imprisoned be freed'. The personal touch paid off. On 17 January he wrote to Vambersky to confirm the release of all five: 'I'm happy that my new and somewhat energetic intervention worked immediately.'[32] Zrno is number thirty-four on the Nuremberg list.

By now there was a Gestapo report on Albert's activities that had been circulated widely among the Nazi leadership: 'It said that I persisted in helping Jews', and ended by asking, 'How long is this public gangster going to be allowed to continue?'[33] Two warrants for his arrest were issued. Though Hermann stopped them going into effect, he was far from pleased with Albert: 'He made representations to me, and told me that the Gestapo had a file on me several inches thick; and he said I should stop this stupidity.'[34]

* * *

The biggest headache Albert caused Hermann concerned affairs of the heart. Albert had fallen for Mila Klasarova, a former teenage beauty queen who worked in a Prague department store. She was extremely pretty, over twenty years younger, and smitten by this sophisticated, successful businessman. This was the final straw for Albert's long-suffering wife. She got a divorce and the apartments in Vienna and Prague plus an income. Relations remained amicable. Albert was very fond of her two sons from her previous marriage, now grown men. He was their mentor and patron, getting one of them a job at a film studio. They remained close for the rest of his life.

The way was clear for a whirlwind romance and speedy union between Albert and his Czech maiden, but Heydrich was horrified that a Goering was going to marry a Slav, an *Untermensch*, intended for servitude or extinction, and was determined to prevent it. Albert had no choice but to appeal to Hermann: 'He had to help me . . . the Gestapo would not tolerate the fact that I was going to marry a Czech woman.' The situation was acutely embarrassing for Hermann. Even so, he could not deny his brother and gave his grudging consent. The crime of mixing blood was so heinous that he stayed away from the wedding. As Albert recalled, 'He did not even give me a present.'[35]

The marriage confirmed Albert's status as the black sheep of the family. Most of the others, if not already active supporters of Hermann's cause, were happy to jump on the bandwagon. There was his favourite nephew, Friedrich Karl Goering, who became a Luftwaffe officer in 1936 despite failing his exams. Hermann was delighted that Friedrich trained to be a fighter pilot, and distraught when he was shot down and killed in November 1941.

Hermann's cousin, Matthias Heinrich Goering, represented the older generation. A conservative nationalist and leading psychotherapist, he established the German Institute for Psychological Research and Psychotherapy in 1936 with a mix of state and private funding. *Mein Kampf* was a set text. Freudian psychoanalysis had been identified as Jewish science and stamped out, while Jungian psychotherapy endorsed the Nazis' racist interpretation of human development. In 1937 the institute had 128 members; by 1941 there were 240. When Hermann took over the Reich Research Council in 1942, he secured Matthias's funding through the Medical Division.

The institute earned its keep. Studies into a possible 'cure' for homosexuality were of particular interest to the Luftwaffe and the SS. Research was done on battle stress and combat fatigue. Hermann's pilots were acutely vulnerable to mental breakdown. In 1940 Matthias oversaw the creation of psychotherapy units at Luftwaffe hospitals in Cologne, Brussels and Paris. By 1943 they were all over Europe, from Athens to Oslo. By 1944 Matthias and his fellow therapists were assessing officers for signs of cowardice or treasonous thoughts. He was taken prisoner by the Soviets at the end of the war and died in a detention camp a few weeks later.

Albert was bucking the trend. He believed Hermann was able to protect him because 'Whenever a member of the family of one of the prominent men was to be arrested . . . the head of the family was given notice of that.'[36] This was true, but it was still up to Hermann what happened next. He was fiercely loyal to his family but was not above punishing miscreants.

Another cousin, Herbert Goering, a minor businessman, was a case in point. In 1936, Hermann got him a post at the Four Year Plan office to revive trade with the Soviet Union. Herbert also joined the Freundeskreis Reichsführer SS, an organisation of businessmen and industrialists allied closely to Himmler; this earned Herbert an honorary SS rank. He expedited shady deals for Hermann and dabbled with insurance fraud in his spare time. Hermann thought Herbert was abusing his privileges and sullying the family name. In 1943 he cut Herbert off and asked Himmler to strip him of his SS title.

Herbert did not take kindly to this and became a 'confirmed opponent of Hermann Goering'.[37] His name popped up in connection with the July 1944 bomb plot against Hitler. Herbert was arrested and imprisoned at Gestapo HQ in Berlin, where he remained for the duration of the war.

Albert never felt Hermann's wrath, despite all the discomfort he caused: 'People said that if the brother of the Reichsmarschall refused to become a member of the party, he must be an enemy of the state.' Even so Hermann continued to indulge him. There was no question of throwing him to the wolves. However, if the truth had been discovered about some of the company Albert was keeping, not even Hermann could have saved him from the Gestapo.

* * *

Karel Staller, number thirty-two on Albert's list, was a head engineer at Zbrojovka, a Slovakian weapons manufacturer that was part of the Skoda conglomerate. Zbrojovka produced the ZB26 light machine gun, and shared its design with the British, who reproduced it as the Bren gun. In 1938 Staller helped 120 engineers from the company get to the UK. He travelled widely across Europe and South America, knew Bruno Seletsky well, and was a fine pianist and energetic socialiser, nicknamed 'Whizz' by his friends. Through their mutual acquaintances, Albert and Staller quickly became close. When Albert visited Brno, where Zbrojovka was based, he stayed at Staller's apartment, hanging out with his family, drinking good cognac, smoking good cigars, bashing away at the piano and listening to the news on the BBC.

On the surface Staller was no different from Albert's other anti-Nazi friends. But Staller was engaged in highly dangerous espionage work. He was an irreplaceable agent of the resistance, smuggling top secret microfilm containing information on the armaments industry out of

Bohemia-Moravia and into Slovakia, where he handed it to an exporter who visited Switzerland five times a year. From there, it was sent to London. Receipt of Staller's microfilms was acknowledged via a coded message embedded in a BBC broadcast. At the same time Staller had one of the few active radio transmitters in Slovakia, maintaining vital communication with the government in exile: 'I lived through many dangerous situations being the radio-telegraphic contact from Silac in Slovakia to London.'[38]

Staller had met Vojtech Luza in 1933. Luza was a highly regarded general in the Czech Army who became military commander of the province of Moravia-Silesia in 1937 and held the post until occupation. His senior position marked him out for resistance leadership, and he formed R3, the Council of Three. Staller smuggled microfilm for Luza in his shaving kit and shoes, and was the general's only contact with London after he went into hiding, moving from one isolated farmhouse to another. Staller gave R3 lots of his own money, supplemented by large sums siphoned from the Brno munitions works, and supplied them with weapons. Staller was also a courier for the PRC, an organisation linked to the Communists and made up of writers, artists, academics, and ex-diplomats.

Albert knew nothing of Staller's clandestine activities. The risks were too great, the need for secrecy paramount. Albert may have suspected but preferred to remain ignorant. Had he found out, he would have endangered Staller, his family, friends and all the networks connected to him. The mere knowledge of Staller's true role was enough to get Albert killed. As it was, he provided a valuable service. Albert picked up high-level gossip which he would drop into conversation, like the date of the planned German invasion of France, which Staller would immediately pass to London. Thanks to Albert's patronage Staller was free to go about his business.

Albert met Jan Moravek on the same trip to South America that he met Bruno Seletsky. Moravek was a Skoda engineer trading arms to Bolivia who married and then moved to Buenos Aires. In late 1938 he decided to return to Czechoslovakia. His brother was already involved with the resistance and persuaded him to join. Moravek became 'an organiser' at Skoda: 'He supplied us with information about what we on the shop-floor should do, and we provided him with information from Czech intelligence in London.'[39]

In the summer of 1940 Moravek's parents were accused of keeping a pig, a serious offence, and their farm was searched. While Moravek was in Yugoslavia his house was ransacked. The Gestapo found weapons, documents, including 'the blueprint of a submachine gun', and evidence of a substantial deposit in the National City Bank, Buenos Aires. Punishment for having a foreign bank account was death. Albert was alerted. Time was short and Moravek's escape was going to cost. Luckily a vacancy had suddenly appeared at a Skoda factory near Bucharest. Albert secured Moravek the job and a salary that would cover the required sum. Moravek headed for Romania, leaving his wife, Elsa, and their daughter in Prague, with no idea where he had gone.

Elsa did not know who to trust. Her lawyer had double-crossed her and helped the Gestapo loot the Buenos Aires account. In this climate of fear, she was even wary of Albert. Only later did she realise that, 'He was so brusque with me because . . . he knew that in the room where he was receiving me, the walls had ears.'[40] However, after a formal meal, and many glasses of cognac, 'He spoke about Germany's defeat as something positive. I was impressed by his courage, when he confessed he was ashamed of the atrocities committed . . . Our friendship started from that day, coloured by fear and reserve.'[41]

She continued to wait for news of her husband. Finally she was summoned to Albert's office: 'Goering told her she was a German citizen, and she would take a German passport and leave with two suitcases.'[42] Elsa and her daughter joined Moravek in Romania, at his rented house, safe from the reach of the Gestapo. Albert became part of the family: 'All those four years Albert Goering came to visit us. In winter we went skiing, in summer we went mushroom picking. He knew how to cook very well . . . he did a very good omelette.'[43]

* * *

On the morning of 27 May 1942, a few months after Albert bailed out the Omnipol directors, two Czech agents, parachuted in some months earlier from the UK, attacked Heydrich's car at a junction in a Prague suburb that was on his daily route to and from work. After one agent's gun jammed the other threw a bomb. The blast broke one of Heydrich's ribs, and fragments of horsehair and wire from the car's upholstery were driven into his spleen. After a brief shoot-out the agents fled the scene. A state of emergency was declared and a curfew imposed. House-to-house searches began. Every male over the age of fifteen had to register at a police station within three days or be shot. Meanwhile the agents and their two comrades holed up in the catacombs of a Greek Orthodox church in Prague.

On 4 June Heydrich died of blood poisoning after an unsuccessful operation. Five days later, following Heydrich's state funeral in Berlin, Hitler authorised the destruction of Lidice, a small village which had vague links to the resistance. The men were to be killed, the rest sent to camps. Children considered racially pure enough were to be placed in SS orphanages. The operation started that evening; 199 men were shot in groups of ten and put in a mass grave dug by Czech Jews from a local camp; 195 women were removed with 87 children. Only eight were adopted by the SS. Lidice was burnt to the ground and bulldozed to nothing.

But there was still no sign of the agents. On 13 June, a proclamation was issued offering immunity to anyone who provided information within five days. Sergeant Curda, a parachutist who had been in hiding since he lit fires to guide British bombers to Skoda, cracked. First he wrote a letter, which went unanswered. Then, two days before the official amnesty expired, he walked into a Gestapo HQ. He was interrogated. Arrests followed. On the 18th 700 Waffen SS men surrounded the church. After six hours of sporadically intense fighting, the four agents took their own lives rather than be captured. The traitor Curda became a Gestapo spy.

The breaking of the Czech resistance accelerated. That summer over 3,000 were arrested, over 1,000 killed, and 252 friends and relatives of the agents were executed at Mauthausen in Austria. Many Skoda workers were seized. Undeterred by the horror unfolding around him, Albert 'insisted on their release. He made sure the families of those arrested received the full salary even though it was forbidden.'[44]

CHAPTER TEN

All or Nothing

In 1936, Hermann created a secret reconnaissance unit. Violating international treaties and air space, his pilots flew over 'enemy' territory taking snaps of military bases and fortifications. Supplied with advanced aerial cameras they ranged across the fringes of the UK, Poland, France, Czechoslovakia and the Soviet Union. Their pictures were analysed by the Main Photo Centre which was attached to Fifth Branch, Luftwaffe Intelligence.

In the meantime, transcripts of tens of thousands of phone-calls, radio transmissions and telegrams were being processed by Hermann's personal eavesdropping service, the FMT, during the pre-war diplomatic crisis which lasted from the Munich conference to the invasion of Poland. The airwaves were buzzing with chatter and Hermann was privy to every word.

All this information convinced him that a great deal could be achieved through negotiation. He was worried about triggering a wider conflict which Germany was not yet ready for: 'I didn't want war against Russia in 1939 but I was certainly anxious to attack them before they attacked us, which would have come in '43 or '44 anyway.'[1] The Molotov–Ribbentrop Pact, signed on 24 August 1939, secured Soviet neutrality and allowed for a joint carve-up of Poland. Ignoring the agreement, Hermann's reconnaissance planes entered Soviet air space several hundred times before hostilities began in June 1941.

Hermann's other chief concern was the British. During 1939 he used his Swedish connections to explore a peaceful settlement.

Hermann had known Axel Wenner-Gren, the head of Electrolux, for many years. Wenner-Gren had strong contacts with the Conservative Party and British industry. However, all he came up with was a self-penned twenty-year armistice plan which Hermann promptly binned.

Another Swede, Birger Dahlerus, who had spent a decade in England working for the likes of SKF, the ball-bearing manufacturer, and Ericsson, the telecommunications company, arranged a meeting at a remote farmhouse in Schleswig-Holstein between Hermann and seven English businessmen, one of whom reported the proceedings to the Foreign Office. There was good food, convivial chat, but nothing substantive. Hermann persevered with Dahlerus, who met both Halifax and Chamberlain. Fruitless exchanges continued until May 1940, seven months into the war.

Hermann's caution clashed with Hitler's aggression. It was a bruising experience: 'Every-time I stand before the Führer my heart drops into the seat of my pants.'[2] In March 1939 an inflammation of the jaw led to an abscess and he excused himself from Berlin and diplomatic errands in favour of a pleasure cruise aboard his yacht, *Karin II*, idling along the waterways of Germany and Holland, Wagner booming out of especially installed speakers.

Just days before Hitler took action against Poland, Hermann had tea in Berlin with Sir Nevile Henderson, still the British ambassador, and 'made much of the horrors of a war between England and Germany. For instance, he would be compelled to have England bombed. Henderson replied that in that case he would probably die by Goering's hand. If that was to happen, Goering said he would fly over to England in person and drop a wreath on Henderson's grave.'[3]

Whatever Hermann's reservations – 'Everybody is for war, only I, the soldier and field marshal, am not'[4] – once committed, he showed no mercy. On 24 September 1939, the Luftwaffe mounted a thousand-plane raid on Warsaw. After three days of bombing by high explosives and incendiaries that killed 10,000 civilians, the city surrendered. Norway followed, then the Blitzkrieg in the west, featuring the Luftwaffe's devastation of Rotterdam, and the fall of France.

Conquering the UK presented a more significant challenge: 'We knew literally nothing of amphibious operations ... accounts of the campaigns of Caesar, Britannicus and William the Conqueror were being read.'[5] A meeting on 15 November 1939 got preparations started.

However, over six months later, there was 'still only a plan', that was 'not yet . . . decided upon'.[6]

A report submitted to Hitler on 11 July 1940 was equally ambivalent: 'Britain can be made to ask for peace simply by cutting off her import trade by means of submarine warfare, air attacks on convoys and heavy air attacks on main centres.' Hitler agreed: 'The Führer also views invasion as a last resort, and also considers air superiority a prerequisite.'[7]

* * *

Hermann could not resist the chance to prove that his air force was capable of delivering victory on its own. Any doubts about the outcome were assuaged by his conviction that the British would cave in after a good beating and by faulty intelligence from Fifth Branch. Their detailed assessment of the RAF's readiness for battle concluded that the Luftwaffe was 'clearly superior' in all areas. They were wrong.

Other members of Fifth Branch were guilty of sloppy work. Operators of the top secret encryption and decryption device, the Enigma machine, frequently made errors which enabled the British at Bletchley Park to crack the Luftwaffe's general purpose code key on 6 January 1940 and then repeatedly afterwards, with increased efficiency, until they were able to decode messages in 'real time', as they were sent.

This breakthrough gave an additional advantage to an air defence system developed since 1918 specifically to counter German bombers, which were regarded as the main European threat to British security. Advance warning and speed of reaction were the vital elements. The Observer Corps was set up in 1929. Ten years later 30,000 volunteers manned a thousand observation posts dotted across the country, each one equipped with maps, a height estimator and a telephone. Radio direction-finding, or radar, was developed from 1935. By 1939, there were twenty-one coastal radar stations, with an average range of eighty miles. Incoming data was processed at Bentley Priory in Stanmore and relayed to the waiting pilots in a matter of minutes.

The teetotal Hugh Dowding became head of Fighter Command on 6 July 1936. His philosophy was simple: 'The best defence of the country is the fear of the fighter.'[8] He divided the UK up into sections and assigned a fighter group to each one. They determined tactical response, when, where and with how many to engage the enemy. In the battle to come,

11 Group, defending London and the south-east and based in Uxbridge, would bear the brunt. Air Marshal Keith Park, a First World War ace, took command on 20 April 1940. He operated rotating squadrons to maximise his options and preserve his planes from unnecessary deployment.

Crucially Britain produced twice as many fighters in June 1940 as the Nazis and would continue to do so throughout the year, making a nonsense of Hermann's boast to his Luftwaffe commanders: 'Our first objective will be the destruction of the fighter force . . . This . . . will be attained within two or three days.'[9]

* * *

Hermann's perception of air warfare was completely governed by his First World War experiences. Victory came down to the individual skill and bravery of the pilots: 'Personal heroism must always count for more than technical novelties.'[10] Aces were singled out for special treatment. Hermann gave medals, promotions, and celebrity to the highest-scoring heroes. Wealth and fame beckoned, as it had in his glory days. One ace was paid handsomely to endorse three different brands of cigar.

During August 1940, at the height of the battle, Hermann dismissed seven senior squadron leaders and replaced them with young aces. The top scorer, Werner Mölders, was invited hunting with Hermann. They were joined by another young ace, Adolf Galland, who had just received the prestigious Oak Leaves. Both pilots had learnt their dog-fight tactics in Spain.

As in the First World War, a competitive star system gave rise to false and exaggerated claims, but on a much larger scale due to the vast number of planes in action. For instance, between 10 July and 11 August, Luftwaffe pilots registered 381 victories. The reality was only 178. This degree of misinformation about RAF casualties had serious consequences. Nicolaus von Below, the Führer's Luftwaffe aide, noted that, 'Goering reported this fantastic success rate to Hitler: he calculated that the British must already be scraping the bottom of the barrel for aircraft.'[11]

In an effort to clear the way for a quick invasion, the Luftwaffe campaign began with attacks on coastal towns and the British Navy which lasted from 10 July until early August. While British fighters inflicted heavy losses, Bomber Command battered the French ports where preparations for Sealion were under way. Next, the Luftwaffe launched Operation Eagle, to crush the British by drawing them into mass aerial combat. Over five days of intense fighting the RAF established a kill ratio of 2:1.

The Luftwaffe switched focus again. Between 24 August and 6 September, the Germans concentrated on hitting airfields and their related infrastructure. This was the point at which Fighter Command was at its most vulnerable. Damage was considerable, but Hermann had already announced that, 'It is doubtful whether there is any point in continuing the attacks on radar sites',[12] thereby taking the sting out of the operation.

After the first British raid on Berlin, Hermann changed tack. An all-out assault on the British capital was ordered: 'Goering wants to use innumerable incendiary bombs . . . to create scores of fires in all parts of London.'[13] For him, it was a battle of wills with the British people. He firmly believed they could not withstand the punishment heading their way. On 7 September, 350 bombers hit the East End docks. The next eight days were decisive. The Luftwaffe lost 298 aircraft, the RAF 120. During October 365 German planes were destroyed compared to 146 British. Sealion was postponed and in effect abandoned on the 12th.

The Blitz continued. Other towns like Liverpool and Portsmouth were targeted. Coventry suffered 3,000 incendiary bombs on the night of 14 November; 60,000 buildings were ruined. Historic parts of central London suffered firestorms over Christmas. The early part of 1941 saw a decline in attacks, followed by a massive push during April and May. By June Hitler was about to invade the Soviet Union and Britain had won a reprieve. Since the bombing began 40,000 civilians had been killed but Britain was no nearer to giving in.

* * *

The Luftwaffe's defeat was not terminal. It was exceedingly costly in terms of skilled pilots – the Germans lost 2,698 – and bad for Hermann's reputation, but he still longed to demonstrate the Luftwaffe's value as a strike weapon. An opportunity arose thanks to Mussolini's disastrous invasion of Greece, launched on 28 October 1940. By the end of November the Italians were back at their starting line in Albania, with the Greeks poised to counter-attack. Hitler decided to bail out his beleaguered ally. In order to intervene in Greece the Germans needed to use Yugoslavian territory. Hitler convinced the Yugoslav king to cooperate. High-ranking members of the Yugoslav Army denounced the agreement and staged a coup on 27 March 1941 in defiance of Hitler.

Retribution was swift. On 6 April, the bombing of Belgrade began, orchestrated by Baron Wolfram von Richthofen, the Red Baron's cousin. Three days later 17,000 lay dead. Yugoslavia fell apart. On the 10th, pro-Nazi Croatian extremists declared independence. The day after, Slovenia did the same. British troops were sent to mainland Greece, but by the end of the month they were leaving for Crete.

General Kurt Student, Inspector of Paratroop Forces, had a plan for an attack on the island that would be spearheaded by a parachute assault on three airstrips. Once they were secured, Junkers transport planes would land and unload troops, artillery and supplies. Hermann liked the idea and proposed it to Hitler, who also approved. Hermann's very own 7th Paratroop Division would lead the attack. It was formed in 1935 after the Prussian militarised police were absorbed into the Army and Hermann was allowed to keep a regiment for himself. The bulk in due course became the elite *Hermann Goering* Panzer Division. The rest began parachute training.

They dropped out of the skies over Crete on 20 May. The British were waiting for them. The Luftwaffe's Enigma code had been broken again by Bletchley Park and details of Student's plan were forwarded to Crete a week before the operation began. The British commander knew exactly what to expect; 2,000 men of the 7th Paratroop Division were killed in the first few hours, many before they hit the ground.

Student gambled to avert disaster. Hermann backed him. A transport plane crash-landed on an unsecured airstrip and spewed out reinforcements, followed by another, and another until a foothold was established after forty-eight hours' fierce fighting. Between 28 May and 1 June the British abandoned the island. Though the Nazis' objective had been achieved it was at a frightful cost. Hitler was unimpressed: 'Crete proves that the days of the paratrooper are over.'[14]

Even so, a similar operation was contemplated against Malta, which had increased in strategic importance since Mussolini had become embroiled in North Africa. The Italians had invaded British-held Egypt from their Libyan colony and been swiftly routed. Tens of thousands were taken prisoner as the British advanced 400 miles in two months. During January 1941, a large Luftwaffe force arrived in Sicily and

Rommel's Afrika Korps soon started to appear in the desert. Until the spring Malta was subjected to remorseless raids. Temporary relief came when the Luftwaffe bombers were transferred to the Crete operation and then the Eastern Front.

They returned at the beginning of 1942 with the task of paving the way for invasion: 'Goering has taken all the measures for the attack on Malta. In a few days the intensive air bombardments will begin, then it will be decided whether we can or cannot land.'[15] Four months of terror followed. In March more bombs were dropped on Malta than on the UK during 1940. April was worse. Supplies of food, fuel, and ammunition were perilously low. Since January, thirty-one merchant ships had tried to reach Malta. Of the ten that made it, three were then sunk in the harbour. In June, only two got through out of eleven. August saw a convoy of fourteen merchant ships set out with a 100-strong escort, including two battleships. They were met by twenty-one U-boats and 540 aircraft. Five supply ships and a sinking oil tanker got through, providing just enough to keep Malta alive. The Nazi invasion plan was shelved. Within weeks the Luftwaffe force based on Sicily was needed elsewhere, over El Alamein's sand dunes and the snowy wastes of Stalingrad.

The Luftwaffe campaign against the Soviet Union had got off to a spectacular start. On 22 June 1941 a massive strike force attacked thirty-one airfields, destroying around 2,000 Soviet planes by lunchtime, three-quarters of which were sitting ducks. However, as fighting dragged on into winter, the strain was beginning to tell. Hermann was feeling it too. That summer he suffered from headaches, heart palpitations, and stomach upsets. He undertook a regime of rest and exercise, riding, swimming, walks, and the occasional game of tennis.

* * *

Continued military victory enabled Hermann to extend his economic empire. The Balkan nations were already closely tied to his armaments programme, supplying nearly half of its lead and aluminium requirements, plus 90 per cent of its tin. Romanian oil kept the Nazi war machine running. Hermann ordered his Four Year Plan office to carry out capital penetration in the usual manner and begin creating cartels to monopolise all Europe's oil, textile, iron, coal and steel industries. By 1942 the HermannGoeringWerke had swollen to mammoth proportions. The coal, iron and steel block contained twenty major companies. The munitions block consisted of nine. A separate block dealt with the Soviet Union. Six commissars were needed to administer the Ukraine alone, handling a plethora of mines and factories.

Hermann saw his colonial aspirations as the only viable solution to the problems affecting the war effort. Labour shortages were chronic as the military sucked up more and more men and nothing was done to increase the number of women at work. Foreigners and prisoners of war were hauled in to plug the gap. During 1940–2, three million were sent to Germany. Hermann convinced Hitler to let them work on farms to increase food production. He was forced to raise taxes and reduce wages. But his measures had little effect on the economic crisis that was exacerbated by his own mismanagement. He critically failed to delegate or appoint talented people lest they might undermine his overall authority. Instead he promoted those whose weaknesses he understood and could exploit. Competence was not an issue. The Transport Ministry was run by two of his yes-men. In 1941 they produced only half of the locomotives and railway wagons needed.

Though Hermann wielded a mass of executive power, he was beset by rivalries and power struggles with the Nazi Party, the SS, the civil service and representatives of German industry, particularly the Ruhr magnates. He was overwhelmed by information. He had to make innumerable decisions on a diverse range of topics. Even if he had had the time, he lacked the patience for considered judgement and was easily diverted by trivial matters, getting involved in a dispute between the Army and Goebbels about a film that depicted a famous singer spending the night with a Luftwaffe officer. The Army said that was no way for an officer to behave, and wanted the film withdrawn. Hermann sided with Goebbels: 'If a Luftwaffe lieutenant didn't make use of such an opportunity, he simply wouldn't be a Luftwaffe lieutenant.'[16]

His chaotic leadership bred inefficiency throughout the production system, severely undermining its ability to convert raw materials into finished weapons. In the crucial period of 1940–3, though the Nazi empire produced on average three times as much coal, three and a half times as much steel, and five times as much aluminium as the Soviet Union, Stalin's factories managed to roll out 10,000 more planes a year, considerably more tanks, and staggeringly more artillery pieces.

Hermann's beloved Luftwaffe was similarly affected by these limitations. Nothing was done to tackle the shortages of skilled labour and dire lack of specialised machine tools. There were no reforms to a manufacturing process that remained decentralised and workshop based. The complex connection between technological innovation and military necessity was befuddled further by the leadership of Udet, the ex-flying ace, drunkard and cartoonist, whom Hermann had leapfrogged into pole position at the Luftwaffe's Technical Department. Totally unsuited to the job, he shot himself on 17 November 1941. General Wilberg, much respected by Hermann, and the fighter hero Werner Mölders were both killed in separate plane crashes on their way to Udet's funeral.

The hard-headed, thoroughly capable Milch, who had constructed the Luftwaffe from scratch only to be marginalised by Hermann, reasserted himself in Udet's absence. He endeavoured to return control back to the designers and manufacturers. He organised a 'ring' system, linking companies together to form a standardised production chain. His methods anticipated the sweeping reforms that Albert Speer would introduce once he had taken the reins of the economy away from Hermann.

On 7 February 1942, Fritz Todt, Minister For Ammunition and Armaments, was killed in a mysterious plane crash, creating a space that Hermann expected to fill. He was furious to discover that Hitler had immediately given the position to his building guru, Speer. The ambitious architect and embryonic technocrat moved quickly to out-manoeuvre Hermann. He secured Milch's support and Hitler gave him full backing. On 3 March, at Karinhall, he got Hermann to sign off on the formation of a Central Planning Committee for the whole war economy which Speer would run. Hermann's grip on power was beginning to slip.

A serious contender for Hitler's affections had emerged in the shape of Martin Bormann, 'the brown eminence', described by Speer as 'the maggot in the apple of the Reich'.[17] Hermann was fully aware that Bormann hated him: 'my mortal enemy, the man is just waiting for a chance to bring me down'.[18]

The son of a postal clerk, Bormann saw action at the end of the First World War before getting involved with the Freikorps and providing the gun used in a murder. He spent a year in jail and joined the Nazi Party in 1926. He was placed in charge of an aid fund for injured or sick SA men, which amounted to 3 million marks by 1932. A year later he was attached to Rudolf Hess's Party Office which gave him direct daily access to Hitler. According to Hermann, 'Bormann knew all about the Führer's most personal affairs.'[19] He took control of Hitler's finances and began writing down his after-dinner thoughts. In the spring of 1942 he was appointed Secretary to the Führer. Now nobody could get to Hitler except through Bormann. Hitler remarked that he was 'glad to have a doorkeeper like that, because Bormann keeps people off my back'.[20]

* * *

On 15 January 1941 RAF Bomber Command received a directive from the Air Ministry stating that 'The sole primary aim of your bomber offensive ... should be the destruction of the German synthetic oil plants.'[21] Seventeen different targets were chosen representing 80 per cent of Germany's oil production. Then another directive appeared in July which identified 'the morale of the civil population ... of the industrial workers in particular'[22] as weak points. A broad campaign of bombing swept over the Ruhr, the Rhine valley and further afield, taking in towns like Hamburg, Frankfurt, and Stuttgart.

Before the war, Hermann had given little thought to the defensive capability of the Luftwaffe, but in June 1940 he created Der NachtJagd, the night fighter arm, under Generalmajor Josef Kammhuber, who quickly took the situation in hand. Radar stations were established at thirty-kilometre intervals between Schleswig-Holstein and Liége, blocking the RAF's routes to Germany, equipped with several types of radar, searchlights, and highly effective 88-mm flak/anti-tank guns. In the major cities, gigantic Speer-designed fortresses were built, each corner tower armed with a huge twin-gunned 128-mm Flakzwilling 40. However, maintaining the 'Kammhuber Line' created a major drain on men and material.

That autumn of 1941, Rommel was readying an offensive against the British with only thirty-five 88-mm guns at his disposal. Hermann's anti-aircraft effort was using nearly 9,000 of them.

Sir Arthur 'Bomber' Harris was put in charge of Bomber Command's next offensive. An Air Ministry directive of 14 February 1942 outlined a new strategy which targeted built-up areas. On the night of 28/29 March, the medieval town of Lübeck was laid waste by fire. A similar fate befell Rostock, another historic landmark. The Luftwaffe retaliated with raids on 'cultural centres'.[23] Bath, Exeter, York, Canterbury, and Norwich were all hit.

Bomber Command's most destructive attacks of the war so far were a mere foretaste for the thousand-bomber raids that followed. The first, code-named 'Millennium', hit Cologne hard. Over 13,000 residential buildings were totally destroyed and 500 civilians died. Essen, Bremen, and Hamburg were next. Throughout the summer of 1942 a range of medium-sized provincial towns were bombed, turning 'every square metre of our territory . . . into a front line'.[24]

The RAF suffered heavily, losing 503 planes between May and mid-August, but reinforcements were on the way in the shape of the Americans, whose armaments industry was beginning to gather a colossal head of steam.

The pummelling of the Reich soured relations between Hermann and his Führer. As Hitler's Luftwaffe adjutant Nicolaus von Below observed in his diary, 'It struck me then that Hitler and Goering no longer talked together as they had done previously.'[25]

* * *

The turning point for the Nazis was Stalingrad. On Sunday 23 August 1942, Richthofen ordered a thousand plane raid on the Soviet city, marking the beginning of sustained carpet bombing which killed thousands in the first week. For the Red Army, the shattered remains acted as impenetrable cover as they defended every inch of ground. For General Friedrich Paulus's Sixth Army it became a nightmare graveyard. While his generals urged retreat, Hitler would not dream of it. To survive, Paulus's besieged troops needed an absolute minimum of 500 tonnes of supplies a day. Though Hermann knew the Luftwaffe could deliver a maximum of 350 tonnes, he recklessly promised Hitler they could land what was needed.

The supply operation was a ghastly farce played out in brutal winter conditions. Planes were buried in snow on the runways, pilots blinded by it in the air. Everything froze. The main airfield was within range of Soviet guns and aircraft, and host to hundreds of incoming wounded. Despite heroic efforts and Hermann's reassurances, the Luftwaffe only managed to supply a daily average of ninety-five tonnes. By the end of January 1943 the Sixth Army had ceased to exist.

Such was the scale of the defeat, and Hermann's ignominious role in it, that he was obliged to broadcast the news to the German people on 30 January 1943. Striking a mournful tone, he offered the hope of redemption: 'A thousand years hence Germans will speak of this battle with reverence and awe . . . Stalingrad will remain the greatest heroic struggle of our history.'[26]

Hermann von Epenstein with his godchildren. Hermann Goering (*far left*) holds hands with Albert (*centre*). *Courtesy of Lungauer Kulturwanderweg – Schloss Mauterndorf*

Castle Mauterndorf as it stands today. *Fotocommunity Support*

A German Army signals unit monitors communications on the Western Front. *Imperial War Museum Q54364*

Albert in uniform as an officer of the signal corps. *Courtesy of 3BM TV*

The demise of the Communist revolt in Munich, May 1919. Freikorps men march their prisoners through the streets. *AKG-Images*

Hermann the air ace, photographed wearing his Blue Max shortly after he replaced the Red Baron as commander of the Richthofen Squadron in 1918. *Getty Images*

Hermann's first wife and one true love, Karin Goering. *Ullstein/AKG-Images*

©Junkers Bildarchiv

Prof. JUNKERS
GAS-WARMWASSER-APPARATE
IN BERUF UND GEWERBE

Vorratsautomaten und Schnellwassererhitzer sind als Spezialapparate für den Arzt, Zahnarzt und für den Friseur ausgebildet. Der Kochend-Wasser-Automat, der ständig kochendes Wasser enthält, dient der Versorgung von Kaffeeküchen in Hotels und anderen Wirtschaftsbetrieben.

An advert for Professor Hugo Junkers's gas-heated boilers, manufactured at the Kaloriferwerke in Dessau, where Albert worked as a technician. *Courtesy of JUMA Verwaltungsges GmbH, Munich*

Albert's passport photo 1939.
Courtesy of 3BM TV

The screen icon Henny Porten in her 1920 movie *Anna Boleyn*. She faced persecution under the Nazis because of her Jewish husband. Both Albert and Hermann protected her.
Ullstein/AKG-Images

Hermann, the Nazi warlord. *Hulton Getty*

Right: Hermann and his nephew Friedrich Karl Goering play with the toy trains in the attic at Karinhall. *AKG-Images*

Below: Hermann, man of the people, enjoys a beer with workers in Berlin. *AKG-Images*

Hermann and Hitler admire a work of art at the German Exhibition in Munich, July 1937. *Ullstein/AKG-Images*

Left: Hermann's Karinhall country estate wrapped in a blanket of snow. *Ullstein/AKG-Images*

Right: Hermann with the result of a successful hunt on his East Prussian estate. *Getty Images*

An artist puts the finishing touches to a bust of Hermann as his subject holds the pose of serious statesman. *Ullstein/AKG-Images*

At the tenth anniversary of the Munich Beer Hall Putsch, Hermann and Hitler stand side by side mourning their fallen comrades. *Getty Images*

Hermann, Hitler and Dr Wilhelm Kessler, Director of Daimler-Benz AG, study a new model at the International Motor Show in Berlin, March 1934. *Ullstein/AKG-Images*

Post-*Anschluss*, Viennese Jews scrub the street as locals enjoy the view. Albert's attempt to rescue an old woman from a similar fate led to his first arrest. *NYP68064*

The streets of Vienna are packed as Hitler arrives in the city on 15 March 1938. Albert stayed in his office. *Getty Images*

Hermann and Emmy at their wedding reception, with Hitler, their guest of honour.
Getty Images

Albert, Hermann and their sisters in a relaxed frame of mind, Vienna 1937. *Courtesy of Dr Christa Hartnigk-Kummel*

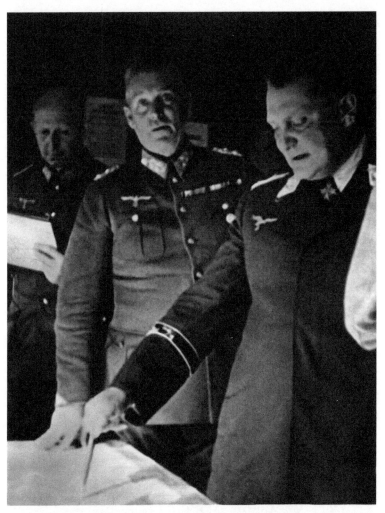

Hermann appears next to General Keitel, chief of staff of Hitler's Armed Forces High Command, in *Feuertaufe*, a drama-documentary about the invasion of Poland, which was released in 1940. *AKG-Images*

The women of Prague greet the arrival of the Nazis with tears in their eyes.
Imperial War Museum NYP68068

Hermann and his cronies are impressed by a scale model of Hermann's
steel plant at Salzgitter. *Ullstein/AKG-Images*

Above: Hermann and Marshal Antonescu in Vienna, March 1941, reaching
agreement on Romanian oil supplies to the Reich.
Imperial War Museum HU39473

Above: A GI admires paintings retrieved from Hermann's collection during May 1945 and put on show at a Luftwaffe barracks near Königsee. *Getty Images*

SKODAWERKE
ŠKODOVY ZÁVODY
PRAG · PRAHA

Ausweis-Průkazka

ZUA   282

Oberdir. Ing.
G ö r i n g Albert
geb. 9.3.1895
nar Berlin
in
v

P

Š₳₣-G.............tion Prag

Left: Albert's Skoda works pass. His anti-Nazi activities at Skoda helped secure his release after the war. *Courtesy of 3BM TV*

CHAPTER ELEVEN

Agent Albert

When Albert completed his stint at the Pilsen factory, he became 'responsible for the production of peacetime goods in order to ensure that Skoda would not lose their market for post-war times'.[1] Albert dealt with a wide range of commodities – 'locomotives, diesel motors, electric motors, cranes and even whole sugar refineries' – which were 'sold in exchange for foreign currency'.[2]

He was forced to lock horns with the Nazi-appointed chairman of Skoda's executive committee, SS Standartenführer Doctor Wilhelm Voss. Albert thought that Voss was 'absolutely unfitted for the job', and also said that they 'often had personal differences'.[3] During the spring of 1942, only weeks before Heydrich's assassination, Voss promised Himmler that Skoda would 'meet with all the wishes and special wishes of the Waffen SS',[4] which included mountain howitzers, rocket launchers, mortars, machine guns and automatic rifles. But that July, Albert Speer gained jurisdiction over the armaments industry in the province. Voss became a frustrated onlooker as Skoda's output immediately increased.

Managers were given greater freedom. The company, and enterprises linked to it, formed their own production chain, a 'ring' of manufacturers. This system was replicated across the Reich with startling results. In one year Speer managed to double the production of tanks and cut in half the construction time for submarines. Even so, Himmler set about subverting his authority. In October 1943, the SD formed an economic intelligence unit to infiltrate Speer's organisation. The former architect was increasingly vulnerable as factories became reliant on the concentration camp inmates the SS provided.

Nevertheless, at least until 1944, Albert conducted business in a slightly less fractious working environment, especially after General Karl Bodenschatz, Hermann's 'personal friend and intimate', became trustee of Skoda. Albert 'used to see him about once in every six months',[5] either in Berlin or Prague. Bodenschatz generally agreed with Albert and 'always followed his advice after he had consulted with the experts'.[6]

Albert also had other business interests. The Anglo-Prague Credit Bank had been set up on 1 April 1922 to resolve debts on international loans. In 1938 it financed and structured the deal that temporarily stopped Hermann getting 56 per cent of Skoda. Acting again for Skoda, the bank bought out the Czech government's shares in Zbrojovka, the armaments firm which Albert's friend, the resistance agent Karel Staller, worked for. The bank raised the money with assistance from the Czech explosives firm Explosia, which ICI had a stake in. Both were connected to Albert's associates from Vienna, Bickford-Smith and Major Short, purveyors of the Bickford fuse, whose enterprise Albert shepherded through the war.

Given his familiarity with those close to the Anglo-Prague Credit Bank, it was a logical step for Albert to become 'representative and supervisor of the branch offices . . . in Bucharest, Belgrade, and Sofia'. Then, when 'Berlin ordered the parent office of the bank in Prague to be dissolved, and the branch offices incorporated into the Deutschebank and the Dresdner Bank', Albert 'postponed the liquidation for a year, and he even maintained the Bucharest branch up to the end'.[7]

* * *

Albert's official activities for Skoda turned him into a travelling salesman, primarily operating in Bulgaria, Romania, Hungary, Yugoslavia, and Greece. Mutually suspicious and nursing territorial grievances, these countries shared some basic characteristics: authoritarian, anti-Communist regimes that granted democratic rights only on sufferance; a majority that still worked the land – just 11 per cent of the Romanian labour force was in industry, over half Bulgaria's GNP came from agriculture; an elite of major landowners and industrial magnates in a sometimes uneasy alliance with the church and the armed forces, facing internal and external threats; and a heavy dependence on their trade with the Reich.

Albert dealt directly with royalty and heads of state who were used to doing business with the Goering family, having received Hermann as a frequent guest since his first trips to the region in 1934–5. Facing spiralling inflation, shortages, collapsing infrastructure and constant pressure to devote all hands to the Nazi war effort, they welcomed any kind of commerce that benefited the civilian market.

When Skoda was ordered to stop producing machines that made cigarettes, Albert 'succeeded in having this order cancelled, and a further quantity of machines were exported to Romania, Bulgaria and Yugoslavia'.[8] This may seem insignificant but similar machines were being modified by the Nazis to produce bullets. Even getting six trains for the king of Bulgaria, who was a trained locomotive engineer, was an achievement. The foreign currency earned by Albert was vital for Skoda, and the Czech economy as a whole. By keeping up a steady flow of orders Albert was eating into the factory time Skoda could dedicate to weaponry. Within two years of Albert starting as export director, the amount of its output that went to the Wehrmacht fell by 12 per cent.

* * *

From the summer of 1940, Albert's main base was the Romanian capital, Bucharest. On arrival he must have felt a strong sense of déjà-vu. The city was gripped by a political crisis that was spilling onto the streets. The regent, King Carol, having stamped out the left a few years earlier, was facing a direct challenge from the Iron Guard, a violently anti-semitic, nationalist organisation that mixed terrorism with party politics, and had the covert support of Himmler.

The king's authority had been severely undermined by hidden provisions in the Nazi–Soviet pact that awarded a third of Romanian soil and over 3½ million of its citizens to Stalin. The provinces of Bessarabia and Bukovina were occupied by Soviet troops between 28 June and 3 July 1940. King Carol was in no position to offer resistance. Salt was poured into the wound a month later, when he was persuaded by Hitler to grant North-East Transylvania, a hotly disputed region, to Hungary. This further loss of territory, and another 2 million people, inflamed public opinion and gave the Iron Guard a pretext for revolt.

Carol, realising his position was untenable, abdicated on 4 September and handed over power to Marshal Antonescu. The ex-chief of the Army was only able to keep a lid on things by bringing the Iron Guard into his hastily formed government. The Guard were in no mood to cooperate and launched a coup in January 1941. Luckily for Antonescu, he had the full backing of Hitler. The Führer considered him to be 'of Germanic origin . . . a born soldier',[9] and 'a man on a big scale, who lets nothing throw him out of his stride'.[10] Hitler had nothing but contempt for the Iron Guard, despite their chimeric anti-semitism. He wanted order and stability in the country that supplied most of the Nazis' oil.

When Ribbentrop informed him that the SD had conspired in the Guardist putsch, Hitler ordered all their agents to leave Romania immediately. Antonescu seized the initiative. On 14 February 1941, 9,000 Guardists were arrested and their ringleaders executed. The marshal banned all opposition parties, ruled by decree, and welcomed Hitler's upcoming 'holy war' against the Soviet Union.

Caught in the cross-fire of this upheaval were the Jews of Bucharest. On 22–3 January, 120 were murdered by Guardists in a local abattoir. Antonescu carried through the anti-Jewish legislation that had been enacted six months earlier, cutting them out of the professions, education and the arts, and began the process of removing their homes and assets. Albert 'urged all his Jewish friends to leave and afforded them all possible help in the way of passports, visas and money',[11] transferring currency for them to accounts in Switzerland. The Benbassat family had benefited from Albert's help during the *Anschluss* when he had got them out of Vienna and to Bucharest. Now he arranged their passage to Lisbon.

As Hitler's armies invaded the Soviet Union, Romanian soldiers reclaimed Bessarabia and Bukovina. Antonescu branded the province's Jews enemies of the state and sanctioned a vicious pogrom that took around 8,000 lives in the towns of Jassy and Czernowitz. Between July and November 1941, over 250,000 were forced into makeshift camps across the border in newly conquered Transnistria. By the following summer only a handful survived. The Romanian Army continued the destruction, ably supported by the Einsatzgruppen, as they advanced through Odessa.

Over 300,000 Jews were still alive in the historic heartlands of Romania. On 12 October 1942 Antonescu, citing his promise to protect 'the Jews in the Old Kingdom', refused to deport them as well. According to him, the Jews of Moldavia, where he grew up, were 'native' Romanians. The Jews of Bessarabia and Bukovina were aliens who existed outside the nation, tainted by the Soviets' brief occupation and their alleged enthusiasm for Communist rule: 'Even before the appearance of Soviet troops, the Jews of Bessarabia and Bukovina spat upon our officers . . . and when they had the chance beat our soldiers to death with cudgels.'[12]

Antonescu's motives were hardly noble. He could see which way the war was going. His beloved army awaited its fate outside Stalingrad. Peace feelers had already been extended to the Allies via diplomatic contacts in Lisbon and Istanbul. He was under considerable pressure from members of the royal family, the government, church leaders and prominent figures in business and industry.

At Nuremberg Albert claimed that, 'By personal intervention with Antonescu of Romania he alleviated the fate of thousands of Jews there.'[13] It is highly probable that Albert added his voice to the protests. He exercised leverage over an administration run by technocrats and civilian experts. His influence can be measured by the fact that 'He forced the Romanian government to pay their unpaid debts to Skoda in 1943 to the sum of 400 million crowns.'[14]

Albert worked closely with the Resita group, Romania's largest industrial corporation, run by the Jewish magnate, Max Anschnitt. Suspected of having Communist sympathies and links to the Soviet Union, Anschnitt was arrested by King Carol for denying him a commission on a deal and kept in prison by Antonescu for being a Jew. However, under the auspices of the HermannGoeringWerke, which had added Resita to its portfolio, he was released and placed back at the helm. Anschnitt donated huge sums of money to organisations helping Jews escape deportation.

* * *

The experience of war on Albert's patch differed sharply between the countries allied to Hitler and the ones occupied by him. In Greece, the Wehrmacht, working hand in glove with Krupps and IG Farben, ransacked the economy with devastating results. Thousands lost their jobs, prices rose fast, and a poor harvest triggered a full-scale famine that claimed over a quarter of a million lives during the winter of 1941/2. Hermann's Four Year Plan office refused to send any grain from the Reich to prevent the crisis. The black market took over. By 1944 bartering had replaced money. Throughout the country partisans fought an extensive and damaging campaign against the Nazis, who responded with increasing levels of indiscriminate violence. Meanwhile Greece's Jews, concentrated in Salonika and numbering around 75,000, were shipped to the death camps. Only 10,000 survived.

Yugoslavia was a bubbling cauldron of partisans, Nazi reprisals, ethnic hatred and civil war. In Croatia the Ustasha sowed its killing fields with Jews, gypsies and Serbs. Tito's Communist guerillas and the royalist Chetniks fought the Nazis and each other. During 1939–41 Skoda had produced a lot of weapons 'for Yugoslavia and for the Soviet Union', so when the Nazis invaded the company already had links with the emergent resistance. Skoda's chairman, Hromadko, made regular trips to Belgrade, where he was able to 'pass confidential news to the Allies', and arrange funding 'for the support of the independence struggle'.[15]

The Nazis were naturally suspicious. The SS man, Doctor Voss, 'had the chairman watched during his travels abroad'. When Voss's spy broke his leg, 'This task was given to Albert Goering'. Albert had no intention of carrying it out: 'He waited for the chairman at the train station or else the airport and after a short time he gave him unlimited freedom of movement. In that way he allowed him to pursue his resistance activities.'[16]

The Bulgarians committed to Hitler on 1 March 1941 but from the start, the king and his ministers sought to limit their participation in the war. They were content to let their troops occupy neighbouring Macedonia, but fearful of sending them to the Eastern Front. Communist partisans were soon troubling the capital Sofia. Despite the usual gamut of anti-semitic laws there was little enthusiasm for the Final Solution. When the SS demanded that Bulgaria's 49,000 Jews be collected and put on trains there was widespread opposition. Sixty-three eminent figures presented their objections to King Boris. Again, Albert had the chance to express his opinion in person, after all he had got the king his trains. On 10 March 1943, Boris drew a line in the sand: no deportations. However, Macedonia's Jews were not spared – 11,400 were sent to Treblinka from where only 70 returned.

Hungary pursued a similar course to Bulgaria. Skoda's business there was initially limited but grew as the war progressed. When the Nazis threatened to halt the company's automobile trade with Hungary, Albert intervened: 'I went all the way up to see Neurath, who was then protector of the country, and I told him it was impossible to stop the export of automobiles . . . and he granted this.'[17] Albert was probably aware of Hungary's efforts to secure peace with the Allies, which gathered urgency after its army was decimated by the Soviets around Voronezh in January 1943. First contacts were made in Lisbon that month. Meetings between British intelligence and Veress, a representative of the 'Hungarian Government Resistance Group', continued in Istanbul throughout the summer. Veress returned to Budapest in September armed with two wireless transmitters and a code book. For the next six months he relayed messages until Hitler acted to prevent Hungary's defection.

The head of state, Admiral Horthy, faced with the threat of invasion, purged the government and filled it with men amenable to the Nazis. Adolf Eichmann arrived in Budapest with a 200-strong task force. Operating out of the Hotel Majestic, they began rapid preparations for the transportation of Hungary's 700,000 Jews. The first trains for Auschwitz left on 14 May 1944. By 8 July over 434,000 had made the hellish journey. Then Horthy, aware of the Soviet military juggernaut heading towards his borders and swayed by international outrage and diplomatic pleading, put the brakes on. Budapest's Jews, already being shoved into ghettos and denuded of their rights and their property, were given a temporary reprieve.

Eichmann's measures reached out to embrace Hungarian Jews living abroad, like Albert's friend, Doctor Kovacs, whom he had met in Rome before the war. A letter was sent to the Hungarian legation demanding they strip Kovacs of his citizenship. This was the least of his worries. Only a year earlier the situation had seemed so hopeful. Having triumphed in North Africa, the Allies invaded Sicily in July 1943, prompting a coup against Mussolini, who was arrested later that month. On 3 September, as the Allies crossed the Straits of Messina and landed on Italian mainland soil, the new government under King Victor Emmanuel signed an armistice and promptly fled Rome – the Nazis were coming to town. On the 12th German airborne troops liberated Mussolini from the ski resort where he was being held.

These were nervous times for Italy's Jews, who had so far suffered only relatively mild discrimination. Now it was open season. Doctor Kovacs turned to Albert. He was 'frightened that his furniture would be requisitioned, and explained his position to Goering. Whereupon Goering gave them a certificate to the effect that all of the furniture in the flat belonged to him.'[18] Meanwhile, one of Kovacs's circle, Vitez Szasz, who had been head of the Hungarian Legation in Rome for over twenty years, saved '280 Jews from the clutches of the Nazis, and continued that work'.[19] After Kovacs was given sanctuary at the Hungarian Embassy by Szasz, it seems likely they made use of the Swiss bank account opened by Albert in 1939 to finance escape routes.

Though Naples was liberated on 1 October, it would be another eight months before the Allies got to Rome, their advance hopelessly blocked by the German defensive line built around the medieval monastery of Monte Cassino, located high in the central ridge of mountains that divides Italy. The first attacks against this fortress were launched in December. The defenders finally surrendered on 18 May 1944. During that time 7,500 Italian Jews were deported, of whom 610 made it home.

* * *

The demonic energy invested in the Final Solution reached a fever pitch of intensity as the Nazi empire contracted, creating a whirlpool effect that sucked in millions. Though Albert managed to get a few people out of the camps, including a Czech and two Soviet prisoners from Seckenheim, he understood how futile and petty his efforts were when stacked against the enormity of the Nazis' crimes.

According to Elsa Moravek, whose family owed him their lives, Albert 'repeatedly said it was a shame what the Gestapo were doing, and that all the trees of Europe could not hide all the Germans that were part of it'.[20] Albert realised that the retribution, though thoroughly deserved, would be devastating: 'Deep inside Albert was suffering. He was a sincere German and he was scared of the consequences of the war.'[21]

Yet he remained defiant in public. An arrest order was issued when he called Himmler a 'lustmerder . . . somebody who likes to kill for fun'. He managed to insult the Nazis' man in Bucharest, Manfred von Killinger. The SA general invited Albert 'several times to come to dinner, or come to a lecture, or something of that sort, but I refused . . . One day, one of the counsellors of the Legation . . . asked me why . . . I told him that I would rather sit down with a chauffeur of a taxi than sit down with a murderer, because Killinger was the murderer of Rathenau.'[22]

Walter Rathenau, a prominent Jewish politician, had been gunned down in 1922 during a wave of attacks orchestrated by a terrorist cell which Killinger belonged to. A former Navy officer who had fought with the Freikorps in Munich during 1919, he joined the SA, survived the Night of the Long Knives and was based at the German Consulate in San

Francisco between 1936 and 1938, where he ran an espionage network along the US West Coast. He loathed the kind of people that Albert associated with: 'If it were up to me, I would douse the entire Romanian bourgeoisie in gasoline.'[23]

Albert's remark 'got back to Killinger, and he was very, very furious, and he denounced me to the Gestapo'. Hermann was alerted and he got Albert out of trouble again, even though he 'had a terribly difficult time'. The same thing happened when Albert 'in conversation with some friends, called Hitler the greatest criminal of all times'.[24]

Albert's attitude can be summed up by an incident recalled by Jacques Benbassat. One evening in Bucharest, 'He played the piano and sang some Viennese songs with my father.' From across the street someone sang back in German, 'So Albert went to the balcony to see who it was and there were two German officers on a balcony.' A few words were exchanged, 'And the Germans asked, "Who are you? What's your name?" He said "Albert Goering". They said, "Are you related?" So he said, "Yes, he's my brother." So they snapped to attention, "Heil Hitler", and he raised his glass and he said, "Kiss my arse."'[25]

* * *

As the war entered its final year, any semblance of normality clinging to the daily lives of civilians across central Europe and the Balkans was mercilessly stripped away. Infernal chaos, monotonous horror and random slaughter marched hand in hand with disease, homelessness and hunger. After the invasion of Italy, Allied bombers and their stockpiles of incendiaries were within range of Sofia, Bucharest and Belgrade, which soon felt the heat.

The Red Army was coming. Towards the end of the summer of 1944 it launched a massive offensive, entering Romania and Hungary. In Bucharest, on 23 August, Antonescu resigned. Killinger shot himself to avoid capture. The king sued for peace and declared war on Germany. Bulgaria followed soon after. By October Tito's partisans were on the verge of entering Belgrade and British paratroops were landing in Athens. In Hungary, Horthy tried to jump ship but the Nazis would not release their stranglehold. The Arrow Cross, Hungary's equivalent of the Iron Guard, assumed power in Budapest and set about murdering Jews. As the world caved in around him, Albert left Bucharest and headed for Prague.

While Slovakia was torn by a massive anti-Nazi uprising, Bohemia-Moravia descended into chaos as resistance fighters, Nazi troops, SS death squads and Soviet soldiers roamed the countryside. Albert's good friend, Karel Staller, was still performing missions for his controllers in London. During April 1944 he brought the venerable General Luza a microfilm containing a list of questions for him about the likelihood of revolt. Soon after Staller delivered another communiqué which asked Luza to organise and lead an insurrection. However, in October, while heading for the capital, Luza was shot dead in a tavern by local police. On 10 April 1945, the Gestapo dumped his corpse by a deserted roadside.

The Skoda factory at Pilsen had led a charmed life. Despite two major Allied bomber raids in the spring of 1943, each involving over 200 planes, none had hit their target. The company's armament production peaked in 1944. This dubious achievement did not stop the Gestapo making one last attempt to get Albert behind bars. The final arrest order was issued in Prague on 31 January 1945. Hermann, whose reputation by this point was in tatters, was still able to get Albert's head off the chopping block, but only just: 'When I saw him he told me that this would be absolutely the last time he could help me . . . because he had very great trouble getting me out.'[26]

CHAPTER TWELVE

Destruction

As the lice-ridden, freezing German soldiers trapped in Stalingrad waited for the deliverance of death or surrender and dreamt only of bread, Hermann celebrated his fiftieth birthday at Karinhall in lavish style, prompting 'revolting stories' about the extravagant gifts he received, including a French hunting lodge and three medieval statues. The occasion was seen by many of his contemporaries as symptomatic of how corrupt, narcissistic and out of touch he had become. Goebbels summed up the general feeling: 'One can no longer really depend on Goering. He is tired and somewhat washed out.'[1]

Hermann's performance in the last two years of the war was certainly erratic. He was often lethargic, remote and lost in his private obsessions, whether it be hunting or art collecting. He frequently withdrew to his various homes. In addition to Karinhall, Hermann had a villa built at Obersalzberg, on the same bit of mountain as Hitler's Berchtesgaden retreat, near other prominent Nazis' properties. When Epenstein's widow, Lilli, died in 1938 he had also inherited both Veldenstein and Mauterndorf castles, and poured money into their restoration and redecoration, carrying on the work his godfather began.

Hermann was an intelligent man, and reason dictated that the war was lost. But if he was hiding from this painful truth, dulling it with drugs and beautiful objects, he still refused to relinquish his power or Hitler's cause. At Nuremberg he claimed it was only after the Battle of the Bulge in the winter of 1944–5, that he felt the game was truly up: 'The situation was not bad at all until the Ardennes. It was only then that things began to look dangerous.'[2] He remained as ruthless and quick to act when someone threatened his authority: 'The other day he said . . . that he was taking note of all those who pissed on him or just lifted a leg.'[3]

Hans Jeschonnek, the Chief of the Luftwaffe General Staff, begged Hitler to let him replace Hermann. Hermann responded by accusing him of insubordination. Jeschonnek agreed to soldier on but had lost all heart. On 19 August 1943 he shot himself in the head. To avoid a scandal Hermann recorded the cause of death as a stomach haemorrhage and falsified the date.

When a clique of officers plotted his removal in early 1944, Hermann had Adolf Galland, commander of his fighter force, sacked and charged with treason. Speer managed to save Galland from a court martial, but Hermann, with Hitler's approval, came up with another solution. Galland was put in charge of test-flying prototype jet planes, with the expectation he would be killed doing so. That summer, Milch's constant criticism of Hermann finally got him fired too.

As the Führer interfered more and more in the day-to-day running of the Army and the Luftwaffe, down to the tiniest details, Hermann operated on the basis that Hitler's word was law, whatever the consequences. On 24 June 1943, General Kammhuber, the man responsible for almost single-handedly organising the Nazis' anti-aircraft defences, met Hitler and asked for more night fighters and more money to improve radar technology. Hitler angrily rejected him. Soon after, Hermann removed Kammhuber from his post and sent him to Norway.

After the war, when an American psychiatrist suggested to him that he was nothing but a 'yes-man', Hermann replied, 'That may be, but please show me a "no-man" in Germany who is not six feet under today.'[4]

* * *

Much of the criticism levelled at Hermann was a result of the Allied bombing campaign, which reached new levels of intensity in 1943. Between March and the end of July a huge offensive was launched against industrial and urban targets, the weight of which was directed at the Ruhr. Though RAF Bomber Command lost over a thousand planes during this period, this did little to dent the numbers massing nightly over Germany or their terrifying impact. Hamburg, the Reich's second city and largest port was singled out for particularly fearsome treatment. A big raid on 24 July killed 1,500 people and 140 animals in the city zoo. Three nights later, 787 aircraft attacked in waves, generating an unholy firestorm. Those it did not burn alive it suffocated to death in basement shelters. An estimated 40,000 died.

The cost of trying to combat Bomber Command and the daylight attacks of the burgeoning American bomber forces was not just measured in civilian casualties and flattened buildings. Luftwaffe personnel and resources were stretched to breaking point; valuable factory hours were sacrificed; 7,000 searchlights were required to scan the skies; half of the electronics industry and a third of the optics business were engaged in making equipment for air defence.

Hermann's standing was further diminished by reversals in the U-boat war, a conflict that Churchill referred to as 'the only thing that really frightened me'.[5] A naval conference attended by Hitler concluded that, 'The substantial increase in the enemy air forces is the cause of the present crisis in submarine warfare.'[6] 1942 had been a spectacular year for the U-boat commanders who increased their tally from 457 ships in 1941 to well over a thousand. But in 1943 their score fell by more than 50 per cent. The Luftwaffe's lack of a truly long-range bomber helped give the Allies air superiority over the oceans. In 1943 their planes accounted for over half the U-boats destroyed at sea.

On 9 March Goebbels jotted in his diary that, 'The utter failure of the Luftwaffe has reduced Goering's prestige with the Führer tremendously.'[7] Below had 'gained the impression that Hitler had had enough of him, speaking of him in terms harsh and dismissive'.[8] Hermann was well aware of his Führer's change in attitude towards him. At Nuremberg he characterised it as part of an overall shift in Hitler's personality: 'To me there are two Hitlers ... The man I knew until the end of the French war had much charm and goodwill. The second Hitler, who existed from the beginning of the Russian campaign until his suicide, was always suspicious, easily upset, and tense. He was distrustful to an extreme degree.'[9] Bearing the brunt of Hitler's displeasure took its toll: 'He could be cruel and hateful ... He would scream about the inefficiency of the Luftwaffe with such contempt and viciousness, that I would actually blush and squirm.'[10]

Despite the recriminations, Hitler would not get rid of him: 'He believes ... that Goering's authority is indispensable to the supreme leadership.'[11]

After Hermann visited the bombed-out cities of the Ruhr in October 1943, and the Junkerswerke at Dessau a month later, even Goebbels was pleased: 'Goering, thank God, is showing himself once more in public. He has evidently recovered from his recent bout of stagnation.'[12]

Hitler was not motivated by pragmatism alone. His attachment to Hermann ran deep. When Mussolini was overthrown that July, Hitler was prompted to remind his cohorts that Hermann 'has come through a great many crises with me . . . One cannot have a better adviser in times of crisis . . . both brutal and ice cool.'[13] A year later, though Hermann's defects had multiplied in Hitler's eyes, he continued to rely on his old colleague: 'It was clear to him that Goering had failed with the Luftwaffe . . . but when it really mattered, Hitler said, he would want Goering at his side.'[14]

* * *

Hermann understood that survival in Hitler's entourage meant an absolute denial of the possibility of defeat, regardless of the facts. This came relatively easy given his flair for deluded fantasy. Hermann would refuse to acknowledge any photographic evidence produced by Colonel Rowehl, head of the Luftwaffe's secret reconnaissance unit, which showed the true extent of Allied air strength. Totally frustrated, Rowehl resigned in December 1943.

Hermann was able to sustain his faith in victory by devoting his energies to the development of wonder weapons. To make this vision real, Hermann became an enthusiastic supporter of underground factories. He wanted at least eight 'bombproof manufacturing sites as rapidly as possible', situated in 'large caves, cellars, non-operating mines and unused fortress facilities'.[15]

In October 1943 he instructed Speer to begin work, but Speer dragged his feet. Then, in January 1944, Speer was admitted to an SS-run clinic suffering from exhaustion. The sharks began to circle, Hermann included. For perhaps the last time, his interests coincided with Himmler's, who also advocated an extensive underground system, knowing full well that the concentration camp labour needed to build it would be controlled by the SS. In March the two met and agreed to put an SS man in charge of the construction industry.

When Speer became aware of their intentions he threatened to resign. Hitler was incensed by his apparent disloyalty and overweening arrogance. Hermann was quick to phone Speer and advise him to go quietly. But Hitler calmed down and in an act of rare magnanimity pardoned Speer. Nevertheless, Hermann and Himmler got their way on the underground assembly lines. Prisoners toiled in conditions of soul-destroying, flesh-eating, bone-crushing degradation which matched anything in the long and terrible history of slavery.

Hermann hoped that the planes manufactured in these caverns would turn the course of the war. High on the agenda was a high-speed bomber capable of reaching the east coast of America. During 1944, nine different companies turned out competing designs. Though both Junkers and Messerschmitt got close to winning Hermann's backing, it was the Horten brothers who landed the contract, getting the go-ahead on 23 March 1945. The EF 132 jet bomber, which had a whole new wing design, was still undergoing tests at Dessau when the Soviets arrived.

Low-tech options were also popular with Hermann, like the so-called 'people's fighter'. In September 1944 he gave leading manufacturers twelve days to come up with a single-engined jet plane that could be churned out in great numbers and flown by the teenagers enrolled in the Flieger Hitler-Jugend, the Flying Hitler Youth. Heinkel got the commission, and made a prototype that was test flown on 6 December. The production schedule was set at a thousand per month, and the wheels of industry set in motion. However, the plane, made of wood and salvaged material, proved to be a death trap, falling apart in flight.

These efforts paled in comparison to the Nazis' rocket programmes. Hermann had first got involved back in 1935, commissioning experiments which led the Argus Motorwerke and the Fieseler company to develop the FZG-76 or V-1, a cheap, easy to manufacture, pilot-less monoplane made of steel and plywood which could be launched from a movable 50-metre long ramp with a curve at the end, a kind of ski-jump. It had a 480-km/hr cruising speed, a 320-km range, and a pre-set guidance system. Hermann was impressed.

The V-1 went into production during the spring of 1943. By November allied intelligence had identified eighty-two launch sites. On Christmas Eve American Flying Fortress bombers attacked nearly a quarter of them, but the Luftwaffe moved the rest and designed a simple launcher that could be assembled in minutes. The first missile landed on London on 12 June 1944. Between then and 5 September, over 8,500 were launched at the British capital, of which around a third reached their targets. A third crashed in the sea or the countryside, while the remainder were shot down by fighters or anti-aircraft guns. The missiles that got through damaged over a million homes and killed nearly 6,000 people. Bomber Command struck back immediately. Almost nightly raids began on 16/17 June and continued until mid-August, when the V-1 sites in northern France were overrun by Allied troops after the Normandy landings.

The focus of V-1 activity switched to the port of Antwerp, captured in September by the advancing Allied troops. Starting the next month, Antwerp suffered 175 days of uninterrupted attack and over 8,000 casualties. Meanwhile London also remained in the Nazi sights. Between September 1944 and January 1945 608 V-1s were launched from the air by Heinkel bombers but only sixty-three got through. The final offensive, which lasted until March, saw 124 V-1s catapulted from ski-jumps in north-western Holland. A mere thirteen hit home.

In December 1944, an American general wrote a study that compared the main V-1 onslaught with the Blitz.[16] Though the missiles caused just a quarter of the casualties, he found that they destroyed virtually the same amount of property, for the loss of exactly zero German aircrew, while the Blitz cost over 7,000. The report underlined the potential of the V-1 and its effectiveness as a weapon. However, Hermann's ambitious plans to produce a thousand a month were never fulfilled.

Hitler had other priorities, namely the V-2 rocket, which he believed was the ultimate terror weapon. There is no doubt the V-2 represented a major breakthrough, and became the basis for post-war missile development. However, it was ruinously expensive, much more costly than the V-1, and immensely complicated. Even after a successful test flight in December 1942 the rocket still needed 65,000 separate adjustments.

* * *

By 1945, a considerable amount of the blame for impending defeat fell on Hermann. Men who distrusted and ceaselessly sought to undermine each other were unanimous on the subject. Ribbentrop wrote that he 'last spoke to Hitler one week before his death, and he said that the Luftwaffe problem was the real military cause of the defeat'.[17]

Martin Bormann told his wife that, 'The whole war situation would be different if the enemy did not have complete domination of the air ... but the Reichsmarschall's style of living has transmitted itself, quite naturally to the air force.'[18] Goebbels warmed to the theme: 'The Führer gives vent to the most violent criticism of Goering ... He regards the Luftwaffe merely as a great junk shop.'[19]

With the Soviets mustered on the frontiers of the Reich and the Allies bridging the Rhine, with no fuel for tanks or ammunition for guns, and troop reinforcements consisting of the old and very young, the Luftwaffe's collapse was hardly the Nazis' most serious problem, but the laying waste of German cities was the most potent, an inescapable fact that grimly illustrated their predicament. As Sir Arthur 'Bomber' Harris, a man who never shrunk from the consequences of his actions, pointed out, 'In the last three months of 1944 Bomber Command had dropped as great a weight of bombs as in the whole of 1943.'[20]

On New Year's Day 1945, a thousand Luftwaffe planes made a surprise attack on Allied airfields and sustained significant casualties. The failure of this last desperate throw of the dice gave the Anglo-American air forces free reign over Germany. For the next four months death rained down on the Reich, obliterating what was left of its urban centres.

Since 1942 Hitler had taken root in one bunker after another before reaching his final resting place in Berlin. Sealed away from unpalatable realities, it was possible to keep the dream alive. He pored over maps, deployed phantom divisions, and hatched counter-attacks. But what he could not deny was the relentless ferocity of the bombing that shook the walls of his concrete coffin. Even so, Hitler would not dismiss Hermann: 'The Führer will never drop him ... In the true German way he must remain loyal to Goering.'[21]

* * *

On 12 January 1945 Hermann celebrated his birthday at Karinhall with family and close associates. Caviar, duck, venison, Danzig salmon and paté de foie-gras were washed down with endless bottles of champagne and brandy from Hermann's vast cellar. On the 30th a Soviet jeep was spotted in the nearby forests. It was time for the womenfolk to leave. Hermann shot four of his favourite bison and started packing one of the most valuable art collections ever assembled into crates.

Eighteen years after the war ended, Speer reflected in his prison diary on the Nazis' paradoxical obsession with art: 'The ruthlessness and inhumanity of the regime went hand in hand with a remarkable feeling for beauty.'[22] In 1945 it was estimated that a fifth of the world's art was in Germany. Hitler worshipped at the altar of culture: 'Wars pass by. The only things that exist are the works of human genius. That is my explanation for my love of art.'[23] In his will he wrote that 'his most heartfelt wish' was to have his massive collection placed in 'a picture gallery in my home town of Linz.'[24]

Hermann shared his passion: 'I am so artistic in temperament that masterpieces make me alive and glowing inside.'[25] Though Hitler always got first choice, Hermann was next on the pecking order. Thanks to their different tastes, he had a relatively free hand. According to Hermann, Hitler 'leaned toward the antique and classical – Romantic . . . Greek or Renaissance, such as was found in the beginning of the nineteenth century . . . I preferred the German masters and the early Italians . . . Hitler . . . was an enthusiast of bronze or stone. I prefer wood . . . In art I preferred the work of the Dutch masters, the Scandinavians, Dürer and Holbein.'[26]

In May 1945, the Art Looting Investigation Unit, which was run by Allied intelligence, analysed Hermann's procurement methods: 'He wanted the works of art and so he took them, always managing to find a way of giving at least the appearance of honesty.'[27] At Nuremberg, faced with the charge of wholesale art theft, Hermann reacted with indignation: 'None of my so-called looting was illegal. I paid a small price – smaller than the articles were worth . . . but I always paid for them.'[28] He used his own agents and art dealers to locate what he wanted and negotiate the price. The most prominent was Andreas Hofer, whom Hermann had met in 1936. During March 1941 he appointed Hofer Director of the Art Collection of the Reichsmarschall.

Hofer would set a price with the gallery or private individual who owned the art. Then he would quote a higher price to Hermann and pocket the difference. This was common practice. One of Hermann's agents in Amsterdam bought the whole of the renowned Goudstikker collection of Dutch masters with 3.5 million Reichsmarks of Hermann's money, but kept back some paintings to sell to Hitler.

The arrival of the Nazis in France caused immense upheaval in the art world. Already the Louvre had transported over 3,000 pictures, including the *Mona Lisa*, down south in trucks, and hid them in an abbey. Hundreds of Impressionist and Cubist paintings were stashed away or shipped out of the country. Back in Paris the art market absorbed the initial shock and went into business with its greedy new masters. The world famous auction house at the Hôtel Drouot reopened on 26 September 1940. During the 1941–2 season it broke all records. Next year was even better.

Trade was booming, buoyed by Hermann's frequent visits and the direct access he enjoyed to state funds. When he needed extra for a piece he contacted the Reichsbank. Money was no object and the dealers knew it, causing Hermann to complain that they would 'triple the price, quintuple it, if it is the Reichsmarschall buying'.[29] An exhibition of medieval and Renaissance work was held especially for him at the Galerie Charpentier. Hermann bought the lot.

At Nuremberg he insisted that he had not 'accumulated art treasures in order to sell them or to become a rich man'.[30] This caveat did not apply to 'degenerate' art, the modernism that the Nazis so loathed, Hermann included: 'I am generally very sceptical about modern paintings. Picasso, for instance, nauseates me.'[31] Nevertheless, when the Nazis removed 16,000 modernist works from galleries all over Germany and dumped them in a warehouse, Hermann saw them as a potential asset. He had a few set aside, paid the museums they came from a nominal sum, and then sold a Cézanne and two Van Goghs to a Dutch banker for half a million Reichsmarks. He re-invested the cash in paintings he liked.

Hermann also realised that the works could be sold to earn foreign currency. An official agency, the Commission for the Exploitation of Degenerate Art, was formed to sell as much as possible. Those it could not shift, over a thousand paintings and sculptures, nearly 4,000 drawings and watercolours, were piled together in the courtyard of the Berlin Fire Department HQ on 20 March 1939 and burnt. The cream of the storehouse, 126 paintings and sculptures, went under the hammer ten days later in Switzerland. These masterpieces were paid for in Swiss francs which the Nazis converted into sterling and buried in German accounts in British banks.

Hermann continued to use 'degenerate art' as a form of exchange. Between March 1941 and November 1943 he organised sixteen swops. He gave a German dealer paintings by Picasso, Matisse and others, and received a Titian in return. A month later he got a Rembrandt and two tapestries for twenty-five pictures and a fee of 250,000 Swiss francs.

Hermann reserved the outright banditry for Jewish-owned art. The *Anschluss* offered rich pickings. Nearly 3,500 pieces were taken from Baron Alphonse de Rothschild alone. Leading the confiscations was the Austrian art historian Katejan Mühlmann, who had been given the innocuous title of Representative for State Art Policy and Foreign Tourism, and dealt for both Hermann and Hitler. In September 1939 Hermann offered Mühlmann the chance to extend his operation. On 9 October Mühlmann became Special Delegate for the Reichsmarschall for the Securing of Artistic Treasures in the Former Polish Territories, with a mandate from Hermann systematically to divest the country of its treasures, without any compensation. Mühlmann exploited the situation to his advantage while making sure he kept Hermann happy, sending him a gift of thirty-one drawings by Albrecht Dürer.

The expansion of the Nazi empire opened up possibilities that could not be adequately exploited by a small task force like Mühlmann's. Hitler chose Alfred Rosenberg, the regime's self-consciously academic and much ridiculed philosopher, to manage the wholesale piracy. Hermann gave Rosenberg his full support against any competing interests, provided Luftwaffe transport, and in May 1941 signed a decree that gave Rosenberg absolute power to seize Jewish cultural assets. In return for his help, he got unique access to the huge art repository in Paris that housed Rosenberg's haul. Between 3 November 1940 and 27 November 1942 Hermann visited it twenty times and walked away with 700 paintings.

During January 1942 Rosenberg launched the M-Aktion, the furniture project, to strip Jews of their remaining belongings. House-to-house checks were carried out across Paris; 38,000 dwellings were sealed, and their contents removed, stored and catalogued. By 15 July 1944, 21,000 items had been categorised as art and stored in the Jeu de Paume. An art historian working for Hermann sifted through it all and organised private exhibitions for his benefit.

It is impossible to argue with the Art Looting Investigation Unit's conclusion that Hermann was 'cruel, grasping, deceitful and hypocritical',[32] despite his protests that he got the collection fairly and kept it safe for the next generation to enjoy: 'If I had not taken them they would be in the hands of those damned Russians.'[33]

Trains carrying Hermann's possessions from Karinhall started arriving at Berchtesgaden in early April 1945 under Hofer's supervision. Some of the freight cars had already been damaged by the Allies. Mobs helped themselves to anything they could carry. Witnesses reported seeing people staggering off, drunk on Hermann's wine, weighed down with bits of tapestry, or clinging to hefty sculptures.

By the time the Americans and French marched into town on 4 May, Hofer had stashed half of Hermann's cargo in an underground shelter sealed with thick concrete. It took three days for the Allies to break through and three days to remove the contents of this Aladdin's cave, which were temporarily kept in a local building before being moved to the Munich collecting point, along with other spectacular finds of Nazi treasure. Eventually over 1,000,000 objects were stored in Munich and slowly returned to their previous owners.

Allied art experts began the mammoth job of constructing an exact inventory of Hermann's collection. They were enthusiastically assisted by Hofer, who was hoping to keep himself out of jail. Together they counted over 1,375 paintings, 250 sculptures, 108 tapestries and 175 other *objets d'art*.

* * *

On the morning of 20 April 1945, Hermann left Karinhall forever. Luftwaffe engineers had planted explosives throughout the mansion. Some say Hermann solemnly pushed the plunger himself and watched his beloved home blow up. The truth, as so often with Hermann, is less romantic. He took one last look, got in his limousine and drove away, leaving the demolition teams to do their work.

It was the Führer's birthday. Hermann headed for Berlin to join the other top-rank Nazis for muted celebrations, during which Hitler declared he would stay in the capital. Hermann had other plans. He was on his way south to set up an alternative command base at Berchtesgaden, with mixed blessings from Hitler. He doubted Hermann's motives, though fell short of calling him a coward to his face. This, their final meeting, ended with a curt farewell. On the 22nd Hitler confirmed that he was not leaving Berlin and ordered his faithful generals, Jodl and Keitel, to join Hermann: 'There is no question of fighting now, there is nothing left to fight with. If it is a matter of negotiating, Goering can do that better than I.'[34]

The next day, Hermann sent a telegram to Führer headquarters: 'In view of your decision to remain at your post in fortress Berlin, do you agree that I take over, at once, the total leadership of the Reich, with full freedom of action at home and abroad, as your deputy, in accordance with your decree of 29 June 1941?'[35] Berlin was given until 10.00 p.m. to reply.

Anticipating Hitler's suicide, the second man in the Reich had jumped too soon to claim his inheritance. Bormann intercepted the telegram, showed it to Hitler and demanded Hermann's head. Hitler screamed treason for a while then slumped into depression. Bormann maintained the pressure, and Hitler, stirred up once again, ordered Hermann's arrest. The SS barracks near Obersalzberg was alerted and Hermann's villa surrounded. Hitler did not forgive him: 'Before my death I expel the former Reichsmarschall Hermann Goering from the Party.'[36]

On the night of the 25th, 359 Lancaster bombers attacked Berchtesgaden. Hermann and his captors retreated into the tunnels thirty metres below his villa. They emerged from hiding on the 28th to find the house completely wrecked. Hermann suggested they all decamp to Castle Mauterndorf, a mere sixty-five kilometres away. The SS commander, whose enthusiasm for his task was already waning, agreed. Holed up there, they heard the news of Hitler's death broadcast on the radio a few days later. On 6 May the SS guards melted away. Hermann and his entourage set off to greet the Americans, having dispatched a letter to Eisenhower. Hermann was looking forward to meeting the American general on equal terms, 'without any obligations . . . as soldier to soldier . . . to prevent further bloodshed'.[37]

* * *

Albert Goering also expected good treatment from the Americans. After Hermann had saved him from the clutches of the Gestapo at the end of January 1945, he was ordered by Himmler to leave Prague and head for Salzburg. Albert arrived first in Vienna. When Budapest fell to the Soviets on 14 February after a bitter siege, their way was open to the Austrian capital. Albert managed to keep one step ahead and was gone before the Soviets reached Vienna's suburbs on 4 April. It took another ten days of bombardment and harsh street fighting to subdue the fanatical defenders.

Albert was already in Salzburg, laid low by a serious liver condition and waiting in a military hospital for the war to end. In Czechoslovakia the fighting continued. On 5 May US tanks entered Pilsen, Skoda's home town. The following day, encouraged by Czech radio and the BBC, partisans in Prague launched an uprising. Within forty-eight hours the SS had brutally repressed the revolt, slaying several thousand. Though General Patton's men were closest to the city, it had been promised to Stalin. Patton remembered that he 'was very anxious to go and assist them' but, 'It was definitely established that we were not to pass beyond the stop line passing through Pilsen.'[38]

On 8 May, the same day the war was officially declared over, the Soviets attacked Prague. The agony of its citizens was prolonged for nearly a week before Nazi resistance finally ceased.

PART FOUR

We weren't a band of criminals meeting in the dead of night to plan mass murders like figures in a dime novel.

Hermann Goering, January 1946

The fact that I am the brother of Hermann Goering is hardly criminal.

Albert Goering, 19 September 1945

She compared history to a big crossword puzzle. For every little square you fill, there are three more empty, she said, and even if you manage to fill them, new ones open up immediately, even emptier.

David Albhari, *Gotz and Meyer*

CHAPTER THIRTEEN

Judgement

On 13 May 1945, four days after Hermann, Albert arrived at the US Seventh Army interrogation centre at Augsburg. On the 18th, the acting commander of the Intelligence unit stationed there, Major Paul Kubala, invited Hermann and his accordion over to the officers' mess, hoping that a boozy evening might loosen his tongue. Hermann drank his fill, chatted away merrily, but never lowered his guard, 'at all times an actor that does not disappoint his audience'.[1] A few days later he was transferred to new quarters at Bad Mondorf, an isolated spa resort in Luxembourg.

The brothers were at Augsburg together for a week. After the war Albert spoke of their final meeting: 'Through the bars of his prison cell, he had spotted Hermann taking a walk. He had asked to see him ... The brothers were allowed to walk a few paces together ... Hermann said: "I am very sorry that it is you who has to suffer so much because of me. You will be free soon."'[2]

* * *

By 28 June Albert had compiled his list of thirty-four names and been interrogated twice. Kubala found him 'very talkative and willing to cooperate'.[3] At the beginning of July he was moved to Hersbruck Civilian Internment Camp No. 4, where he underwent a thorough physical examination and an arrest report was filled out. On 1 August he arrived at Seckenheim and was confined in a room with five other prisoners until the 17th when he was transported to Nuremberg jail.

Soon afterwards he was questioned by John Harlan Amen, a tough New York prosecutor who specialised in corruption cases. He asked Albert about Hermann's money, his investments in America and his art acquisitions. Albert denied any knowledge of these activities.

On 6 September, a desperate Albert wrote to the commandant of the prison, spelled out his aversion to Nazism and described his confusion: 'I have to suppose that my transport to Nuremberg . . . is based on a misunderstanding'; his suffering: 'I get destroyed physically and psychologically'; his ill-health: 'I will suffer permanent damage if I am not placed as soon as possible in a hospital under treatment of a specialist'; and the fact that: 'The Seventh Army Interrogation Centre . . . made a proposal for my discharge in mid-July.' He ended the letter 'trusting in my belief in God and the American sense of justice'.[4]

His cry for help landed on the desk of Colonel Burton Andrus, who had been in charge at Bad Mondorf before taking over at Nuremberg. He idolised Patton and was a stickler for rules and regulations. Though Andrus could have helped Albert he chose not to and simply forwarded an edited version of the letter to the prosecutors' office, having removed references to Albert's liver condition and his request to speak to an interpreter.

Andrus's unsympathetic treatment of Albert is not surprising given his low opinion of Germans – 'I hate these Krauts'[5] – and personal animosity towards Hermann. Andrus took an instant dislike to him when he arrived at Mondorf, 'with the blubber of high-living wobbling under his jacket', and an addiction to paracodeine: 'Goering, I felt, was to be our first serious problem'.[6] However, under the supervision of a doctor, his intake was drastically reduced. He lost weight and regained his senses. During intensive questioning he was asked about the bribes he received in the form of 'gifts'. Hermann refused to incriminate anyone: 'These are the most private things . . . I will only answer when it concerns me specifically. These things were given on the basis of friendship.'[7]

On 12 August he was flown to Nuremberg where he continued his battle of wills with Andrus. The colonel wanted the prisoners to slop out their own cells after breakfast. When Hermann was handed a bucket and mop he threw a tantrum that triggered heart palpitations. As a result Hermann was excused cleaning duties.

* * *

The main interrogation of Albert took place on 25 September. After Amen got the session started, Bill Jackson took over. Bill, a young Harvard law graduate, owed his post at Nuremberg to his father, Robert Jackson, who had risen through the Justice Department under Roosevelt, served on the Supreme Court and was the chief US prosecutor at the trials. Six months later Robert would go toe to toe with Hermann in the courtroom and take a beating: 'Goering simply wiped the floor with him. He reduced Jackson to such a state of impotence and fury.'[8]

His son Bill had no such difficulties. Albert was a sickly-looking 'hand-wringing type of witness ... highly nervous',[9] with seventy-two carbuncles on his back. The contrast between this wretched specimen and his mighty brother must have been particularly acute for Bill, who had visited one of Hermann's hunting lodges a few weeks earlier looking for evidence and found magnums of champagne, Havana cigars, a cache of Lucky Strike cigarettes and a packing case full of gold coins, furs and silks.

The interrogators focussed on Albert's role at Skoda. They assumed he was Hermann's flunkey, his job mere 'window dressing'. Albert denied the accusation, stating that he only met Hermann every three to six months for a chat: 'He would say, "Well, how is business moving along?" However, he would not be interested in details ... He might also drop a chance remark such as, "Did you see King Boris?" But there were never any reports in the sense that they were detailed reports. It was merely general conversation.'[10] When Hermann wanted more specific information after a meeting at Obersalzberg, 25–6 March 1943, Albert's response had been polite, respectful but totally unhelpful. Could Skoda supply 300 tanks to Bulgaria? What new anti-aircraft guns were in development? What sorts of tank? Was the factory operating at full tilt? Albert answered on 6 April: 'Unfortunately we at Skoda don't have even the smallest free capacity, not even to cover part of the tank delivery.' Designs for a new anti-aircraft gun had been abandoned: 'further works have been stopped', due to technical problems. If Hermann had any other questions he should contact Bodenschatz or general director Vambersky.[11]

Bill Jackson did not have this correspondence to hand. He had virtually no evidence at all, but he ploughed on, despite Albert insisting that he had no connection to the Wehrmacht, or any financial stake in weapons manufactured for the German forces by Skoda: 'I never bought shares, I never sold any shares, and I never possessed any shares.'[12] He had a fixed arrangement dating back to 1939 that gave him $\frac{2}{1000}$ of the proceeds of exports to Romania, and $\frac{1}{1000}$ from sales to Hungary, Greece, Yugoslavia, Italy and Turkey. He declined to profit from trade with the Reich: 'Originally, there was also another provision in the contract, which stipulated that I was to receive $\frac{2}{1000}$ of total sales of the Skoda Works. I did not want this.'[13]

Having discussed Albert's efforts to help the Jews, his arrests by the Gestapo, his general nonconformity and how Hermann kept him out of prison, Bill Jackson returned to the central theme of the Allied case, guilt by association: 'After all he did for you, do you mean to tell us that you did nothing in return for him?' Tired of repeating himself and defeated by the process, Albert simply shrugged his shoulders: 'What was there that I could do for him? . . . He was a great man.'[14]

The interrogation was adjourned for lunch and never continued. Albert was left with no idea of what would happen next. He had still not been charged. In early October, enquiries by British intelligence as to Albert's whereabouts – they thought he might be in either London or Lisbon – prompted an evaluation of his overall status by the administration division at Nuremberg. On the 24th they requested 'instruction . . . with reference to release or disposition of Albert Goering', because they saw no reason 'for his continued detention'. A month later the judge advocate asked the US Army European command centre for guidance: 'A request has been made by the Czechoslovakian government for extradition of subject. Do you object to his being extradited?'[15]

* * *

In another part of the prison, Hermann sat in cell 5, watched twenty-four hours a day by guards. He did his best to fraternise with them, building alliances where he could. He received more mail and 'wrote more letters to friends and relatives . . . than any of the others'[16] held in the same top security wing. He read 'two books a week and always had to be chased by the librarian to return them' and 'sucked incessantly on his huge, hand-carved pipe'.[17]

His most regular visitor was the US Army psychiatrist Doctor David Kelley, with whom he developed an easy rapport. Against his better judgement, Kelley was impressed by Hermann's 'charming manner . . . excellent intelligence' and 'good sense of humour'.[18] On 19 October the doctor was joined by an interpreter, Captain Gustav Mahler Gilbert, a psychologist born in the US but of Austrian Jewish descent. Soon after the pair met, they agreed to collaborate on a book. Gilbert began keeping verbatim notes of their conversations with the Nazi prisoners.

Hounded by the press for juicy details, Kelley broke silence first and went on Armed Forces Network radio to talk about Hermann. Gilbert then felt obliged to approach Reuters and the *Daily Express*. Meanwhile, Kelley negotiated an exclusive deal with Simon and Schuster. On 6 February 1946 he left Nuremberg after rumours that he had stolen official files, taking a copy of Gilbert's notes with him. Gilbert got himself a literary agent and managed to prevent Simon and Schuster from publishing Kelley's work. Eventually, in 1947, both books came out within a week of each other.

Kelley was replaced by Doctor Leon Goldensohn, who was working at a US Army hospital in Nuremberg when the call came. Goldensohn's non-confrontational approach and relaxed manner put Hermann at ease, and he talked more openly and intimately than he had with the intrusive, badgering Gilbert: 'At least you don't lecture me and pry into my affairs. You have a good technique as a psychiatrist . . . you hardly say anything.'[19]

Colonel Andrus had given Gilbert licence to spy on the prisoners, sticking close to them during their journeys to and from court, their lunch breaks and time spent in the exercise yard. He dropped in on them without warning, day or night, including weekends, hoping to provoke a rash admission or a slip of the tongue. Andrus was privy to every word: 'He gave me typewritten reports of all that was being said.'[20] Gilbert paid special attention to unsettling and undermining Hermann's equilibrium. Both he and Andrus were concerned that Hermann's performance in court might persuade his fellow Nazis to unify behind him. Gilbert knew he liked being the first prisoner to get into the lift that went down to the courtroom and made sure he got on last.

In February, Gilbert separated Hermann from his co-defendants during lunch. While the others were sat four to a table Hermann had to sit on his own, causing him to complain bitterly: 'Goering was furious over being put in a small room by himself, and complained of the lack of heat and daylight, though it was obvious his anger was really due to the frustration of losing his audience.'[21]

* * *

On 21 November 1945, the trial began at the renovated Palace of Justice with an opening address by Robert Jackson. After statements from the British, Soviet and French representatives, the prosecution started presenting its mountain of evidence. On 8 January 1946 they got to Hermann. Two months later he finally took the stand to mount his defence, which ended on 22 March with a cross-examination by Soviet and French lawyers.

In the dock Hermann demonstrated all the facets of his personality that had beguiled, entertained and overwhelmed so many. A British journalist called him a 'jovial Falstaff'.[22] An officer in charge of documents thought that, 'If you were going to have a cocktail party and wanted somebody to be the life of the party, that's the person you'd have.'[23] An Allied administrator remembered Hermann having 'charisma to an extraordinary degree'.[24] The novelist Rebecca West wrote that, 'When his humour was good, he recalled the madam of a brothel'.[25] The RAF officer and war hero Airey Neave, who had been imprisoned by the Gestapo twice and made a successful escape from Colditz and served the indictment to Hermann in his cell, conceded that, 'No one had been prepared for his immense ability and knowledge . . . Murderer he may have been but he was a brave bastard too.'[26]

For three days, beginning on the morning of 13 March, Hermann's lawyer, Otto Stahmer, led him step by step through the history of the Nazi Party. Hermann argued that all he ever wanted was to reverse Versailles. War was the regrettable outcome. He was only standing trial because he was on the losing side, not because he had committed any crimes. He ended with a *coup de théâtre*: 'At this point I should like to say the same words which one of our greatest, most important and toughest opponents, the British Prime Minister, Winston Churchill, used: "In the struggle for life and death there is in the end no legality."'[27]

After the weekend recess Hermann faced Robert Jackson. The American tried to tackle him on the core principles of Nazism, without a clear thrust to the questions and lacking 'familiarity with European history and the workings of European governments'.[28] Hermann tied him in knots, giving long-winded answers, asking for clarification on minor points and causing Jackson to make 'the fatal mistake of losing his temper'.[29]

It was Sir Douglas Maxwell Fyfe, a Tory MP and former Attorney General, who managed to get the measure of Hermann. Fyfe described him as, 'The most formidable witness I have ever cross-examined: he had studied the documents with great care and skill, he knew exactly the points where his case was strong and constantly attempted to steer the examination away from dangerous topics.'[30] However, Fyfe had recognised that 'his blind-spot was vanity' and had 'got up very thoroughly' the case of the seventy-six RAF prisoners of war who had escaped from the camp at Sagan in Silesia. Hitler had personally ordered that they be turned over to the Gestapo. Three made it back to Britain; fifty were executed.

Fyfe's concise, factual and rapid-fire questions made Hermann visibly uncomfortable. Suddenly his much vaunted honour, his image as a noble warrior, was being exposed as a hollow sham: 'After a few hours of this ding-dong duel I noticed a new look of weariness coming into Goering's cold eyes.'[31]

Later on, while the court was hearing the case against the SS, Fyfe confronted Hermann again. Luftwaffe-approved experiments at Dachau conducted by Doctor Sigmund Rascher had used a mobile pressure chamber to simulate the effect of falling without oxygen or a parachute from over 9,000 metres. The 'subjects', drawn from the camp population, invariably died within minutes.

At a conference in October 1942, attended by interested professionals and Luftwaffe personnel, lectures were given on 'Prevention and Treatment of Freezing' and other related topics. Soon after, Dr Rascher recreated the experience of airmen who had crashed in the North Sea or Arctic waters by lowering bodies into tanks filled with icy water. When the prisoners were close to freezing they were removed and given either warm or tepid water to revive them. Some were given a naked female to lie against. Between 80 and 300 died, mostly of convulsions. Fyfe had documents and witnesses that pointed to Hermann's involvement. Shame-faced, he denied any knowledge.

On 31 August 1946, Hermann made his final statement to the court: 'I deny most emphatically that my actions were dictated by the desire to subjugate foreign peoples by wars, to murder them, rob them, or to enslave them, or to commit atrocities or crimes. The only motive which guided me was my ardent love for my people, its happiness, its freedom, and its life.'[32]

* * *

If Hermann was not guilty, who was? He refused to point the finger at Hitler: 'I can't stand there like a louse and call the Führer a million-fold murderer!'[33] Speer had no such inhibitions and squarely put the blame on Hitler from the moment he took the stand until his last appearance before the court: 'After this trial, the German people will despise and condemn Hitler as the proven author of their misfortune.'[34] He avoided the hangman and earned Hermann's contempt: 'Damn that stupid fool Speer . . . How could he stoop so low as to do such a rotten thing to save his lousy neck! I nearly died of shame.'[35]

Hermann told Goldensohn who he thought was really responsible: 'Himmler and Goebbels . . . must have influenced him to go ahead with such an idiotic scheme as gas chambers and crematoriums to eliminate millions of people.'[36] There was never much love lost between Hermann and the propaganda chief. Goebbels thought Hermann was too bourgeois, 'that repulsive old roué', while Hermann described Goebbels as 'that club-footed fanatic',[37] and blamed him for the atrocities: 'He influenced Hitler to be more anti-semitic than Hitler had been before.' Hermann thought this had as much to do with ambition as it did with ideological conviction: 'I think Goebbels was using anti-semitism as a means of achieving personal power. Whether he had a deep-seated hatred against the Jews is questionable.'[38]

Hermann found Himmler much harder to characterise: 'I would never have expected it of him . . . He didn't seem to be the murderer type.'[39] Hermann was deceived by his innocuous manner, his tedious pedantry and self-importance, more akin to a slightly dull schoolteacher than a man intent on constructing a Nazi utopia out of the bones of the racially inferior: 'Himmler appeared as an ambiguous puzzle. He was always a psychological puzzle to me.'[40] Hermann failed to grasp the depths of Himmler's psychosis, his inverted moral world where putting a bullet through a child's head could be considered beneficial to mankind: 'That Himmler! I just wish I could have him alone for an hour and ask him a few things.'[41]

* * *

On 30 September 1946, Hermann was found guilty and sentenced to death. When he discovered he was going to hang, he sat down and penned four letters: one to his wife, one to the prison chaplain and two to the authorities. He wrote to the Allied Control Council, 'I would have no objection to being shot. However, I will not facilitate execution of Germany's Reichsmarschall by hanging . . . For this reason, I have chosen to die like the great Hannibal',[42] and to Colonel Andrus, 'I have had a poison capsule with me since the beginning of my imprisonment . . . None of those responsible for searches are to be blamed.'[43] Hermann had decided to exonerate his old sparring partner, while drawing attention to his failures.

Hermann claimed that he had three cyanide capsules with him when he arrived at Bad Mondorf and concealed one in his clothes so it could be found, which it was, and another in a pot of skin cream that was discovered among his baggage at Nuremberg after his death. Tests done on the capsule he actually used, which was found between his teeth at 10.45 p.m. on 15 October as he gurgled his last breath, showed it had spent time up his anus.

An official one-page statement issued on the 26th endorsed Hermann's version. Ever since, people have questioned how he kept the poison hidden for nearly seventeen months. It has been assumed that one of the guards passed it to him. Lieutenant Jack 'Tex' Wheelis seemed to be the likely culprit. According to a fellow soldier, Tex 'would have been the perfect model for a Marlboro cigarette commercial'.[44] Hermann forged a bond with this keen hunter. As Tex's wife admitted years later, 'My husband liked Goering. They became friends.'[45] Tex did little favours for Hermann and was rewarded with a solid gold fountain pen, an engraved Swiss wristwatch and a cigarette case. Each item was retrieved by Tex from Hermann's personal affects that were stored in the prison baggage room. But Tex never admitted to anything. Then, on 7 February 2005, the *Los Angeles Times* ran an interview with Herbert Lee Stivers. Nineteen years old at the time of the trial, he had been assigned to guard duty at Nuremberg, escorting prisoners to and from court: 'Goering was a very pleasant guy . . . we'd talk about sports, ballgames . . . about Lindbergh.' According to Stivers, he fell under the spell of a sexy stranger. After boasting to her about his access to the Nazi big-wigs and getting her Hermann's autograph, he was introduced to her friends. They told him Hermann was very sick and not getting the right care. Stivers agreed to help and twice passed notes contained in a fountain pen. On the third occasion, the pen carried a capsule. He never saw the girl again: 'I guess she used me.'[46]

Hermann took the truth to his grave, an unknown spot, perhaps by a road or a river, or deep in the forest, where his ashes were scattered in secret by unsuspecting Allied soldiers, along with those of the eleven Nazis who were hanged in the early hours of 16 October 1946 for their crimes against humanity.

* * *

Hermann never recognised the legitimacy of the International Military Tribunal: 'The death sentence ... that doesn't mean a thing to me – but my reputation in history means a lot.'[47] Hitler remarked that, 'A man who is indifferent to history is a man without hearing, without sight.'[48] The Nazis turned German and world history into a carnival hall of mirrors, where they peered at grotesquely distorted images of the past and took them to be authentic representations of themselves. The only picture in Hitler's sparse room in his Berlin bunker was a portrait of Frederick the Great, which he would gaze at for hours, trying to see his reflection there.

Himmler directly identified with King Heinrich I, a Saxon warrior who vanquished the Slavs during the tenth century. Every year at midnight he visited Heinrich's tomb to pay homage. The SS elite stayed in a castle near the site of a famous victory by Armenius (dubbed Hermann by German nationalists), chief of the Cherusci tribe. In AD 9, he trapped a Roman legion in the Teutoburg forest and over three days slaughtered thousands of them.

In 1936 Himmler set up the Society for the Promotion and Preservation of German Cultural Monuments, with priority given to fortresses built by the Teutonic knights. The SS-run Research and Teaching Foundation Ancestral Heritage, or Ahnenerbe, sponsored archaeological and anthropological projects and dispatched agents across the globe to search for signs of the Germanic race in ancient and prehistoric man.

Hermann had a more modern disposition. He liked to style himself as the 'last Renaissance man', a vision that flattered his ego but had only a passing resemblance to the truth. A more accurate self-assessment can be found in Gritzbach's biography of Hermann, which he practically dictated to the author: 'Hermann Goering is not merely a soldier – he is not merely a statesman. He is always simultaneously both statesman and soldier.'[49] The first half of the twentieth century witnessed the hey-day of soldier-statesmen, men who had entered the military and wound up running their countries. Most had been called upon to save or resurrect the nation. Hermann waited until 1945 to make his bid for the throne, when defeat was staring him in the face. Only then did he briefly seize supreme power to have it snatched away again.

Hermann was a soldier-statesman without a state. He was a warlord. He thought like one and acted like one. He travelled around war-torn Europe in his luxurious private train which was furnished with velvet upholstery and serviced by his own hand-picked staff, which included cooks from his favourite restaurant in Berlin. Attached to the carriages were two freight cars armed with flak guns, and trailers for his cars, a Buick, a La Salle, two Ford Mercuries, a Citroën and two Mercedes. On board the train there was a darkroom for Hermann's personal photographer, an operating theatre and a barber's shop. This was first-class travel, warlord style.

He had a total disregard for human life and an insatiable appetite for power. His decisions produced hundreds of thousands of innocent corpses: 'In earlier times you pillaged. He who conquered a country disposed of the riches of that country. At present things are done in a more humane way. As for myself, I still think of pillage comprehensively.'[50] Tragically for the people of Europe this was not an off-the-cuff remark or an idle threat.

He had much in common with his contemporaries in China, the warlords of the 1920s and 1930s. A Western writer described them as being 'gifted with peculiar personal charm' and 'a sense of high drama . . . The warlord is a creature of emotion, cruel or merciful . . . dangerous and unstable as friend or enemy, licentious and unusually fond of luxury.'[51] Though some began as bandits, they all served in the Imperial army and were appointed military governors of provinces sometimes as large as western Europe. When central authority collapsed they took control of local industry, the tax system, the food supply, the opium trade, and the transport infrastructure. Like Hermann, they preferred to travel by private train. They constructed cults of personality and home-spun political philosophies, combining influences as diverse as Fascism, American Liberalism, Communism, Confucianism and Christianity. They believed in modernisation and industrialisation. The 'Model Governor' of Shansi province built a 900-kilometre long railway with German steel and launched a Ten Year Plan of factory construction to produce weapons, textiles, bricks, cement, paper, cigarettes and alcohol. The 'Old

Marshal' of Manchuria controlled 90 per cent of China's heavy industry and lived in a palace with five wives, seventy kitchen staff and a cellar full of French wine.

They used Western military advisors and armaments. Their soldiers ran amok while the peasants starved. They valued loyalty over ability, and rewarded their families and followers accordingly, operating vast networks of graft and corruption. The methods of the 'Dog-Meat General', who ruled part of northern China, were not as sophisticated as Hermann's but they shared the same spirit: 'His trouser pockets were always stuffed with money, and when people came to him for help he would pull out a bank-roll and give a handful to those that asked.'[52]

The grand ambitions of these Chinese warlords were frustrated not just by their incompetence and megalomania, but by technological and material inadequacy. Thanks to the fact that Germany was one of the most advanced nations on earth, Hermann could be a warlord on a grand scale. He made extensive use of slave labour. In 1942, between 80 and 90 per cent of the 600,000 people working for the Hermann-GoeringWerke were provided by the SS, compared to an average of 20 per cent in the rest of German industry. By 1945, 100,000 prisoners of war from all over Europe had died at Salzgitter, Hermann's showpiece steel factory.

Shortly before invading the Soviet Union, he contemplated the outcome: 'The war can be continued only if all the armed forces are fed by Russia in the third year of the war ... There is no doubt that as a result many millions of people will be starved to death if we take the things we need.'[53] Eighteen months later he made this assessment of the situation: 'This year between 20 and 30 million persons will die in Russia of hunger. Perhaps it is well that it should be so, for certain nations must be decimated.'[54] These staggering figures were never achieved, but not for want of trying.

CHAPTER FOURTEEN

Verdict

Still under arrest simply for being Hermann's brother, Albert was moved from Nuremberg and placed in a series of civilian internment camps before arriving at Darmstadt on 17 June 1946. Two weeks later he applied for his release, stating on the form that he was 'no party member and did not take part in political activities'. His conduct was rated as 'good'.[1] Further questioning ensued. Albert faithfully repeated his litany of anti-Nazi activities. This time it fell on receptive ears: 'The above-mentioned story is believed to be the truth because this interrogator knows personally that subject has helped Franz Lehar who is the uncle of this interrogator.'[2]

The world-renowned Austrian composer Franz Lehar was number fifteen on Albert's list. Speer wrote that Hitler 'regarded Franz Lehar as one of the greatest composers in the history of music. Hitler ranked *Die Lustige Witwe* ['The Merry Widow'] as the equal of the finest operas.'[3] Lehar's distinctive style inspired the hit films coming out of Viennese film studios during the 1930s. Albert met Lehar when he was at Tobis-Sascha, and they became friends.

The composer's wife, Sophie Pashkis, was Jewish. Because of his reputation the authorities turned a blind eye until 1942, when Lehar received an official letter: 'I was either to get divorced immediately or they would consider me a Jew which would have meant a ban on all my works . . . They let me know that they were not prepared to let me leave the country.' Lehar immediately turned to 'the only man who had come to the aid of his friends . . . Albert Goering in Bucharest. Three days later he was with me in Vienna . . . next day he had already departed for Berlin.'[4]

Albert visited Hermann and explained Lehar's predicament. Hermann phoned Goebbels and reminded him about Hitler's admiration for the composer's music. Goebbels asked to see Albert. According to Albert and 'a close colleague of Goebbels', he was given a warm welcome: 'With such a small problem you should have come directly to me, my dear friend. The lower ranks have acted without thinking.'[5] Goebbels promptly presented Albert with an honorary Aryan certificate for Lehar's wife.

Albert repeated this tale to Victor Parker, his American interrogator at Darmstadt, whose surname had been Pashkis. He was Sophie's nephew and could confirm that Albert had saved her life and Lehar's career. Parker signed off on Albert's release at the end of July, unaware that three months earlier the judge advocate's office at Nuremberg had recommended Albert's transfer to the 'Czech war crimes liaison detachment'.[6] Instead of going free, Albert was extradited to Prague and thrown in the ghastly Pankras prison. This former Gestapo torture chamber and temporary home to many of those whom Albert had helped, was now crammed with 'SS members . . . robbers and murderers, Germans under arrest, of whom barely 10 per cent survived the inhumane prison conditions',[7] and policed by a brutalised mix of Soviet partisans, resistance fighters, and ex-concentration camp inmates.

* * *

The post-war Czech government, a National Front coalition of four parties under President Eduard Benes, previously head of the exile administration in London, issued the Great Decree on 19 June 1945, which established a legal framework for punishing 'Nazi criminals, traitors and their accomplices'. Twenty-four Extraordinary People's Courts were set up, each with a judge and a panel of four pre-selected civilians.

Their word was final: 'Against the verdict . . . there are no means of legal redress.' The decree laid down a mandatory sentence of between five and twenty-five years or the death penalty, which was 'to be carried out within two hours of the pronouncement of the verdict',[8] with a proviso that 'the time limit may be extended for an additional hour'. The danger to Albert was very real. Of the 723 sentenced to death by the

People's Courts, 686 were executed; 487 of them were German, as were 70 per cent of those imprisoned, including 455 for life.

At the beginning of October, Albert was interviewed in Pankras prison for two days by officers of the US Chief of Counsel Subsequent Proceedings Division. They asked him about Doctor Voss, the SS man at Skoda, 'vain and inept'; about Hermann; and about Krupp, the pro-Nazi steel baron. Albert had nothing new to add to his previous testimony, only to say that Krupp's prominent place in the Nazi war economy was due to his faith in Hitler and not his business acumen. Under questioning at Nuremberg a few weeks earlier Hermann had said almost exactly the same thing.[9]

Albert finally came before a People's Court on 6 November. A steady stream of Skoda personnel, from the shop floor to the boardroom, testified in his defence, detailing his efforts to keep the company out of Nazi hands and its directors out of jail. An international effort to bombard President Benes with telegrams and letters was coordinated from Paris by Albert's old friend, the film director Ernst Neubach, who sent his appeal in February 1947: 'We, his friends, are unable to believe that in Prague it has been forgotten what Albert Goering did for the Czech workers.'[10]

This pressure, combined with witness statements and lack of evidence, proved enough. Albert was acquitted on 14 March. The People's Courts were disbanded a couple of months later. Albert was handed over to the Austrian Embassy in Prague and by mid-April he was in Vienna. On learning of his release American officials requested that he 'be taken into US custody and transferred to Nuremberg as a witness (non-voluntary)'.[11]

Albert eluded them and was reunited with his wife Mila and his three-year-old daughter Elizabeth for the first time since she had been born. Any joy they felt must have been mixed with sadness. Albert's health was in ruins. Captivity had aged him, the poor food, the cramped conditions, the frequent beatings by both his American and Czech jailers. All his assets had been seized. Virtually penniless, they rented a tiny flat in Salzburg and waited for things to improve.

If anything they got more precarious. The Cold War was spreading its icy tentacles across Europe. The Communists in Prague, who had won 40 per cent of the vote in the 1946 election, staged a coup. In late February 1948, after a massive general strike, they secured control of the cabinet. More than 28,000 state employees were dismissed. Members of resistance groups that were not affiliated to the Communists during the war were now under threat.

Refugees made for Austria, where spies were already thick on the ground and Vienna was a divided city. Radomir Luza, son of General Luza, leader of the Council of Three network, fled Prague and ended up in Salzburg, where he engaged in cross-border operations, including an aborted attempt to smuggle out President Benes, before heading to Paris in September 1948.

Albert's close associate, Karel Staller, had been General Luza's link-man with London and his organisation's cash machine. Though Staller was the District Director of Metal Industry in Slovakia it was too dangerous to stay. Using forged papers he escaped with his family on Christmas Day 1949. In Vienna they met up with Albert's friend Bruno Seletsky, the former exports director at Skoda. They moved on to Salzburg. Karel was recruited by the Americans as an informer and put in a safe-house in the mountains. During their stay, his family spent time with Albert and he gave them some crockery for their new home. After three months they left; someone had been rifling through their mail.

Albert lived in fear of the knock on the door. The Americans had turned over his flat a number of times already. His job prospects were zero. Worst still his young wife had discovered he was cheating on her. It was bad enough that the successful, debonair older man she had married was now a walking wreck, and that she and her daughter had only a future of penury and insecurity to look forward to, but this was the final straw. She took their daughter Elizabeth and went to Peru.

Albert moved in with his new mistress and ex-housekeeper, Brunhilde Siebaldstaetter. The Americans came looking. Brunhilde kept them at bay. Albert hid 'under the bed, quaking. They wanted to take him away. That is what it was like then.' Life was hard: 'He got food parcels . . . and a bit of support . . . otherwise he couldn't have survived.'[12] Some relief was provided by holidays spent in Innsbruck with the Benbassat family: 'My father had each time invited Albert to spend these vacations with us . . . We used to sit in the comfortable hotel lobby, drinking coffee together.'[13]

In 1952 Albert went to Argentina, having been offered a job at a German-run factory. Judging by letters he wrote at the time this was to be a permanent move. It wasn't. The reasons for his change of heart are not known. Perhaps he was put off by the high percentage of Nazis in the ex-pat community. There may also have been a failed attempt at reconciliation with his wife and daughter but Elizabeth has no memory of any meeting. She claims she wrote to Albert for seven years after the separation and never received a reply or 'a single cent . . . he never had any consideration for his only child'.[14] It is possible he saw Mila and she decided not to tell Elizabeth, who was only six. But even if he did make contact nothing came of it.

He did spend a day with Jan Moravek, the ex-Skoda engineer he had spirited away from the Gestapo and into Romania, whose family had returned to Prague when the Soviets entered Bucharest, and then left again after the Communist take-over. This encounter is the only evidence we have of Albert's time in Argentina. He returned to Salzburg and Brunhilde. Finally things were looking up. In 1955 he was offered a job at a construction company in Munich. He was going home.

But German society was not ready to accept a Goering. The 400-strong work-force 'found out that he was Hermann's brother so he was sacked. The head of the company called him into his office and said, "I'm sorry but they all said it's either him or us."'[15] Albert spent his last decade in Brunhilde's apartment, his health shaky, existing off the odd bit of translation work, donations from friends, and state benefits.

Brunhilde's daughter thought that Albert was 'embittered' and 'in turmoil' and that, 'He liked to live in the past, a man who had been in such a high position in life, who had actually done good.'[16] Yet he could have capitalised on his extraordinary experiences. Many individuals who had relationships with the Nazi leadership, no matter how tenuous, felt compelled to share their thoughts with the world. Publishers were happy to help. After his release from prison in 1966, Speer became a best-selling celebrity author. Albert chose to remain silent: 'After the war he could have written his memoirs or sold his story. But instead he lived modestly, with his conscience at peace.'[17]

Albert had good days and bad days, moments of regret and recrimination, of pride and satisfaction, of despair and loss. His faith provided comfort. He kept his dignity. Shortly before his death in 1966 he married Brunhilde to ensure she got a full widow's pension.

* * *

Edda Goering, Hermann's daughter, believed that 'on a personal level' her father and Albert 'liked each other very much'.[18] Albert's daughter had the same impression: 'They used to visit one another, and I think yes, they were very close.'[19] Yet Hermann described Albert as 'quiet, reclusive, melancholy and pessimistic',[20] while his friends knew him as a bon viveur. Perhaps Albert was unable to relax, fearful of being compromised, to be seen making merry with Hermann? 'He was caught between the war and his brother and the Nazis and the people he cared about so much . . . like a double personality.'[21]

Jacques Benbassat recalled how Albert's 'sense of humour was one of the things that I enjoyed very much . . . We exchanged jokes . . . Very few of mine were new to him.'[22] Gritzbach wrote that Hermann was 'very fond of wit and humour. The many jokes that are in circulation about his person have always caused him much merriment.'[23] He jotted down his favourites in a leather-bound book, like the one about a motorist who crashed into Hermann's car one night and claimed in court that he was dazzled by the glare from Hermann's medals. He often raided his store of jokes, from the obscene to the genuinely witty, using them to shock and seduce. At Nuremberg he kept up a steady flow of anti-British wisecracks, which were always going to raise a smile from his American captors: What do you get if you have one Englishman? An idiot. If you have two? A club. And three? An Empire. But if he heard a gag that upset him the hapless comic would end up in a concentration camp.

The brothers also shared a preference for plump women. Albert 'definitely preferred the better nourished beauties and once startled me with the statement, "A woman cannot be too fat."'[24] Emmy told the British ambassador that Hermann 'likes women who are fat'.[25] Otherwise they viewed them very differently. Albert was a serial philanderer, cheating on all his wives except Brunhilde. Even marriage to a young Czech beauty did not still his wandering eye.

Hermann took his vows seriously. He was devoted to Emmy – 'He has been so good to me . . . He has always protected me'[26] – especially after she bore him a daughter in June 1938. Hermann doted on his little Edda, treating her like a princess. Though Karin still haunted him – on his first trip to Paris in 1940 he wrote to her son Thomas about how, 'In the hush of the early evening I strolled along the Champs Elysées and I felt that your dear mother's hand was in mine'[27] – her spectre did not diminish his feelings for Emmy. From his Nuremberg cell he wrote her passionate letters: 'Sometimes I think my heart will break with love and longing for you. That would be a beautiful death.'[28]

Albert's loyalty to his friends was exceptional. They formed a vast extended family. An inveterate letter writer, his correspondence included hundreds of people. Hermann ran a system of patronage which embraced, among many others, his First World War comrades, the Luftwaffe officers that he spared from widespread retribution after the bomb plot against Hitler, the kitchen staff at his favourite restaurant whom he kept out of the Army, and his business colleagues whose nefarious conduct he refused to discuss with his Allied interrogators.

Sir Nevile Henderson wrote that he had 'never seen greater loyalty or devotion than his to Hitler'.[29] Hermann's commitment was stretched to breaking point at times, and finally snapped, causing Hitler to brand him a traitor. This undoubtedly hurt Hermann, but he blamed Bormann, 'that dirty swine . . . I would strangle the son-of-a-bitch with my bare hands',[30] and stood by his Führer: 'It has not always been easy for German heroes . . . but they kept their loyalty just the same.'[31]

His pre-modern disposition – 'I am not a moralist, although I have my chivalric code'[32] – made loyalty an unqualified virtue. But his 'code' was always a fanciful ideal and, in the context of his Nazism, utterly meaningless. Hermann vainly tried to explain away his rampant amorality. It was not his fault. His principles had fallen prey to a cruel world: 'I am not a callous monster . . . but I have seen so much already – the thousands of maimed and half-burnt bodies in the First World War – the starvation – and in this war women and children burnt to death in air attacks.'[33]

Albert was a liberal who believed in tolerance and individual freedom. His ethical code was founded on his religious beliefs. A friend called him 'a moral man living in an immoral time'.[34] The Nazis despised what he represented, what they saw as conventional bourgeois morality. Hermann declared that, 'The German revolution, in contrast to the French, is not being made in conformity with this science of liberal enlightenment, but against it.'[35] Hitler called Christianity 'the heaviest blow that ever struck humanity', and described the bourgeoisie as 'riff-raff'.[36] Near the end of the war he remarked that, 'We should have brushed aside, rudely and without pity, the fossilised bourgeoisie, as devoid of soul as it is denuded of patriotism.'[37]

This hostile attitude dovetailed neatly with their assault on the Jews of Europe. Statistics collected for the delegates at the Wansee conference showed that the Jewish population was predominately middle class. Some 32.7 per cent were in the arts and the professions – doctors, lawyers, scientists, academics – 20 per cent in trade, and 20 per cent in the civil service. A mere 14.8 per cent came from the urban working class, and only 9.1 per cent from agriculture.

Nazi aggression placed enormous strains on loyalty and personal morality. The rewards were as enticing as the punishments were severe. All those empty desks had to be filled. Collaboration could make your fortune. Kurt Prufer trained as an engineer at a Technische Hochschule in the 1920s and gained a place at a leading furnace manufacturer, Topf and Sons. By 1940 Topf had won several SS contracts to build concentration camp crematoriums. Prufer was the company's head engineer. He improved on the latest designs and lowered fuel costs. To accommodate a new crematorium at Mauthausen, he increased furnace capacity to sixty bodies an hour. Five more facilities were ordered for the Auschwitz-Birkenau complex. Topf went into overdrive. All the while Prufer received a 2 per cent commission.

* * *

At Skoda, Albert was responsible for the 'high volume of exports' of peace goods. His interests – 'He wanted to carry on working for Skoda after the war'[38] – coincided with the company's plan to use his sales to offset the 'losses for the enterprise in terms of half-done orders and unpaid bills',[39] which would occur if the Nazis went into rapid decline. As it was, Albert 'heard it repeated many times that Skoda was the best factory in the Reich'.[40]

By helping Skoda to prosper, Albert was indirectly helping the Nazi war machine. He could argue, as he did, that he also undermined it. But some of his other business decisions were less defensible: 'I received monthly between 100 and 200 marks from the Tobis Film Company in Berlin, and I was on the board of directors.'[41] On 7 October 1938, Tobis-Sascha, Albert's employer in Vienna, was disbanded. The Austrian studios became part of Wien Film AG, while Tobis re-consolidated in Germany.

Tobis did make some relatively innocuous period pieces, but also produced a pro-euthanasia film about a young doctor whose wife had multiple sclerosis, at a time when the nation's disabled and mentally ill were being massacred by the regime, some anti-British propaganda movies, two about the Irish liberation struggle and one about the Boer War, and three features celebrating Hermann's Luftwaffe. Why did Albert associate himself with this Nazi bilge? Where did he draw the line between self-preservation and outright collusion?

A film director visiting Albert in early 1937 noticed 'in front of the Tobis-Sascha head office . . . a brown Steyr cabrio which I remembered seeing at the studios. The whole of Vienna knew that Hermann Goering had given this beautiful car to his brother.'[42]

Steyr AG specialised in luxury cars and motorbikes. In 1934 it amalgamated with the German corporation, Daimler-Puch AG. The automobile industry was obviously vital to the Nazis, providing vehicles for the Army and engines for the Luftwaffe, and they invested heavily. During 1932 German manufacturers produced a total of 2,851 cars. In 1936 they produced 244,640. After the *Anschluss*, Steyr-Daimler-Puch AG became part of the HermannGoeringWerke. On 15 November 1938, Hermann appointed a Plenipotentiary for the Automobile Industry and instructed him to standardise models and complete the conversion to military production, which accounted for 93 per cent of output by 1943.

Albert became a Steyr representative: 'Skoda had an agreement with Steyr-Daimler-Puch AG in Vienna regarding the sale of cars and trucks . . . soon he was in charge of the combined sales agencies in Yugoslavia, Romania and Bulgaria. The general manager of the Steyr works in Vienna was Herr Meindl, an Austrian Nazi of the old Beer Hall putsch days.'[43] Meindl was Hermann's ally. In June 1943 Hermann put him in charge of a massive new factory near Vienna against the wishes of the Daimler management. Himmler's man was the ubiquitous Doctor Voss, chairman of the board at Steyr. Albert operated in their midst, within parameters set by Speer.

Daimler's companies started using slave labour in 1941. During the spring of 1942 they received a massive influx from the Soviet Union. Female prisoners on starvation rations regularly sold their bodies for bread. Abortions were compulsory. In May 1943 Daimler agreed to send all the Jewish workers at its factory in Poland to the death camps. The chairman of the conglomerate had committed suicide a year earlier. His replacement had a half-Jewish wife, as did another board member, while the director at their Mannheim factory was married to a full Jew. This caused inevitable grumbling but the firm was sufficiently important for Himmler to approve a compromise. The new chairman stayed, the other two were seen to be fired, but only one was actually dismissed and both retained their influence.

* * *

Sven Wingquist, the Swedish industrial magnate and playboy socialite, first met Hermann shortly after the first war. Wingquist had invented the self-aligning ball-bearing. His company, SKF, had 185 outlets world wide. As a result of Hermann's marriage to Karin, Hugo von Rosen, co-director of SKF USA and its huge factory in Philadelphia, became his second cousin.

Without ball-bearings the Nazi war machine would cease to function. One Luftwaffe fighter plane needed as many as 4,000. Tanks and all other motorised vehicles ran on them. Rosen and SKF USA directly supplied Hermann up until the war and continued some trade with the Reich through outlets in South America, shipping the ball bearings via Sweden until 1944. SKF's main financier was the Swedish Enskilda Bank, part of the Wallenberg empire. Hermann dealt closely with Jacob Wallenberg, who controlled most of Sweden's heavy industry, including its oil and iron ore production. Jacob was a partner with Axel Wenner-Gren, another of Hermann's Swedish contacts, in the electronics firm Ericsson.

In the late 1930s Jacob agreed to help his young cousin, Raoul Wallenberg, with his stalled career. Jacob introduced him to a shipping tycoon who was setting up an import–export business with Kalman Lauer, a Hungarian Jew. Raoul was made co-partner.

Stockholm, June 1944: Iver Olsen, an American diplomat, intelligence agent and representative of the War Refugee Board, was looking for a Swede to rescue Hungarian Jews from deportation. He asked Lauer to recommend somebody. Lauer suggested Raoul Wallenberg, and arranged a meeting. Olsen approved of Raoul, as did the US ambassador. Both were reassured by the Wallenberg family name.

Raoul appeared in Budapest armed with diplomatic status and a clear mandate. He quickly learned that the Swedish Red Cross had begun to issue provisional Swedish passports to Jews which preserved them from the camps. Raoul seized on this idea. To get a Schutzpass, as they were called, you had to show some kind of connection to a Swedish citizen. By August he had 4,500 to give out and 20,000 applicants.

On 15 October 1944, the violently anti-semitic Arrow Cross party took power with Nazi assistance. Mass executions of Jews began on the banks of the Danube. Eichmann arrived three days later and moved into the Royal Hotel. Thousands were sent on death marches towards Mauthausen in Austria. Raoul went to the border with his team and issued as many Schutzpass as they could type, bluffing the SS guards to release their captives. Hundreds were saved.

The Red Army began its siege of Budapest on 26 December. By the end there was no water, no electricity and the only things left to eat were the 30,000 horses trapped in the city, which the fighting had turned into a stinking pile of refuse, rubble and corpses. The Arrow Cross were on the rampage. Raoul was a marked man. As the Nazis faced defeat, an order went out to kill all the Jews collected in the Central Ghetto. Wallenberg intervened and got it cancelled; 70,000 were spared. On 17 January 1945, Raoul was snatched by the Soviets, who thought he was a spy. He is believed to have died somewhere in the Soviet Union.

Raoul Wallenberg is rightly regarded as a hero. But he would never have been able to achieve what he did without his cousin Jacob, whose readiness to do business with the Nazis made it possible for them to go to war.

* * *

It will never be known exactly how many Albert saved. There were the thirty-four names on his list. Many others went on record, plus unnamed hundreds from Vienna, Prague, Bucharest and Rome, furnished with money, papers and an escape route. For reasons of safety, and perhaps character, Albert often stayed incognito: 'Nobody knew it was him . . . not even those who were receiving the money knew where it came from or who was sending it.'[44] His relationship with the rulers of Romania and Bulgaria may have saved thousands. There are rumours about his activities on behalf of the Jews of Budapest, using Wallenberg's methods. Much of the relevant documentation was either destroyed by the war or taken by the Soviets and buried in archives, where it remains today.

British and American intelligence did not know what to make of him. In early 1940, when Albert sailed from Trieste to Athens on Skoda business, the British considered kidnapping him on the off-chance he might be a Nazi spy. A plan was kicked around between the Admiralty and the Foreign Office, but as he made the return journey it was dismissed as 'idiotic' and not worth the trouble for 'a nonentity like Albert Goering'.[45] After the war the Allies locked him up, thought about recruiting him and perpetually confused him with his cousin Herbert, the insurance fraudster.

Though Albert earned his living in a murky, blood-drenched arena, he paid a price greater than his contribution. He suffered two years' grim imprisonment. Compare this to the fate of Erhard Milch. From 1926 until 1944, Milch concentrated his talents and energies on building an air force that would make Germany a military superpower again. Despite Hermann's mismanagement, he nearly achieved his goal. In April 1947 he was sentenced to life. In 1952 his term was reduced to fifteen years. In 1954 he was released on parole.

Without question, Albert deserves to stand alongside Raoul Wallenberg and Oskar Schindler. If this means accepting the unpalatable truth that a Nazi warlord protected his renegade brother out of the kindness of his heart, then so be it. When Allied interrogators asked Albert whether Hermann was a 'hard man', he replied, 'on the contrary, he is very soft'.[46]

That an evil man is capable of good and a good man capable of evil, is hardly a startling revelation. Albert was neither saint nor martyr, yet his bravery sprang from a similar source, that precious reservoir of selfless courage which gives someone the strength to risk everything for the sake of others.

In the words of Ernst Neubach, who orchestrated the campaign to free Albert from Pankras jail, 'The victory over the Nazis would not be a victory if Albert Goering did not count as one of the victors.'[47]

Notes

Chapter One: Siblings *(pages 3–16)*

1. 28 June 1945, NA SAIC/PIR/67 ref SAIC/FIR/48
2. W. Henderson, *The German Colonial Empire 1884–1914* (UK 1993) p. 44
3. General von Trotha, 2 October 1904, in T. Pakenham, *The Scramble for Africa, 1876–1912* (UK 1991) p. 611
4. Hans Thirring, in L. Mosley, *The Reich Marshal: A Biography of Hermann Goering* (UK 1974) p. 6
5. Sir H. Channon, *Chips – The Diaries of Sir Henry Channon* (UK 1967) pp. 110–11
6. G. Gilbert, *Nuremberg Diary* (USA 1947) p. 210
7. Nuremberg 25 September 1945, PRO FO box 645/156
8. Hans Thirring, in Mosley, p. 6
9. D. Irving, *Goering: A Biography* (UK 1989) p. 27
10. Mosley, p. 9
11. *Ibid.*
12. *Ibid.*
13. A. Cecil, *The Myth of the Master Race: Alfred Rosenberg and Nazi Ideology* (UK 1972) p. 157
14. I. Kershaw, *Hitler 1889–1936: Hubris* (UK 1998) p. 249
15. Irving, p. 32
16. L. Goldensohn, *The Nuremberg Interviews: An American Psychiatrist's Conversations with the Defendants and the Witnesses* (USA 2004) p. 106
17. Elsa Moravek Perou de Wagner, from *The Real Albert Goering*, 3BM TV broadcast Channel 4, 5 December 1998
18. Goldensohn, p. 104
19. Doctor L. Kovacs, 4 July 1944, PRO HS 4/101

Chapter Two: Cataclysm *(pages 17–31)*

1. F. von Papen, *Memoirs* (UK 1952) p. 293
2. Mosley, pp. 16–17
3. Richthofen, in P. Kilduff, *The Red Baron: Beyond the Legend* (UK 1994) p. 79
4. Kilduff, p. 93, citing *Die Kolnische Zeitung* (1916)
5. Richthofen, in Kilduff, p. 198

6. *Ibid.*, p. 157
7. I. Passingham, *All the Kaiser's Men: The Life and Death of the German Army on the Western Front, 1914–1918* (UK 2003) p. 129
8. Richthofen, in Kilduff, p. 120
9. *Ibid.*, p. 54
10. Irving, p. 33
11. A. Fokker and B. Gould, *Flying Dutchman* (USA 1931) p. 217
12. Kilduff, pp. 109–10
13. *Ibid.*, p. 119
14. *Ibid.*, p. 7
15. Mosley, p. 18
16. Kilduff, p. 88
17. Irving, p. 35
18. Kilduff, p. 129
19. Mosley, p. 37
20. G. Sereny, *Albert Speer: His Battle with the Truth* (USA 1995) p. 374
21. Kershaw, *Hitler 1889–1936: Hubris*, p. 87
22. Passingham, p. 87
23. *Ibid.*, p. 234
24. Ernst von Salomon, in N. Jones, *The Birth of the Nazis: How the Freikorps Blazed a Trail for Hitler* (UK 2004) p. 135
25. Mosley, p. 41
26. *Ibid.*, p. 45
27. *Ibid.*

Chapter Three: Munich *(pages 33–47)*

1. Kershaw, *Hitler 1889–1936: Hubris*, p. 133
2. Goebbels diary, 6 November 1925, in R. Evans, *The Coming of the Third Reich* (UK 2003) pp. 205–6
3. *Ibid.*, 18–20 July 1926, in Kershaw, *Hitler 1889–1936: Hubris*, pp. 283–4
4. P. Padfield, *Himmler: Reichsführer SS* (UK 1990) p. 68
5. Mosley, p. 64
6. *Ibid.*, p. 67
7. Goldensohn, p. 132
8. *Ibid.*, p. 133
9. *Ibid.*
10. G. Gilbert, *Nuremberg Diary*, p. 400
11. Irving, p. 66
12. *Ibid.*
13. J. Fest, *The Face of the Third Reich* (UK 1970) p. 118
14. Mosley, pp. 70–1
15. Letter to Colonel B. Andrus, 6 September 1945, Justice Robert Jackson, Main Office Files, NA RG 238 Box 180
16. Ernst Neubach, *Deutsches Wochenmagazin*, 24 February 1962
17. Nuremberg, 3 September 1945, PRO FO box 645/156

18. Goldensohn, pp. 121–2
19. *Ibid.*
20. *Ibid.*
21. Nuremberg, 25 September 1945, PRO FO box 645/156
22. E. Neubach, *Deutsches Wochenmagazin*, 24 February 1962
23. Nuremberg, 25 September 1945, PRO FO box 645/156
24. Jacques Benbassat, *The Real Albert Goering*, 3BM TV
25. Evans, *The Coming of the Third Reich*, pp. 182–3
26. Irving, p. 46
27. *Ibid.*, p. 48
28. *Daily Telegraph*, 29 June 1923, cited in Evans, *The Coming of the Third Reich*, pp. 105–6
29. Irving, p. 48
30. M. Burleigh, *The Third Reich: A New History* (UK 2000) p. 212
31. Röhm, quoted in Kershaw, *Hitler 1889–1936: Hubris*, p. 502
32. Hermann Goering, January 1934, in Irving, p. 141
33. Padfield, p. 99
34. *Ibid.*, p. 158
35. *Ibid.*, p. 161

Chapter Four: Going Up, Going Down *(pages 49–61)*

1. B. F. Egenberger Agent CIC, Seventh Army HQ Salzburg, 9 May 1945, NA 5200/30
2. *Ibid.*
3. 28 June 1945, NA SAIC/PIR/67, ref SAIC/FIR/48
4. G. Knopp, *Hitler's Warriors* (UK 2005) p. 264
5. Mosley, p. 89
6. Letter to Karin's mother, 25 May 1924, Irving, p. 70
7. Irving, p. 63
8. *Ibid.*, p. 78
9. *Ibid.*, p. 80
10. Mosley, p. 96
11. Letter to Karin's mother, 22 October 1924, Irving, p. 77
12. Irving, p. 84
13. *Ibid.*, p. 86
14. *Ibid.*, pp. 87–8
15. *Ibid.*, p. 88
16. *Ibid.*
17. *Ibid.*
18. *Ibid.*, pp. 91–2
19. Colonel B. Andrus, in Mosley, p. 326
20. D. Kelley, *22 Cells in Nuremberg* (USA 1947) pp. 48–9
21. Goldensohn, p. 128
22. Irving, pp. 95–6
23. *Ibid.*

Chapter Five: Power *(pages 65–76)*

1. Mosley, p. 147
2. H. Goering, *The Political Testament of Hermann Goering: A Selection of Important Speeches and Articles* (UK 1938) p. 115
3. Evans, *The Coming of the Third Reich*, p. 270
4. Letter to Karin's mother, May 1928, Irving, p. 93
5. Goebbels in *Der Angriff*, 20 August 1928, Kershaw, *Hitler 1889–1936: Hubris*, p. 303
6. H. Goering, *Germany Reborn* (UK 1934) p. 70
7. F. Thyssen, *I Paid Hitler* (USA 1941) p. 100
8. Mosley, p. 113
9. *Ibid.*, p. 115
10. H. Schacht, *My First 76 Years: The Autobiography* (UK 1955) pp. 278–9
11. Irving, p. 115
12. Goering, *Germany Reborn*, p. 73
13. Sir N. Henderson, *Failure of a Mission, 1937–1939* (UK 1940) p. 87
14. Letter to Karin's mother, 21 February 1929, Mosley, p. 114
15. Martin Sommerfeldt, in Irving, p. 106
16. Goldensohn, p. 121
17. Goering, *Germany Reborn*, p. 51
18. *Ibid.*, p. 79
19. *Ibid.*, p. 101
20. Goebbels diary, January 1933, Mosley, p. 147
21. Mosley, p. 117
22. *Ibid.*, p. 130
23. *Ibid.*, pp. 131–2
24. *Ibid.*
25. Countess Fanny von Möllendorff, *ibid.* p. 184

Chapter Six: Ski Bunnies and Bolsheviks *(pages 77–93)*

1. Victor Adler speech, 1918, quoted in G. Kinderman, *Hitler's Defeat in Austria 1933–1934: Europe's First Containment of Nazi Expansionism* (UK 1988) p. 50
2. Edda Goering, *The Real Albert Goering*, 3BM TV
3. *Ibid.*
4. Jacques Benbassat to author, 2005
5. Jacques Benbassat, *The Real Albert Goering*, 3BM TV
6. Jacques Benbassat to author, 2005
7. Jacques Benbassat, *The Real Albert Goering*, 3BM TV
8. Jacques Benbassat to author, 2005
9. Nuremberg, 25 September 1945, PRO FO box 645/156
10. 28 June 1945, NA SAIC/PIR/67, ref SAIC/FIR/48
11. Elsa Moravek Perou de Wagner, *The Real Albert Goering*, 3BM TV
12. Goering, *Germany Reborn*, foreword
13. *Ibid.*, p. 9
14. *Ibid.*, p. 10
15. *Ibid.*, p. 13

16. *Ibid.*, p. 19
17. *Ibid.*, p. 34
18. *Ibid.*
19. *Ibid.*, p. 71
20. *Ibid.*, p. 40
21. *Ibid.*, p. 29
22. *Ibid.*, pp. 66–7
23. *Ibid.*, p. 74
24. *Ibid.*, p. 58
25. *Ibid.*, p. 63
26. *Ibid.*, p. 78
27. *Ibid.*, p. 114
28. *Ibid.*, p. 25
29. *Ibid.*, p. 43
30. *Ibid.*, p. 25
31. *Ibid.*, p. 73
32. *Ibid.*, p. 40
33. *Ibid.*, p. 159
34. *Ibid.*, p. 134
35. *Ibid.*, p. 129
36. *Ibid.*, p. 158
37. *Ibid.*, p. 121
38. *Ibid.*
39. *Ibid.*
40. *Ibid.*, p. 124
41. *Ibid.*, p. 125
42. Irving, p. 116
43. Goering, *Germany Reborn*, p. 132
44. Interrogation of Hermann by Dr R. Kempner at Nuremberg, in Mosley, p. 159–60
45. Goering, *Germany Reborn*, p. 133
46. Evans, *The Coming of the Third Reich*, pp. 330–1
47. Goering, *Germany Reborn*, p. 127
48. *Ibid.*, p. 129
49. Padfield, p. 142
50. G. Gilbert, *Nuremberg Diary*, p. 422
51. Fritsch, in Irving, p. 196
52. Goldensohn, pp. 129–30
53. Goering, *Germany Reborn*, p. 158
54. Dollfuss at rally, 11 September 1933, from Kinderman, Appendix 17
55. Dollfuss speech in Vienna, 10 May 1934, from Kinderman, Appendix 18
56. Kinderman, Appendix 20
57. R. Bosworth, *Mussolini* (UK 2002) p. 280
58. *Ibid.*, p. 275
59. *Ibid.*, p. 281
60. *Ibid.*, pp. 284–5

Chapter Seven: Showbusiness *(pages 95–117)*

1. Nuremberg, 3 September 1945, PRO FO box 645/156
2. *Ibid.*
3. George Pilzer, interview with Adam LeBor, 1998
4. Goebbels, in *Film-Kurier*, 28 April 1935, cited in D. Welch, *Propaganda and the German Cinema, 1933–1945* (UK 2001) p. 80
5. Goebbels press conference, 15 March 1933, cited in Evans, *The Coming of the Third Reich*, p. 355
6. G. Knopp, *Hitler's Henchmen* (UK 2000) p. 29
7. Goebbels, in *Volkischer Beobachter*, 9 February 1934, cited in Welch, p. 74
8. Goebbels, as recalled by W. von Oven, *ibid.*, p. 189
9. Goebbels diary, 1 December 1944, *ibid.*, p. 190
10. Goebbels diary, 19 March 1945, *ibid.*, p. 192
11. Knopp, *Hitler's Henchmen*, pp. 35–6
12. *Ibid.*, p. 37
13. Goebbels diary, 21 May 1931, cited in T. Gunning, *The Films of Fritz Lang: Allegories and Visions of Modernity* (UK 2000) p. 192
14. Welch, p. 83
15. Gerhard Renner, 'The Anschluss of the Film Industry after 1934', in K. Seyar and J. Warren (eds), *Austria in the Thirties: Culture and Politics* (USA 1991) p. 255
16. E. Neubach, *Deutsches Wochenmagazin*, 24 February 1962
17. Welch, pp. 173–4
18. Christina Neubach, *Deutsches Wochenmagazin*, 24 February 1962
19. E. Neubach, *ibid.*
20. *Ibid.*
21. Dispatch to Foreign Office, 17 April 1935, Mosley, p. 200
22. Schacht, p. 368
23. Von Hassel, 14 February 1943, U. von Hassel, *The Von Hassel Diaries, 1938–1944* (UK 1994) p. 285
24. Kelley, p. 56
25. Oberstjagermeister Ulrich Scherping, Irving, p. 180
26. Channon, pp. 106–7
27. *Ibid.*
28. E. Gritzbach, *Hermann Goering: The Man and his Work* (UK 1938), p. 226
29. Hermann's hunting diary, Library Of Congress AC. 9342; or Irving, pp. 188–90
30. Goering, *Political Testament*, pp. 170–6
31. *Ibid.*
32. *Ibid.*
33. *Ibid.*
34. Gritzbach, p. 60
35. *Ibid.*, p. 57
36. *Ibid.*
37. P. Schmidt, *Hitler's Interpreter* (UK 1951) p. 29
38. *Ibid.*, p. 32
39. *Ibid.*, p. 30

40. Goldensohn, p. 102

41. G. Gilbert, *Nuremberg Diary*, p. 47

42. I. Kershaw, *Making Friends with Hitler: Lord Londonderry and Britain's Road to War* (UK 2004) pp. 155–6

43. *Ibid.*

44. Lord Halifax, PRO FO box 371/2736

45. Earl of Birkenhead, *Halifax: The Life of Lord Halifax* (UK 1965) p. 372

46. Schmidt, p. 54

47. N. Henderson, p. 80

48. *Ibid.*, p. 91

49. *Ibid.*

50. Birkenhead, p. 357

51. N. Henderson, p. 90

52. H. von Etzdorf, in M. Bloch, *Ribbentrop* (UK 1994) p. 14

53. J. von Ribbentrop, *The Ribbentrop Memoirs* (UK 1954) p. 29

54. *The Times*, 29 October 1936, cited in Bloch, p. 120

55. G. Gilbert, *Nuremberg Diary*, p. 13

56. *Ibid.*

57. Ribbentrop, pp. 207–8

58. Kershaw, *Hitler 1889–1936: Hubris*, p. 444

59. Goering, *Political Testament*, p. 177

60. Knopp, *Hitler's Warriors*, p. 234

61. F. Taylor, *Dresden: Tuesday 13th February 1945* (UK 2004) p. 84

62. *Ibid.*, p. 85

63. Hermann, 29 April 1937, J. Killen, *The Luftwaffe: A History* (UK 1967) p. 156

64. Ribbentrop, p. 60

65. Killen, p. 74

66. Memo, 4 September 1936, Irving, p. 167

67. Report of meeting of Estimates Committee, 15 May 1936, R. Overy, *Goering: The Iron Man* (UK 1984) p. 43

68. Hermann letter to von Blomberg, 19 June 1936, *ibid.*, p. 46

69. Meeting of Council of Ministers, 4 September 1936, *ibid.*, p. 47

70. I. Kershaw, *Hitler 1936–1945: Nemesis* (UK 2000) p. 161

71. Hermann interrogated by Herbert Dubois, 25 June 1945 and 5 August 1945, Irving, p. 164

72. Overy, *Goering: The Iron Man*, p. 42

73. Schacht, p. 455

74. Irving, p. 164

75. Hermann speech broadcast on radio, 28 October 1936, Goering, *Political Testament*, p. 206

76. *Ibid.*

77. Overy, *Goering: The Iron Man*, p. 42

78. Hermann speech, 28 October 1936, Goering, *Political Testament*, p. 202

79. *Ibid.*, p. 203

80. Hermann, 15 July 1937, Overy, *Goering: The Iron Man*, pp. 127–8

81. Egon Lanske Austrian Film Minister, G. Renner, 'The Anschluss of the Film Industry after 1934', in Seyar and Warren, *Austria in the Thirties: Culture and Politics*, pp. 261–2

82. *Ibid.*

83. E. Neubach, *Deutsches Wochenmagazin*, 24 February 1962

84. *Ibid.*

85. *Ibid.*

86. *Ibid.*

87. George Pilzer, *The Real Albert Goering*, 3BM TV

88. *Ibid.*

89. William Szekely, *Deutsches Wochenmagazin*, 24 February 1962

90. War Crimes Branch 21, US Zone – Office of Military Government, NA NND88/077-CIB, file DS/CFA/JG

Chapter Eight: Death March *(pages 119–39)*

1. Schmidt, p. 64

2. *Ibid.*

3. Bosworth, p. 320

4. J. Fest, *Hitler* (UK 1974) p. 809

5. Schuschnigg speech to Federal Diet, 24 February 1938, K. von Schuschnigg, *Farewell Austria* (UK 1938) p. 280

6. Schuschnigg speech, Vienna, 9 March, *ibid.*, p. 316

7. Kershaw, *Hitler 1936–1945: Nemesis*, p. 76

8. N. von Below, *At Hitler's Side: The Memoirs of Hitler's Luftwaffe Adjutant, 1937–1945* (UK 2001) pp. 89–90

9. Schuschnigg radio broadcast, 11 March 1938, Schuschnigg, p. 327

10. Letter from US Chargé d'Affaires H. R. Wilson to President F. D. Roosevelt, 12 March 1938, FDR Library, PSF box 45; or Irving, pp. 211–12

11. Lord Halifax telegram, Kershaw, *Hitler 1936–1945: Nemesis*, p. 78

12. Hitler speech, Vienna, 15 March 1938, G. Shepard, *The Austrians: A Thousand Year Odyssey* (UK 1996) p. 328

13. Letter to Hermann from his sister Paula, 15 March 1938, Irving, p. 211

14. E. Neubach, *Deutsches Wochenmagazin*, 24 February 1962

15. William Szekely, *ibid.*

16. Greta Wolfe, *The Real Albert Goering*, 3BM TV

17. William Szekely, *Deutsches Wochenmagazin*, 24 February 1962

18. Albert Goering recalled by Szekely, *ibid.*

19. *Ibid.*

20. Nuremberg, 24 September 1945, PRO FO box 645/156

21. Edda Goering, *The Real Albert Goering*, 3BM TV

22. Nuremberg, 25 September 1945, PRO FO box 645/156

23. *Ibid.*

24. G. Gedye, *Fallen Bastions: The Central European Tragedy* (UK 1939) p. 295

25. William Szekely, *Deutsches Wochenmagazin*, 24 February 1962

26. Nuremberg, 25 September 1945, PRO FO box 645/156

27. Mosley, pp. 219–20

28. Hubert Butler, Burleigh, p. 327
29. Walter Darre, 16 May 1945, NA SAIC/X-PS, or Irving, p. 235
30. Irving, p. 236
31. R. Manvell and H. Fraenkel, *Goering* (USA 1962) p. 191
32. G. Gilbert, *Nuremberg Diary*, pp. 437–8
33. *Ibid.*, p. 68
34. *Ibid.*, p. 60-61
35. *Ibid.*, p. 152
36. *Ibid.*, p. 290
37. *Ibid.*, p. 187
38. Goldensohn, p. 118
39. *Ibid.*, p. 117
40. Emmy Goering, 23 March 1945, cited in G. Gilbert, *Nuremberg Diary*, p. 213
41. Mosley, p. 234
42. G. Gilbert, *Nuremberg Diary*, p. 213
43. Nuremberg, 3 September 1945, PRO FO box 645/156
44. Nuremberg, 25 September 1945, *ibid.*
45. *Ibid.*
46. *Ibid.*
47. *Ibid.*
48. *Ibid.*
49. *Ibid.*
50. Nuremberg, 3 September 1945, PRO FO box 645/156
51. Mosley, pp. 300–2
52. *Ibid.*
53. Goldensohn, p. 116
54. Goering, *Germany Reborn*, p. 130
55. Goldensohn, p. 114
56. Heydrich, 31 July 1939, C. Browning and J. Matthias, *The Origins of the Final Solution: The Evolution of Nazi Jewish Policy, 1939–1943* (UK 2004) pp. 16–17
57. Himmler, *ibid.*, p. 69
58. Goldensohn, p. 113
59. NA T-501/214/269, or Browning and Matthias, p. 158
60. Irving, p. 344
61. Von Hassel diary, 1 November 1941, von Hassel, p. 222
62. Wansee Protocol, copy no. 16, cited in M. Roseman, *The Villa, the Lake, the Meeting: Wansee and the Final Solution* (UK 2002) pp. 108–12
63. *Ibid.*
64. *Ibid.*
65. *Ibid.*
66. Goebbels diary, 23 March 1942, L. Lochner (trans.), *Goebbels Diaries* (UK 1948) p. 173
67. Padfield, pp. 468–70
68. G. Gilbert, *Nuremberg Diary*, p. 107
69. Goldensohn, p. 116

70. G. Gilbert, *Nuremberg Diary*, p. 371
71. C. Browning, *Ordinary Men: Reserve Battalion 101 and the Final Solution in Poland* (UK 2001) p. 199
72. Hermann at Nuremberg, 11 March 1946, M. Marrus (ed.), *The Nuremberg War Crimes Trial, 1945–1946: A Documentary History* (USA 1997) pp. 207–9
73. *Ibid.*
74. G. Gilbert, *Nuremberg Diary*, p. 371
75. *Ibid.*, p. 67
76. Browning and Matthias, pp. 340–2
77. Hitler, 13 February 1945, F. Genoud (ed.), *The Testament of Adolf Hitler: The Hitler–Bormann Documents, February–April 1945* (UK 1959)
78. Goldensohn, p. 105
79. Padfield, pp. 176–7
80. Goldensohn, p. 132
81. Albert Guérisse GC (aka 'Pat O'Leary') quoted in, M. Gilbert, *The Dent Atlas of the Holocaust: The Complete History* (UK 1993) p. 233

Chapter Nine: Resistance *(pages 143–55)*

1. British Intelligence report, 4 July 1944, PRO HO box 4/101
2. Albert Goering, as recalled by E. Neubach, *Deutsches Wochenmagazin*, 24 February 1962
3. L. Kovacs, 4 July 1944, PRO HO box 4/101
4. *Ibid.*
5. *Ibid.*
6. *Ibid.*
7. 25 July 1939, Overy, *Goering: The Iron Man*, p. 82
8. Hans Modry, 7 February 1947, Notes from the Trial, Special People's Court Prague, Testimony in Defence of Albert Goering, SKA
9. *Ibid.*
10. Nuremberg, 25 September 1945, PRO FO box 645/156
11. *Ibid.*
12. Recollections of a Czech student in report from British Embassy, Prague, 8 December 1939, PRO HS4/37
13. E. Neubach, *Deutsches Wochenmagazin*, 24 February 1962
14. Alexandra Otzoup, statement under oath, Camp Monschof, 9 January 1947, *ibid.*
15. Elsa Perou de Moravek, *ibid.*
16. Vladislav Kratky, *The Real Albert Goering*, 3BM TV
17. Hans Modry, 7 February 1947, Notes from the Trial, Special People's Court Prague, Testimony in Defence of Albert Goering, SKA
18. *Ibid.*
19. Vladislav Kratky, interview with Adam LeBor, May 1998
20. *Ibid.*
21. Jan Stupka, *ibid.*
22. Miloslav Hejma, *ibid.*
23. Jacques Benbassat, *The Real Albert Goering*, 3BM TV
24. Walter Schellenberg, quoted in C. MacDonald, *The Killing of SS Obergruppenführer*

Reinhard Heydrich (UK 1989) p. 5

25. *Ibid.*, pp. 20–1

26. Hans Modry, 7 February 1947, Notes from the Trial, Special People's Court Prague, Testimony in Defence of Albert Goering, SKA

27. Nuremberg, 25 September 1945, PRO FO box 645/156

28. 28 June 1945, NA SAIC/PIR/67, ref SAIC/FIR48

29. Hans Modry, 7 February 1947, Notes from the Trial, Special People's Court Prague, Testimony in Defence of Albert Goering, SKA

30. *Ibid.*

31. Albert letter to Bodenschatz, 5 January 1942, BA-Berlin

32. Albert letter to Vambersky, 17 January 1942, BA-Berlin

33. Nuremberg, 25 September 1945, PRO FO box 645/156

34. *Ibid.*

35. *Ibid.*

36. *Ibid.*

37. Schacht, p. 421

38. Karel Staller, interview at Hotel Metropole, 11 July 1973, *History of Zbrojovka*

39. Vladislav Kratky, interview with Adam LeBor, May 1998

40. E. Perou de Moravek (writing as E. Permora), *El Frente Desarmado* (Buenos Aires 1952) pp. 207–10

41. *Ibid.*

42. *Ibid.*

43. Elsa Moravek Perou de Wagner, interview with Adam LeBor, 1998

44. Alexandra Otzoup, statement under oath, Camp Monschof, 9 January 1947, *Deutsches Wochenmagazin*, 24 February 1962

Chapter Ten: All or Nothing *(pages 157–68)*

1. G. Gilbert, *Nuremberg Diary*, pp. 67–8

2. Irving, p. 220

3. B. Dahlerus, *The Last Attempt* (UK 1948) p. 114

4. Von Hassel, p. 71

5. General Günther von Blumentritt, R. Overy, *The Battle* (UK 2000) pp. 108–9

6. Memo of Naval Supreme Command, 7 July 1940, J. Showell (ed.), *Führer Conferences on Naval Affairs, 1939–1945* (UK 1990) p. 112

7. Report of Commander-in-Chief Navy (Raeder) to Hitler, 11 July 1940, *ibid.*, p. 113

8. H. Dowding, in S. Bungay, *The Most Dangerous Enemy: A History of the Battle of Britain* (UK 2002) p. 59

9. Luftwaffe Conference, The Hague, July 1940, Killen, p. 120

10. Hermann speech, 1 March 1938, Overy, *Goering: The Iron Man*, p. 177

11. Von Below diary, 11–13 August 1940, von Below, p. 70

12. Conference at Karinhall, 15 August 1940, Killen, pp. 134–5

13. A. Speer, *Inside The Third Reich* (UK 1970) p. 388*f*

14. Hitler to Student, 20 July 1941, J. Keegan, *The Second World War* (UK 1989) pp. 138–9

15. G. Ciano, 29 January 1942, G. Ciano, *The Ciano Diaries, 1939–1943: The Complete, Unabridged Diaries of Galeazzo Ciano* (USA 1946)

16. Goebbels diary, 23 May 1942, Lochner, *Goebbels Diaries*, p. 173

17. G. Knopp, *Hitler's Hitmen* (UK 2002) p. 123

18. *Ibid.*, p. 168

19. *Ibid.*, p. 141

20. *Ibid.*, p. 154

21. M. Middlebrook and C. Everitt (eds), *Bomber Command War Diaries: Operational Reference Book, 1939–1945* (UK 1985) p. 123

22. Directive from Air Ministry, 9 July 1941, *ibid.*, pp. 175–6

23. Goebbels diary, 27 April 1942, Taylor, pp. 128–9

24. Albert Speer, in R. Neillands, *The Bomber War: Arthur Harris and the Allied Bomber Offensive, 1939–1945* (UK 2001) p. 384

25. Von Below, p. 158

26. Hermann speech broadcast on radio, 30 January 1943, in Killen, p. 214, and Overy, *Goering: The Iron Man*, p. 189

Chapter Eleven: Agent Albert *(pages 169–78)*

1. Hans Modry, 7 February 1947, Notes from the Trial, Special People's Court Prague, Testimony in Defence of Albert Goering, SKA

2. Nuremberg, 3 September 1945, PRO FO box 645/156

3. Hans Modry, 7 February 1947, Notes from the Trial, Special People's Court Prague, Testimony in Defence of Albert Goering, SKA

4. Voss letter to Himmler, 30 March 1942, A. Speer, *The Slave State: Heinrich Himmler's Masterplan for SS Supremacy* (UK 1981) p. 87

5. Nuremberg, 25 September 1945, PRO FO box 645/156

6. 28 June 1945, NA SAIC/PIR/67, ref SAIC/FIR/48

7. *Ibid.*

8. Nuremberg, 25 September 1945, PRO FO box 645/156

9. Hitler, in H. Trevor-Roper (ed.), *Hitler's Table Talk: His Private Conversations* (UK 1953) p. 49

10. *Ibid.*, p. 67

11. Jacques Benbassat, *The Real Albert Goering*, 3BM TV

12. Marshal Antonescu, in Burleigh, p. 610

13. 28 June 1945, NA SAIC/PIR/67, ref SAIC/FIR/48

14. Hans Modry, 7 February 1947, Notes from the Trial, Special People's Court Prague, Testimony in Defence of Albert Goering, SKA

15. Josef Voracek, *ibid.*

16. *Ibid.*

17. Nuremberg, 25 September 1945, PRO FO box 645/156

18. L. Kovacs, 4 July 1944, PRO HO box 4/101

19. British intelligence notes on interview with Vitez Szasz, *ibid.*

20. E. Permora (Elsa Perou de Moravek), pp. 207–10

21. *Ibid.*

22. Nuremberg, 25 September 1945, PRO FO box 645/156

23. Killinger press conference, 19 November 1941, cited in R. Ioanid, *The Holocaust in Romania: The Destruction of the Jews and Gypsies under the Antonescu Regime, 1940–*

1944 (USA 2000) p. 241

24. Nuremberg, 25 September 1945, PRO FO box 645/156
25. Jacques Benbassat, *The Real Albert Goering*, 3BM TV
26. Nuremberg, 25 September 1945, PRO FO box 645/156

Chapter Twelve: Destruction *(pages 179–91)*

1. Goebbels diaries, 9 May 1943, Lochner, p. 285
2. Goldensohn, p. 111
3. Bormann letter to his wife, 4 November 1944, M. Bormann, *The Bormann Letters: The Private Correspondence between Martin Bormann and His Wife from January 1943–April 1944* (UK 1954)
4. Kelley, p. 60
5. Keegan, *The Second World War*, p. 83
6. Minutes of conference between Commander-in-Chief Navy (Dönitz) and Hitler, 5 June 1943, Showell, pp. 331–43
7. Goebbels diary, 9 March 1943, Lochner, p. 201
8. Von Below, p. 169
9. Goldensohn, p. 112
10. G. Gilbert, *Nuremberg Diary*, p. 78
11. Goebbels diary, 20 April 1943, Lochner, p. 262
12. Goebbels diary, 9 November 1943, *Ibid.*, p. 411
13. Führer conference, 25 July 1943, Overy, *Goering: The Iron Man*, p. 44
14. Von Below, p. 214
15. 10 October 1943, Speer, *Slave State*, p. 217
16. General Bissel, in R. Irons, *Hitler's Terror Weapons: The Price of Vengeance* (UK 2002) pp. 198–9
17. Ribbentrop, p. 175
18. M. Bormann letter to his wife, *The Bormann Letters*, 4 October 1944
19. Goebbels diary, 4 March 1945, H. Trevor-Roper (ed.), *Goebbels Diaries: The Last Days* (UK 1978) p. 44
20. Sir A. Harris, *Bomber Offensive* (UK 1947) p. 265
21. Goebbels diary, 11 March 1945, Trevor-Roper, *Goebbels Diaries*, pp. 106–8
22. Speer, 1 December 1963, A. Speer, *Spandau Secret Diaries* (UK 1976) p. 419
23. Trevor-Roper, *Hitler's Table Talk*, p. 251
24. Night 28/29 April, H. Trevor-Roper, *The Last Days of Hitler* (UK 1947) p. 213
25. Goldensohn, p. 129
26. *Ibid.*, p. 106
27. OSS Art Looting Investigation Unit Consolidated Interrogation Reports, cited in Irving, p. 303
28. Goldensohn, p. 128
29. Hermann, August 1942, in Irving, p. 303
30. Goldensohn, p. 129
31. *Ibid.*, p. 106
32. OSS Art Looting Investigation Unit Consolidated Interrogation Reports, cited in L. Nicholas, *The Rape of Europa: The Fate of Europe's Art Treasures in the Third Reich and the Second World War* (USA 1994) pp. 378–9

33. Goldensohn, p. 129

34. Trevor-Roper, *The Last Days of Hitler*, p. 161

35. Hermann, telegram to Hitler, 23 April 1945, in A. Beevor, *Berlin – The Downfall, 1945* (UK 2002) p. 289

36. Hitler's will, 29 April 1945, in Knopp, *Hitler's Hitmen*, p. 161

37. Hermann to General Eisenhower, 6 May 1945, Irving, p. 20

38. General G. Patton, *War as I Knew It* (UK 1948) p. 327

Chapter Thirteen: Judgement *(pages 195–206)*

1. Major Paul Kubala, in Mosley, pp. 322–3

2. E. Neubach, *Deutsches Wochenmagazin*, 24 February 1962

3. 28 June 1945, NA SAIC/PIR/67, ref SAIC/FIR/48

4. Albert letter, 6 September 1945, Chief Justice Robert Jackson, Main Office Files, NA RG 238 Box 180

5. Colonel B. Andrus letter to friend, in J. Persico, *Nuremberg: Infamy on Trial* (USA 1994) p. 50

6. Colonel B. Andrus, *The Infamous of Nuremberg* (UK 1969) pp. 29–31

7. Interrogation at Mondorf, 24 May 1945, NA SAIC/X/5

8. Seaghan Maynes (Reuters journalist), in H. Gaskin, *Eyewitnesses at Nuremberg* (UK 1990) p. 78

9. Dick Sonnenfeldt (Allied interpreter), in *The Real Albert Goering*, 3BM TV

10. Nuremberg, 25 September 1945, PRO FO box 645/156

11. Albert–Hermann meeting, 25–6 March 1943, and Albert letter, 6 April 1943, BA-Berlin

12. Nuremberg, 25 September 1945, PRO FO box 645/156

13. *Ibid.*

14. *Ibid.*

15. Chief Justice Robert Jackson, Main Office Files, NA RG 238 Box 180

16. Andrus, p. 129

17. *Ibid.*, pp. 131–2

18. Kelley, pp. 42–3

19. Goldensohn, pp. 103–4

20. Andrus, p. 139

21. G. Gilbert, *Nuremberg Diary*, pp. 158–9

22. R. Cooper, *The Nuremberg Trial* (USA 1947) p. 175

23. Roger Barret, Officer in Charge of Documents, in Gaskin, p. 79

24. Alfred Steer, Administrative Head of Language Division, *ibid.*, p. 86

25. R. West, *A Train of Powder* (UK 1955) p. 6

26. A. Neave, *Nuremberg: A Personal Record of the Trial of the Major Nazi War Criminals* (UK 1978) p. 318

27. Marrus, p. 182

28. Sir D. M. Fyfe, *Political Adventure: The Memoirs of the Earl of Kilmuir* (UK 1964) p. 111

29. *Ibid.*, pp. 113–14

30. *Ibid.*

31. *Ibid.*

32. Marrus, p. 220
33. G. Gilbert, *Nuremberg Diary*, p. 371
34. Speer, 31 August 1946, in Marrus, p. 224
35. G. Gilbert, *Nuremberg Diary*, p. 102
36. Goldensohn, p. 131
37. *Ibid.*, p. 114
38. *Ibid.*, p. 115
39. G. Gilbert, *Nuremberg Diary*, p. 39
40. Goldensohn, p. 115
41. G. Gilbert, *Nuremberg Diary*, p. 107
42. Persico, p. 418
43. Andrus, pp. 505–6
44. B. Swearingham, *The Mystery of Hermann Goering's Suicide* (UK 1987) p. 160
45. *Ibid.*, p. 170
46. Herbert Lee Stivers, interview with staff writer B. Pool, *Los Angeles Times*, 7 February 2005
47. G. Gilbert, *Nuremberg Diary*, p. 80
48. Trevor-Roper, *Hitler's Table Talk*, p. 384
49. Gritzbach, p. 192
50. Overy, *Goering: The Iron Man*, p. 120
51. Pearl Buck, *Saturday Evening Post*, 2 April 1933, cited in J. Sheridan, *Chinese Warlord: The Career of Feng Yu-hsiang* (USA 1966) p. 20
52. Lin Yu-tang, 'The Dog Meat General', in E. Snow (ed.), *Living China: Modern Chinese Short Stories* (UK 1936) p. 224
53. Memo 2 May 1941, Manvell and Fraenkel, p. 256
54. Hermann, 24–27 November 1942, in Malcolm Muggeridge (ed.), *Ciano's Diplomatic Papers* (UK 1948) pp. 464–5; or Manvell and Fraenkel, p. 262

Chapter Fourteen: Verdict *(pages 207–18)*

1. Application for Release, Civilian Internment Camp Darmstadt, 5 July 1946, NA NND 88/077
2. Preliminary Interrogation Report, CIC Darmstadt, 31 July 1946, *ibid.*
3. Speer, *Spandau Secret Diaries*, p. 119
4. Franz Lehar, *Deutsches Wochenmagazin*, 24 February 1962
5. *Ibid.*
6. Nuremberg Judge Advocate's Office, 15 March 1946, NA FSI/G2 8092
7. E. Neubach, *Deutsches Wochenmagazin*, 24 February 1962
8. The Great Decree, 19 June 1945, Clause 31, cited in B. Frommer, *National Cleansing: Retribution against Nazi Collaborators in Postwar Czechoslovakia* (USA 2005) pp. 348–63
9. Office of US Chief of Counsel Subsequent Proceedings Division – interrogation summary no. 106, 11 September 1946, and interrogation summary no. 113, 13 September 1946, NA
10. E. Neubach, *Deutsches Wochenmagazin*, 24 February 1962
11. Lieutenant Martin Kent, 21 April 1947, NA NND 88/077

12. Brunhilda Lohner, *The Real Albert Goering*, 3BM TV
13. Jacques Benbassat to author, 2005
14. Elizabeth Goering, *The Real Albert Goering*, 3BM TV
15. Brunhilda Lohner, *ibid.*
16. *Ibid.*
17. George Pilzer, interview with Adam LeBor, 1998
18. Edda Goering, *The Real Albert Goering*, 3BM TV
19. Elizabeth Goering, *ibid.*
20. Goldensohn, p. 122
21. Elsa Moravek Perou de Wagner, interview with Adam LeBor, 1998
22. Jacques Benbassat to author, 2005
23. Gritzbach, p. 213
24. Jacques Benbassat to author, 2005
25. Sir N. Henderson, p. 83
26. G. Gilbert, *Nuremberg Diary*, p. 214
27. Mosley, p. 253
28. Kelley, p. 51
29. Sir N. Henderson, p. 84
30. G. Gilbert, *Nuremberg Diary*, p. 215
31. *Ibid.*, p. 401
32. Goldensohn, p. 131
33. G. Gilbert, *Nuremberg Diary*, p. 171
34. George Pilzer, interview with Adam LeBor, 1998
35. Speech to Prussian Diet, 18 May 1933, Goering, *Political Testament*, p. 51
36. Trevor-Roper, *Hitler's Table Talk*, p. 7
37. Hitler, 14 February 1945, in Genoud, p. 69
38. Vladislav Kratky, interview with Adam LeBor, May 1998
39. Hans Modry, 7 February 1947, Notes from the Trial, Special People's Court Prague, Testimony in Defence of Albert Goering, SKA
40. *Ibid.*
41. Nuremberg, 25 September 1945, PRO FO box 645/156
42. E. Neubach, *Deutsches Wochenmagazin*, 24 February 1962
43. 28 June 1945, NA SAIC/PIR/67, ref SAIC/FIR/48
44. Jan Modry, *The Real Albert Goering*, 3BM TV
45. PRO FO box 371/25110 and box 371/25111
46. Nuremberg, 25 September 1945, PRO FO box 645/156
47. E. Neubach, *Deutsches Wochenmagazin*, 24 February 1962

Bibliography

Document Sources

Archives consulted:

BA	*Bundesarchiv*	Berlin
IWM	*Imperial War Museum*	London/RAF Duxford
NA	*National Archives*	Washington
PRO	*UK National Archives*	London
SKA	*Skoda Archive*	Pilsen

Many thanks to Skoda Archivist Vladislav Kratky for digging out material on Albert Goering's time with the company.

Books

Alford, K., *Nazi Plunder: Great Treasure Stories of World War Two* (USA 2001)

Andrus, Colonel B., *The Infamous of Nuremberg* (UK 1969)

Barron, S. (eds), *Degenerate Art: The Fate of the Avant-garde in Nazi Germany* (USA 1991)

Beevor, A., *Berlin: The Downfall, 1945* (UK 2002)

_____, *Crete: The Battle and the Resistance* (UK 1993)

_____, *Stalingrad* (UK 1998)

Bekker, C., *The Luftwaffe War Diaries: The German Air Force in World War Two* (UK 1967)

Below, N. von, *At Hitler's Side: The Memoirs of Hitler's Luftwaffe Adjutant, 1937–1945* (UK 2001)

Bierman, J. and Smith, C., *Alamein: War Without Hate* (UK 2002)

Birkenhead, Earl of, *Halifax: The Life of Lord Halifax* (UK 1965)

Black, E., *IBM and the Holocaust: How America's Most Powerful Corporation Helped Nazi Germany Count the Jews* (USA 2001)

Blair, C., *Hitler's U-Boat War: The Hunters, 1939–1942* (USA 1996)

____, *Hitler's U-Boat War: The Hunted, 1942–1945* (USA 1998)

Bloch, M., *Ribbentrop* (UK 1994)

Bogdanovich, P., *Who The Devil Made It: Conversations with Legendary Film Directors* (USA 1997)

Bormann, M., *The Bormann Letters: The Private Correspondence between Martin Bormann and his Wife from January 1943–April 1945* (UK 1954)

Bosworth, R., *Mussolini* (UK 2002)

Bracher, K., *The German Dictatorship: The Origins, Structure and Consequences of National Socialism* (UK 1970)

Browning, C., *Ordinary Men: Reserve Battalion 101 and the Final Solution in Poland* (UK 2001)

Browning, C. and Matthias, J., *The Origins of the Final Solution: The Evolution of Nazi Jewish Policy, 1939–1942* (UK 2004)

Brozat, M. and Krausnik, H., *Anatomy of the SS State* (UK 1968)

Brustein, W., *The Logic of Evil: Social Origins of the Nazi Party, 1925–1935* (UK/USA 1996)

Bullock, A., *Hitler: A Study in Tyranny* (UK 1952)

Bungay, S., *The Most Dangerous Enemy: A History of the Battle of Britain* (UK 2002)

Burleigh, M., *The Third Reich: A New History* (UK 2000)

Cecil, A., *The Myth of the Master Race: Alfred Rosenberg and Nazi Ideology* (UK 1972)

Cesarani, D., *Eichmann – His Life and Crimes* (UK 2004)

Ciano, G., *The Ciano Diaries, 1939–1943: The Complete, Unabridged Diaries of Galeazzo Ciano* (USA 1946)

Channon, Sir H., *Chips: The Diaries of Sir Henry Channon* (UK 1967)

Christiansen, E., *The Northern Crusades* (UK 1997)

Cocks, G., *Psychotherapy in the Third Reich: The Goering Institute* (USA 1985)

Cooper, R., *The Nuremberg Trial* (USA 1947)

Cornwell, J., *Hitler's Scientists: Science, War and the Devil's Pact* (UK 2003)

Crowe, C., *Conversations with Wilder* (USA 1999)

Dahlerus, B., *The Last Attempt* (UK 1948)

Davies, N., *Europe: A History* (UK 1997)

Dreisziger, N. (ed.), *Hungary in the Age of Total War, 1938–1948* (USA 1998)

Evans, R., *Telling Lies About Hitler: The Holocaust, History and the David Irving Trial* (UK 2002)

____, *The Coming of the Third Reich* (UK 2003)

Farrell, N., *Mussolini: A New Life* (UK 2003)

Fenby, J., *Generalissimo: Chiang Kai-Shek and the China He Lost* (UK 2003)

Fest, J., *Hitler* (UK 1974)

____, *Inside Hitler's Bunker: The Last Days of the Third Reich* (USA 2004)

____, *Plotting Hitler's Death: The German Resistance to Hitler, 1933–1945* (UK 1996)

_____, *Speer: The Final Verdict* (UK 2001)

_____, *The Face of the Third Reich* (UK 1970)

Fokker, A. and Gould, B., *Flying Dutchman* (USA 1931)

Forbes, N., *Doing Business with the Nazis: Britain's Economical and Financial Relations with Germany, 1931–1939* (UK 2000)

Fox, W., *The I.C.I.* (UK 1934)

Franks, N., *Dogfight: Aerial Tactics of the Aces of World War I* (UK 2003)

Franks, N. and Bailey, F., *The Jasta Pilots* (UK 1996)

_____, and Duiven, R., *The Jasta War Chronology: A Complete History of Claims and Losses, August 1916–1918* (UK 1998)

Franks, N. and Gibling, H., *Under the Guns of the German Aces* (UK 1997)

Frischauser, W., *Goering* (UK 1951)

Frommer, B., *National Cleansing: Retribution against Nazi Collaborators in Postwar Czechoslovakia* (USA 2005)

Fyfe, Sir D. M., *Political Adventure: The Memoirs of the Earl of Kilmuir* (UK 1964)

Gallo, M., *The Night of the Long Knives* (UK 1973)

Gaskin, H., *Eyewitnesses at Nuremberg* (UK 1990)

Genoud, F., (ed.), *The Testament of Adolf Hitler: The Hitler–Bormann Documents, February–April 1945* (UK 1959)

Gedye, G., *Fallen Bastions: The Central European Tragedy* (UK 1939)

Gilbert, G., *Nuremberg Diary* (USA 1947)

Gilbert, M., *The Dent Atlas of the Holocaust: The Complete History* (UK 1993)

_____, *The Second World War* (UK 2000)

Gillen, D., *Warlord: Yen Hsi-shan in Shansi Province, 1911–1949* (USA 1967)

Giurescu, D., *Romania in the Second World War* (USA 2000)

Goebbels, J., *Goebbels Diaries* (trans by Lochner L., UK 1948)

_____, *Goebbels Diaries: The Last Days* (trans by Trevor-Roper H., UK 1978)

_____, *Goebbels Diaries 1939–1941: The Historic Journal of a Nazi War Leader* (trans by Taylor F., UK 1982)

Goering, H., *Germany Reborn* (UK 1934)

_____, *The Political Testament of Hermann Goering: A Selection of Important Speeches and Articles* (UK 1938)

Goldensohn, L., *The Nuremberg Interviews: An American Psychiatrist's Conversations with the Defendants and Witnesses* (USAA 2004)

Gregor, N., *Daimler Benz in the Third Reich* (USA 1998)

Griehl, M., *Jet Planes of the Third Reich: The Secret Projects* Vol 1 (UK 2000)

Gritzbach, E., *Hermann Goering: The Man and his Work* (UK 1938)

Graber, G., *The Life and Times of Reinhard Heydrich* (UK 1981)

Grunberger, R., *A Social History of the Third Reich* (UK 1971)

Gunning, T., *The Films of Fritz Lang: Allegories and Visions of Modernity* (UK 2000)

Hake, S., *Popular Cinema in the Third Reich* (USA 2002)

Hamann, B., *Winifred Wagner: A Life at the Heart of Hitler's Bayreuth* (UK 2005)

Handler, A., *A Man For All Connections: Raoul Wallenberg and the Hungarian State Apparatus* (USA 1996)

Harris, Sir A., *Bomber Offensive* (UK 1947)

Hassell, U. von, *The von Hassell Diaries, 1938–1944* (UK 1994)

Hastings, M., *Armageddon: The Battle for Germany, 1944–1945* (UK 2004)

_____, *Bomber Command* (UK 1979)

Hayes, P., *Industry and Ideology: IG Farben in the Nazi Era* (UK 1987)

Heiber, H. and Glantz, D. (eds), *Hitler and His Generals: Military Conferences, 1942–1945* (UK 2002)

Henderson, Sir N., *Failure of a Mission, 1937–1939* (UK 1940)

Henderson, W., *The German Colonial Empire, 1884–1919* (UK 1993)

Herwig, D. and Rode, H., *Luftwaffe Secret Projects: Strategic Bombers, 1935–1945* (UK 2000)

Hiden, J., *The Weimar Republic* (UK 1974)

Higham, C., *Trading with the Enemy* (UK 1983)

Hobsbawm, E., *Age of Extremes: The Short Twentieth Century* (UK 1994)

Hohne, H., *The Order of the Death's Head* (UK 1967)

Homze, E., *Arming the Luftwaffe: The Reich Air Ministry and the German Aircraft Industry* (UK 1976)

Hooton, E., *Eagle in Flames: The Fall of the Luftwaffe* (USA 1997)

_____, *Phoenix Triumphant: The Rise and Rise of the Luftwaffe* (USA 1994)

Hunter, J., *The Blue Max* (UK 1964)

Ioanid, R., *The Holocaust in Romania: The Destruction of the Jews and Gypsies under the Antonescu Regime, 1940–1944* (USA 2000)

Imperial Chemical Industries Ltd., *The History of Nobel's Explosives Company Ltd and Nobel Industries Ltd, Vol I, 1871–1926* (UK 1938)

Irons, R., *Hitler's Terror Weapons: The Price of Vengeance* (UK 2002)

Irving, D., *Goering: A Biography* (UK 1989)

Johnson, E., *The Nazi Terror: Gestapo, Jews and Ordinary Germans* (UK 2000)

Joll, J., *Europe Since 1870: An International History* (UK 1973)

Jones, N., *The Birth of the Nazis: How the Freikorps Blazed a Trail for Hitler* (UK 2004)

Jünger, E., *Storm of Steel* (UK 2003)

Kahn, D., *Hitler's Spies: German Military Intelligence in World War Two* (UK 1978)

Kay, A., *Junkers Aircraft and Engines, 1915–1945* (UK 2004)

Keegan, J., *Intelligence in War: Knowledge of the Enemy from Napoleon to Al-Qaeda* (UK 2003)

_____, *The First World War* (UK 1998)

_____, *The Mask of Command: A Study of Generalship* (UK 1987)

_____, *The Second World War* (UK 1989)

Kelley, D., *22 Cells in Nuremberg* (USA 1947)

Kennedy, P., *The Rise and Fall of the Great Powers: Economic and Military Conflict, 1500–2000* (USA 1988)

Kershaw, I., *Hitler 1889–1936: Hubris* (UK 1998)

____, *Hitler 1936–1945: Nemesis* (UK 2000)

____, *Making Friends with Hitler: Lord Londonderry and Britain's Road to War* (UK 2004)

Kilduff, P., *The Red Baron: Beyond the Legend* (UK 1994)

Killen, J., *The Luftwaffe: A History* (UK 1967)

Kinderman, G., *Hitler's Defeat in Austria, 1933–1934: Europe's First Containment of Nazi Expansionism* (UK 1988)

Kirkpatrick, I., *Mussolini: Study of a Demagogue* (UK 1964)

Knopp, G., *Hitler's Henchmen* (UK 2000)

____, *Hitler's Hitmen* (UK 2002)

____, *Hitler's Warriors* (UK 2005)

Koehl, R., *The Black Corps: The Structure and Power Struggles of the Nazi SS* (USA 1983)

Kreimeier, K., *The UFA Story: A History of Germany's Greatest Film Company, 1918–1945* (USA 1996)

Landy, M., *Fascism in Film: The Italian Commercial Cinema, 1931–1943* (USA 1986)

Lang, J. von, *The Secretary: Martin Bormann – The Man Who Manipulated Hitler* (UK 1979)

LeBor, A., *Hitler's Secret Bankers: The Myth of Swiss Neutrality During the Holocaust* (USA 1997)

LeBor, A. and Boyes, R., *Surviving Hitler: Choices, Corruption and Compromise* (UK 2000)

Liang, H., *The Sino-German Connection: Alexander von Falkenhausen between China and Germany, 1900–1941* (Amsterdam 1978)

Low, A., *The Anschluss Movement* (USA 1985)

Luza, R., *Austro-German Relations in the Anschluss Era* (USA 1975)

Luza, R. and Kella, C., *The Hitler Kiss: A Memoir of the Czech Resistance* (USA 2002)

Lyttelton, A., *The Seizure of Power: Fascism in Italy, 1919–1929* (UK/USA 1973)

McCord, E., *The Power of the Gun: The Emergence of Modern Chinese Warlordism* (USA 1993)

MacDonald, C., *The Killing of SS Obergruppenführer Reinhard Heydrich* (UK 1989)

MacDonagh, G., *The Last Kaiser: William the Impetuous* (UK 2000)

McGilligan, P., *Fritz Lang: The Nature of the Beast* (USA 1997)

Mackensie, W., *The Secret History of the S.O.E.* (UK 2000)

Manvell, R. and Fraenkel, H., *Goering* (USA 1962)

Marrus, M., (ed.), *The Nuremberg War Crimes Trial, 1945–1946: A Documentary History* (USA 1997)

Matyszak, P., *The Enemies of Rome: From Hannibal to Attila the Hun* (UK 2004)

Mazower, M., *Dark Continent: Europe's Twentieth Century* (UK 1998)

_____, *Inside Hitler's Greece: The Experience of Occupation, 1941–1945* (UK/USA 1993)

_____, *The Balkans: From the End of Byzantium to the Present Day* (UK 2000)

Middlebrook, M. and Everitt, C., *Bomber Command War Diaries: Operational Reference Book, 1939–1945* (UK 1985)

Miller, M., *Bulgaria during the Second World War* (USA 1975)

Morton, F., *Thunder at Twilight: Vienna, 1913–1914* (USA 1989)

Mosley, L., *The Reich Marshal: A Biography of Hermann Goering* (UK 1974)

Muggeridge, Malcolm (ed.), *Ciano's Diplomatic Papers* (UK 1948)

Neave, A., *Nuremberg: A Personal Record of the Trial of the Major Nazi War Criminals* (UK 1978)

Neillands, R., *The Bomber War: Arthur Harris and the Allied Bomber Offensive, 1939–1945* (UK 2001)

Nicholas, L., *The Rape of Europa: The Fate of Europe's Treasures in the Third Reich and the Second World War* (USA 1994)

Overy, R., *Goering: The Iron Man* (UK 1984)

_____, *The Battle* (UK 2000)

_____, *The Dictators: Hitler's Germany and Stalin's Russia* (UK 2004)

_____, *Russia's War* (USA 1997)

_____, *Why the Allies Won* (UK 1995)

Padfield, P., *Himmler: Reichsführer SS* (UK 1990)

Pakenham, T., *The Scramble for Africa, 1876–1912* (UK 1991)

Papen, F. von, *Memoirs* (UK 1952)

Parker, M., *Monte Cassino: The Story of the Hardest-Fought Battle of World War Two* (UK 2003)

Passingham, I., *All the Kaiser's Men: The Life and Death of the German Army on the Western Front, 1914–1918* (UK 2003)

Patton, General G., *War as I Knew It* (UK 1948)

E. Permora (E. Perou de Moravek), *El Frente Desarmado* (Buenos Aires 1952)

Persico, J., *Nuremberg: Infamy On Trial* (USA 1994)

Petropoulos, J., *The Faustian Bargain: The Art World in Nazi Germany* (USA 2000)

Pool, J., *Who Financed Hitler: The Secret Funding of Hitler's Rise to Power* (USA 1978/1997)

Powers, T., *Intelligence Wars: American Secret History From Hitler to Al Qaeda* (USA 2002)

Price, A., *Luftwaffe Handbook, 1939–1945* (UK 1997)

Pye, L., *Warlord Politics: Conflict and Coalition in the Modernisation of Republican China* (USA 1971)

Reader, W., *Imperial Chemical Industries – A History*, Vol 2, *The First Quarter of a Century, 1926–1952* (UK 1975)

Ribbentrop, J. von, *The Ribbentrop Memoirs* (UK 1954)

Roberts, A., *Hitler and Churchill: Secrets of Leadership* (UK 2003)

_____, *The Holy Fox: A Life of Lord Halifax* (UK 1991)

Romani, C., *Tainted Goddesses: Female Film Stars of the Third Reich* (USA 1992)

Roseman, M., *The Villa, the Lake, the Meeting: Wansee and the Final Solution* (UK 2002)

Ryan, H. Blood, *Goering: The Iron Man of Germany* (UK 1938)

Schacht, H., *My First 76 Years: The Autobiography* (UK 1955)

Schmidt, P., *Hitler's Interpreter* (UK 1951)

Schuschnigg, K., *Austrian Requiem* (UK 1947)

_____, *Farewell Austria* (UK 1938)

Sereny, G., *Albert Speer: His Battle with the Truth* (USA 1995)

Seyar, K. and Warren, J., (eds), *Austria in the Thirties: Culture and Politics* (USA 1991)

Shepard, G., *The Austrians: A Thousand Year Odyssey* (UK 1996)

Sheridan J., *Chinese Warlord: The Career of Feng Yu-hsiang* (USA 1966)

Showell, J., (ed.), *Führer Conferences on Naval Affairs, 1939–1945* (UK 1990)

Sikov, E., *On Sunset Boulevard: The Life and Times of Billy Wilder* (USA 1998)

Singer, K., *Goering: Germany's Most Dangerous Man* (UK 1940)

Smith, D., *Raoul Wallenberg's Dramatic Quest to Save the Jews of Hungary* (UK 2001)

Smith, D.M., *Mussolini* (UK 1981)

Snow, E., (ed.), *Living China: Modern Chinese Short Stories* (UK 1936)

Speer, A., *Inside The Third Reich* (UK 1970)

_____, *Spandau Secret Diaries* (UK 1976)

_____, *The Slave State: Heinrich Himmler's Masterplan for SS Supremacy* (UK 1981)

Spick, M., *Luftwaffe Fighter Aces: The Jagdflieger and their Combat Tactics and Techniques* (UK 1996)

Stafford, D., *Secret Agent: Britain's Wartime Secret Service* (UK 2000)

Stern, F., *Gold and Iron: Bismarck, Bleichröder and the Building of the German Empire* (USAA 1977)

Stevenson, D., *1914–1918: The History of the First World War* (UK 2004)

Swearingham, B., *The Mystery of Hermann Goering's Suicide* (UK 1987)

Taylor, A.J.P., *Europe: Grandeur and Decline* (UK 1967)

_____, *The Origins of the Second World War* (UK 1964)

Taylor, F., *Dresden: Tuesday 13th February 1945* (UK 2004)

Thyssen, F., *I Paid Hitler* (USA 1941)

Toliver, Colonel R. and Constable, T., *Fighter Aces of the Luftwafffe* (USA 1996)

Trevor-Roper, H., *The Last Days of Hitler* (UK 1947)

_____, (ed.), *Hitler's Table Talk: His Private Conversations* (UK 1953)

_____, (ed.), *Hitler's War Directives* (UK 1965)

Tuchman, B., *The Proud Tower: A Portrait of the World before the War* (UK 1966)

Turner, H., *German Big Business and the Rise of Hitler* (USA 1985)

Ungvary, K., *Battle for Budapest: 101 Days in World War Two* (UK 2003)

Urban, W., *The Teutonic Knights: A Military History* (USA 2003)

Veress, L., *Clear The Line: Hungary's Struggle to Leave the Axis during the Second World War* (USA 1995)

Wagner, E. M. de, *My Roots Continents Apart: A Tale of Courage and Survival* (USA 2005)

Wehler, H., *The German Empire, 1871–1918* (UK/USA 1985)

Welch, D., *Propaganda and the German Cinema, 1933–1945* (UK 2001)

West, R., *A Train of Powder* (UK 1955)

Williams, A., *The Battle of the Atlantic* (UK 2002)

Wilson, J., *Luftwaffe Propaganda Postcards: A Pictorial History in Original German Postcards* (UK 1996)

Zimmerman, D., *Britain's Shield: Radar and the Defeat of the Luftwaffe* (UK 2001)

Index

246   INDEX

Prague 78, 98, 144–6,
148–50, 154–5, 170,
178, 190–1, 208–11, 217
Prussia 5, 12, 20–1, 23,
44, 65, 70, 84–5, 87–7,
103–4, 129, 143, 162

Rascher, S. 201
Rathenau, W. 29, 177
Reemstama, P. 101–2
Ribbentrop, J. von 59, 102,
107–8, 119, 157, 172,
184
Richthofen, Manfred von
20–5
Richthofen squadron 31,
34, 36, 38, 73, 109
Richthofen, Wolfram von
162, 167
Röhm, E. 41, 44–6
Romania 79, 112, 114–15,
149, 154, 163, 170–2,
177, 198, 211, 215, 217
Rome 54, 134, 143–4,
175–6, 217
Rommel, E. 163, 166
Rosen, Eric von 34
Rosen, Hugo von 216
Rosenberg, A. 12, 82, 188
Ruhr 29, 42, 68, 114, 164,
166, 180, 182

SA 29, 41, 44–5, 67, 71,
85, 88–9, 91, 123, 125,
165, 176
Salzburg 4, 8, 191, 209–10
Salzgitter 114, 206
Sascha 95–6, 214
Schacht, H. 69, 112–14
Schleicher, K. von 46, 73
Schmidt, P. 105
Schneider, J. 81–2
Schuschnigg, K. von 92,
119, 120–1, 123–4
SD 45, 122, 127, 132,
147–8, 169, 172
Selassie, Emperor Haile 93,
119
Seletsky, B. 144, 152–3,
210
Shapiro, J. 4

Short, F. 79–81, 170
Sicily 162–3, 175
SKF company 158, 216
Skoda, E. 144
Skoda company 144–9,
152–5, 169–71, 173,
178, 191, 197, 209, 211,
214–15, 217
Slovakia 144, 148, 152–3,
178, 210
Sofia 170, 174, 177
SOE 147
Soviet Union 51–2, 84–5,
98, 108, 110, 112, 128,
134, 138, 152, 157, 161,
163–4, 167, 171–5, 185,
190–1, 200, 206, 215,
217
Spain 79, 110–11, 114
Speer, A. 25, 165–6, 169–
70, 180, 182–3, 186,
202, 207, 211, 215
SS 44–6, 85, 88–9, 91,
121, 127, 131–3, 137–8,
148, 152, 155, 164, 169–
70, 174, 182, 190–1,
201, 204, 206, 208–9,
214, 217
Stalin, J. 98, 171, 191
Stalingrad 163, 167–8,
173, 179
Staller, K. 152–3, 170, 178,
210
Stivers, H. 203
Stockholm 3, 34–5, 55–7,
74, 216
Strasser, G. 46, 68, 84
Student, K. 162
Sweden 3, 34, 36, 39,
53–6, 74–5, 109, 114,
157–8, 216
Szekeley, W. 123

Tannenberg 12, 65
Teagle, W. 115
Technische Hochschulen
13, 35–6, 49–50, 214
Teutonic knights 12, 21,
29, 204
Thalmann, E. 66, 72, 86,
88

Thyssen, F. 68–9
Tito, J. 174, 177
Tobis 99, 214
Tobis-Italiano 143, 145
Tobis-Sascha 99–100, 115,
121, 123, 207, 215
Topf and Sons 214
Trenchard, H. 110
Turkey 114, 198

Udet, E. 109–10, 165
UFA 96, 98–101
Ukraine 102, 134, 164

Vambersky 149–50, 197
Veldenstein castle 8, 10–11,
14, 16, 179
Venice 53–4, 93
Veress 175
Versailles Treaty 30–1,
37–8, 51, 83, 103–4, 200
Vienna 8, 59, 78–81, 92–3,
95–6, 99, 116, 119–21,
123–7, 130, 143, 170,
172, 190, 207–10, 215,
217
V-1 183–4
V-2 184
Vöss, W. 169, 174, 209,
215

Wagner, R. 14, 129, 158
Wallenberg, J. 216–17
Wallenberg, R. 216–18
Wansee conference 135, 213
warlords, Chinese 205–6
Warsaw 130, 133, 158
Wenner-Gren, A. 158, 216
West, R. 200
Wheelis, J. 203
Wilder, B. 96, 98
Windhoek 5, 9
Winquist, S. 216
Wolfe, Greta 123
Wolfe, Max 123

Yugoslavia 114, 154, 162,
170–1, 174, 198, 215

Zbrojovka 152, 170
Zrno, F. 149–50